Strangers With God

Claudio Monge OP

Dominican Series

The Dominican Series is a joint project by Australian Dominican women and men and offers contributions on topics of Dominican interest and various aspects of church, theology and religion in the world.
Series Editors: Mark O'Brien OP and Gabrielle Kelly OP

1. *English for Theology: A Resource for Teachers and Students*, Gabrielle Kelly OP, 2004.
2. *Towards the Intelligent Use of Liberty: Dominican Approaches in Education*, edited by Gabrielle Kelly OP and Kevin Saunders OP, 2007.
3. *Preaching Justice: Dominican Contributions to Social Ethics in the Twentieth Century*, edited by Francesco CampaGenoni OP and Helen Alford OP, 2008.
4. *Don't Put Out The Burning Bush: Worship and preaching in a Complex World*, edited by Vivian Boland, 2008.
5. *Bible Dictionary: Selected Biblical and Theological Words*, Gabrielle Kelly OP in collaboration with Joy Sandefur, 2008
6. *Sunday Matters A: Reflections on the Lectionary Readings for Year A*, Mark O'Brien OP, 2010.
7. *Sunday Matters B: Reflections on the Lectionary Readings for Year B*, Mark O'Brien OP, 2011.
8. *Sunday Matters C: Reflections on the Lectionary Readings for Year C*, Mark O'Brien OP, 2012.
9. Scanning the Signs of the Times: *French Dominicans in the Twentieth Century*, Thomas F O'Meara OP and Paul Philibert OP, 2013.
10. *From North to South: Southern Scholars Engage with Edward Schillebeeckx*, edited by Helen F Bergin OP, 2013.
11. *The ABC of Sunday Matters*, Mark O'Brien OP, 2013.
12. *Restoring the Right Relationship: The Bible on Divine Righteousness*, Mark O' Brien OP, 2014.
13. *Dominicans and Human Rights: Past, Present, Future*, edited by Mike Deeb OP and Celestina Veloso Freitas OP, 2017
14. *Promise of Renewal: Dominicans and Vatican II*, edited by Michael Attridge, Darren Dias OP, Matthew Eaton and Nicolas Olkovich, 2017
15. *A Stumbling Block: Bartolomé de las Casas as Defender of the Indians*, Mariano Delgado, 2019.
16. *Reluctant Prophet: Tributes in Honour of Albert Nolan OP*, edited by Mike Deeb OP, Philippe Denis OP and Mark James OP, 2023

Disclaimer:
Views expressed in publications within the Dominican Series do not necessarily reflect those of the respective Congregations of the Sisters or the Province of the Friars.

Strangers With God

A theology of Hospitality in the Three Abrahamic Religions

Claudio Monge OP

Adelaide
2024

© Copyright remains with Claudio Monge OP

2013 Holy Land Foundation—Milano
Terra Santa Edition—Milano

For information on published works
and programs please contact:

Edizione Terra Santa
Via G. Gherardini 5–20145 Milano (Italy)
Tel.: 39 02 34592679 fax +30 02 3180 `1980
http://www.edizioniterrasanta.it
e-mail: editrice@edizioniterrasanta.it

ISBN:
978-1-923006-30-0 soft
978-1-923006-31-7 hard
978-1-923006-32-4 epub
978-1-923006-33-1 pdf

Published by:

Making a lasting impact
An imprint of the ATF Press Publishing Group
owned by ATF (Australia) Ltd.
PO Box 234
Brompton, SA 5007
Australia
ABN 90 116 359 963
www.atfpress.com

To my Father and Mother
who, with their unconditional love,
have made me understand that
hospitality is a GIFT which enlarges the heart.

Table of Contents

Preface	xi
Foreword	xv
Prologue	xix

Part One
Hospitality in the Traditions of the
Three Abrahamic Religions

Introduction	3

Hospitality in the Jewish Tradition

The Origins of the Chosen People	7
An ontological 'otherness'	7
Integration in a semi-nomadic context	13
Biblical Foundations of Hospitality	17
Historical-Sociological Foundations	17
Theological foundations	20
Welcoming the stranger in the Old Testament:	
between ethnocentrism and universalism	22
Welcoming the stranger according to the legislation of Israel	24
The Major Stages of the History of the Old Testament:	
A Land Lost and Found	33
Exile in a foreign land: Preserving the identity of the	
Chosen People	33
Re-establishing identity in the post-exile	35
The prophetic literature: opening an eschatological	
perspective toward foreigners	39

The myths of origins	43
The saga of the Patriarchs	48
The Hellenistic period: Culture shock and the bias toward	
xenophobia	52

Hospitality According to Rabbinic Literature	59
A religious duty	59
A confessional hospitality	64
The ritual of hospitality in the Jewish world	65
Places of accorded hospitality	69
Conclusion	73

Hospitality in the Arab World

Welcome in the Middle East	77
The Middle East: defining a geographical and cultural area	77
Antonin Jaussen: hospitality in a Bedouin context	79
The sheikh's tent: The heart of the ritual of hospitality	80
The hospitality meal and its service	84
Hospitality is an honour shared with the entire tribe	87

Violations against the rule of hospitality	89
The bawq and the transgression of honor	89
The dakhalah or right of asylum	90

Hospitality in the vocabulary of the Qur'an	93
The ijāra: an extension of divine protection	93
Charity as an ethical requirement of faith	96

A witness of Muslim hospitality: The *Kitāb ādāb al-akl* of	
Al-Ghazali	101
Practical instructions for the benefit of ordinary people	101
Conclusion	105

Hospitality in the Christian World

The Theology of the New Testament	109
The Incarnation: The Son of God pleads for a	
human welcome	109
Hospitality in the Gospels: Welcoming the Father in the Son	113
Festive Gospel meals	118
The apostolic communities: the welcome given the	
messengers of the Gospel	124
Interior dispositions and gestures of welcome	131

The Church's thinking on hospitality: An historical overview	135
The second century: The Fathers of the Church	135
The third century: The development of the	
practice of hospitality	138
Hospitality as an act of justice	140
Hospitality as an institution	147
Evolution or degeneration?	147
Hospitality in the Western monastic tradition	149
Hospitality and charity: An evolution in terms	152
Conclusion	157

Part Two
History of the Acceptance and
Interpretation of Genesis 18

Abraham, The Uncertain Origins of an Ancestor

The keeper of a common memory	**165**
The contested historicity of the biblical cycle of the Patriarchs	165
The example of Abraham in comparative religions	167
Abraham in the theological interpretation of the	
three monotheistic religions	171
Abraham in the Christian tradition	171
Abraham in the rabbinic tradition	173
Abraham in the Islamic tradition	175

Genesis 18:1–15: Abraham ad His Mysterious Guests

The Structure of the Biblical Account	183
The delimitation of the text and its context	184
The narrative structure	187
An exegetical analysis	190
A reward for hospitality?	197
The theophany of Mamre in the Christian interpretation	207
Different versions of the same story	207
The structure of a theophany	210
Genesis 18 and 32: the two 'human theophanies'	213
The identity of the three guests in the history of	
Christian exegesis	217

The theophany of Mamre in the Jewish Tradition	225
Abraham: The man of God	225
The Shekinah and the three messengers	229
The Hellenistic rabbinical exegesis: Josephus and Philo of	
Alexandria	231
Conclusion	237
The theophany at Mamre in the Islamic tradition	239
Occurrences in the Qur'an: similarities and differences	239
Al-Razi and the pedagogy of a transcendent God	243
Conclusion: a God who must be experienced!	247

Epilogue

Theological Paths in the Light of Hospitality	253
A theology of religions as a theology of hospitality	256
To believe hospitably: Truth not as a substance	
but as a relationship	261
Postface	269
List of Boxes	273
A short bibliography	275

Preface

Timothy Radcliffe OP

Claudio Monge addresses one of the key questions of today with an extremely ancient text from the deepest roots of our civilisation, Genesis 18, in which Abraham welcomes the three strangers who come to his tent and announce the conception of Isaac. Today, when millions are in movement, fleeing war and poverty, the question of how we are to receive strangers is urgent and inescapable. Monge explores this text through the traditions of three religions—Judaism, Christianity and Islam—which claim the assent of approximately half of the population of the world. Yet these three religions, all looking back in one way or another to Abraham, are often strangers to each other. If we could offer welcome to each other, what a powerful sign of hope this would be for our conflict torn world!

Monge sketches a 'theology of hospitality' which should, according to the great Jesuit theologian, Henri de Lubac, require 'a firmly rooted openness; the necessity for a discernment that precedes the reception [of the other]; and the demand for a real courage that effects the engagement'. Any true hospitality implies that one's identity is both respected and yet that one is summoned beyond the limits of one's present self-understanding to discover a deeper sense of who one is in relationship with the other. So giving a welcome to the stranger implies both bing an expression of who one is and yet accepting to become more.

Hospitality is open to the discovery of friendship. For Christians this finds its culmination in the improbable friendships of Jesus, who ate and drank with prostitutes and tax collectors, sinners and holy people, lawyers and the marginalised. The story of Abraham's welcome to the strangers who come to his tent in the heat of the day is an invitation to us to reach out in friendship beyond our boundaries to share the gifts of our faith and receive those of others.

At his episcopal ordination in 1981, Blessed Pierre Claverie OP, the bishop of Oran, said to his Muslim friends, 'I owe to you also what I am today. With you in learning Arabic, I learned above all to speak and understand the language of the heart, the language of brotherly friendship, where races and religions commune with each other. And again, I have learned the softness of heart to believe that this friendship will hold up against time, distance and separation. For I believe that this friendship comes from God and leads to God.'[1]

How in hospitable friendship do we remain true to who we are and yet with the courage to become more? The first quality that de Lubac proposes is rootedness, which suggests the image of a tree. The history of salvation stretches from the Tree of Life in the garden of Eden to the tree of the cross. The final chapter of the New Testament gives us again the Tree of Life, 'with its twelve kinds of fruit, producing its fruit each month: and the leaves of the tree are for the healing of the nations.' (Rev 22:2). In Ezekiel, Israel is compared to a great cedar tree (Ezek 17:22–24). Jesus compares the Kingdom of heaven to a mustard seed which becomes a tree which is hospitable to the birds of air which come to make their nests in it (Matt 13:31–32).

So the deeply biblical image of the tree might help us to understand the dynamics of hospitality. Outside my window, there is a beautiful white beam tree. Through the year I observe its changes in each season. It remains itself, a white beam from its highest leaf to his deepest root. It is, one might say, one body, a single nature. If it were not, it would decay and die. But it is also alive in being open to what is not itself. It is open to sun and rain, to the nourishment of the soil and linked with other organisms through a vast underground network of fungal connections, the mycorrhizal network. Without this Wood Wide Web, it would die. It is the home to insects and birds. We witness the flourishing of the tree at these points of interconnection with what is other, especially its leaves, roots and bark. Here it is most itself in its exposure to what is other.

Similarly faith is most alive when it most deeply embraces its own traditions while becoming open to other ways of viewing the world, other religions and even the imagination of creative people who adhere to no faith at all. New life happens most vividly in these

---

1. *A Life poured out; Pierre Claverie of Algeria,* by Jean-Jacques Pérennès OP (Maryknoll: Orbis, 2007), viii

encounters as the welcome offered to the strangers led to the fertility of old Sarah and Abraham and the fulfilment of God's promise to the nations.

Sometimes the challenge for a community of believers is primarily to remain rooted in its own tradition and to cherish the unity of the body, the bonds which unite us to our brothers and sisters in our own faith. At other times, new life is found rather in turning outwards, in the adventure of hospitality those who are 'other', as Pierre Claverie loved to say.

At some moments in the history of all the Abrahamic faiths the imperative has been to befriend the stranger who is a foreigner. At other times, of persecution or division, the stranger might rather be the brother or sister in the faith from whom one is alienated, so that the community can remain strong. Jesus embodied a radical welcome to those who were estranged from the Lord, but we see in the gospels only the beginnings of a reaching out beyond Israel. Monge shows that by the time of the Didache in the second century, the emphasis had turned to the stranger who was a member of the household of faith: 'Welcome anyone coming in the name of the Lord.' Perhaps both forms of hospitality, internal and external, are always needed, with the emphasis changing from time to time.

Should a Christian hope and pray for the conversion of the other to his or her own faith? Or does true hospitality imply that one must renounce that wish? I have heard brethren champion both of these opinions. Pierre Claverie always claimed that all true conversation is conversion, in the first place my own! His friendship for Muslims in Algeria led to a profound conversion of his personal Christian faith. Perhaps all that one can aspire to is to have the confidence to offer the gifts of one's own faith to others, and the humility to receive the gifts they bring. What happens in that encounter is in the hands of the Lord. One cannot anticipate what unexpected fertility will result in, as Sarah and Abraham discovered.

Foreword

by Enzo Bianchi, Prior of Bose

'Civilization took a decisive step, perhaps the decisive step, the day on which the stranger (*hostis*) ceased being an enemy and came to be seen as a guest (*hospes*) . . . The day on which a guest will be recognized in the stranger, something will have changed in the world.' Thus wrote Jean Daniélou, and this affirmation radically qualifies what we call today 'Western civilization'. In fact, hospitality as it was practiced and is practiced among the semi-nomadic populations of the Middle East, seems increasingly more difficult today: we are losing an ancient custom present in all cultures as a sacred duty; the market has even taken ownership of hospitality, depriving it of its quality as a free gift and making of it a commercial enterprise, so that only those who have financial means are able to offer hospitality.

If this is true regarding a hospitality sporadically given and received such as during a visit to a foreign country, what has become of that hospitality which is a localized and the stable acceptance of another, that opening of one's heart, in addition to one's dwelling, to the person who presents himself as a stranger? Today the presence of foreigners in our society is no longer occasional or seasonal but consistent and stable. And, unlike what happened with the migratory fluxes of the last two centuries, foreigners come from countries, cultures, and religions very different from our own and even from each other, thus constituting a pluralistic presence. As a result, many 'autochthons' (those who live where they were born) feel threatened not only in terms of employment and safety, but in their cultural and religious identity as well, to the point that foreigners arouse fear. Thus, a fear of diversity and the renunciation of cultural, moral, religious and social forms different from one's own end are driving us with an ever-increasing speed toward a sphere of privatization, isolation, and the non-acceptance of the other, perhaps by disguising it as a guarding of one's own identity.

It should also be recognized that, gradually, this attitude of mistrust and defence tends to pervert all our relationships, so that we cease the practice of hospitality even with those whom we can literally define as 'a neighbor,' one who is 'closer' to us, who lives with us, sharing the same language and the same culture. So our homes increasingly resemble fortresses: we have become progressively dominated by a mentality that gradually narrows its confines and withdraws from what appears as 'other,' someone unknown, new, and different. We then begin to think of hospitality only as addressed to those we invite, but the invitee is not a guest, nor are the gestures toward him the fruits of hospitality.

The 'Other,' the real other, in fact, is not the one we choose to invite into our home—perhaps with the intimation that we might be invited in return (*cf* Lk 14:13)—but the one who appears, not chosen by us; one who comes to us led by the events of life. The other is one who stands before us as a presence asking for acceptance of his irreducible diversity. It matters little if he or she belongs to a different ethnic group, to another faith, to another culture: they are human beings, and this should be enough to ensure that we welcome them. To give hospitality, in fact, means to humanize our own humanity. We are either aware that each one of us, since coming into the world, is himself/herself a guest of the human condition; or, if not, hospitality becomes relegated as a duty to be fulfilled. This is perhaps a significant gesture at an ethical level, but located on a fundamentally extrinsic level, incapable of responding to the profound vocation of each person to fulfill his or her own humanity by welcoming the humanity of the other.

In fact, the way hospitality is understood and lived reveals the degree of civility of a people; it does not depend on technological capabilities or economic wealth, but on the level of respect for the dignity of every human person. Thus, in practicing hospitality one does *par excellence* the work of humanisation, as St. Benedict so well understood. In his *Rule* he asks the monk to show the guest 'every humanity' (RB 53.9), that is, what is properly human.

Foreword

For all these reasons, the pages proposed by Claudio Monge are extremely valuable. His refined biblical expertise, his knowledge of history and theology, his anthropological and interreligious sensitivity allow him to offer an unpublished 'summa' of hospitality, conceived as a qualifying element in human relationships and the inner dimension and relationship with God that each one of us preserves in his or her own life. The basic reference to God as a guest; the correlation of the revealed and ritualistic aspects of hospitality that situate it in a sacred space; the concept of hospitality as a bridge, fragile yet indispensable, between different worlds; and respect for the distinctiveness of the other—constitute so many opportunities in everyday living which, far from being outdated, are instead essential elements of our human condition. If all this must concur in preventing a 'guest' from becoming an 'enemy', the newfound awareness that emerges with clarity from these pages will in turn free the reader from himself becoming an 'enemy' in an inhospitable society.

Bose, Tuesday of Holy Week
Memorial of the anointing at Bethany

Prologue

These pages represent the compendium of a long journey of more than fifteen years. It would be simplistic to define this journey as exclusively intellectual, because it would be unthinkable without frequent visits to the Middle East, in particular to Turkey, the second Holy Land of Christianity, the ancient Asia Minor of biblical history, with its overwhelming Muslim population today. In short, I could not have even conceived the idea of such a comparative analysis on hospitality without the daily experience of the surprising oriental welcome, which has minimised the significant impact of two worlds so culturally distant, yet so geographically close.

The need to reflect on the idea and practice of hospitality is therefore called for by a stringent existential actuality. The fact is that, for some years now, the theme of hospitality has been the subject of numerous publications, studies, contributions, and gatherings with protagonists of various opinions and expertise convening to give answers to questions related to the challenge of living together in the complex society of our contemporary world. It is precisely by letting ourselves be questioned by these complexities that we become aware that the challenge of hospitality is not merely economic or political but also spiritual. The same permanent reality of an 'existential Exus,' provoked by the precariousness of living in times of crisis, raises a pressing question: How do we preserve hope in these difficult and adverse times? Surely, this hope cannot exist unless it is first supported by the recognition of a fundamental human dignity, because no migrant in search of a safe haven, faced with an uncertain economic system, can be generically reduced to 'a faceless mass condemned by history,' a mere statistical data, an embarrassing dossier among others.

Of course, we must recognise that the fragility of life forces us to take more seriously into account that 'ontological otherness' that characterises us as men and women in search of relationship, without which a credible practice of hospitality would not be possible. This foreignness is minimized, first of all, by the irreducible dissimilarity we encounter when confronted by 'the other than myself', but also with respect to 'that other within myself' whom, at times, we struggle to appropriate in order to be able to offer oneself as a gift to those we meet.

'Writing about hospitality is a vital component in rescuing us from the shipwreck of non-being as we live it today.'[1] This may be precisely because hospitality is woven into the fabric of our life, an ancient and noble word that defines the mutual interdependence of creatures. Existence is not a right; it is first of all a debt. The believer knows that we are indebted to God over and beyond history and the human contributions of so many. In essence, the believer knows that we exist 'in alliance with others' but this is only possible when we resist the temptation of withdrawing into oneself to judge the dialectic between inclusiveness and estrangement, between solidarity and diversity, between civil coexistence and the lack of it.

For these reasons in particular we believe that the theme of hospitality is eminently theological and we will endeavor to illustrate this especially in the final part of this study in particular, the first step in a journey which also becomes a task for the future.

Louis Massignon, the great French orientalist, spoke of hospitality as the great legacy Abraham entrusted to all believers: the theophany of a "God both guest and receiver of the guest" which gives a new and spiritual meaning to the practice of hospitality, a meaning which goes far beyond the phenomenology of the act. Hospitality assumes a sacred character: it is much more than a simple duty among others or a rule of social coexistence.

In the following pages, we want to demonstrate that hospitality, in the tradition of the three monotheistic religions deriving from Abraham, represents and, more often than not, involves the divine. In some verses it is always God himself, or his direct representative, who is welcomed as a mysterious pilgrim: 'Do not neglect to show hospitality to strangers, for thereby some have entertained angels unaware' (Heb 13:2).

---

1. D Puliga, *L'ospitalità è un mito? Un cammino tra i racconti del Medioevo e oltre*, Il Melangolo, Genova 2012, p. 10.

Prologue xxi

Perhaps, it is not excessive to say that hospitality has its own theological as well as dogmatic character because through this practice we discern the very heart of God himself, exceeding the radical identity of the human protagonist of the sacred texts of the Abrahamic religions. More precisely, God is not only the One who heard the cry of the people in a foreign land, but the One who became 'exiled,' a stranger on the earth: (in Ps 119:19: 'I am a sojourner on earth . . .' it is God in person who speaks!) in order to walk with them, to be a companion of all strangers and exiles on the earth. The person, therefore, comes to see himself or herself as welcomed, as being in a gifted space[2] where erring brings one into a new relationship with the truth, where possessing is no longer a dominating element because it is replaced by gratuity, 'where the meaning of existence is no longer merely care for oneself but care of and responsibility for each other's well-being.'[3]

In this work we will strive to explore some social practices characteristic of the Semitic world in an effort to understand in particular the evolution of ideas and practices of hospitality in the geographical cradle common to all three monotheistic religions. We will examine to what extent the practices of hospitality change when the notion of God himself becomes a kind of moral code for man's behavior. But the heart of our research will be to analyze the history of the reception and interpretation of the biblical narrative of Abraham's hospitality at Mamre (*cf* Gen 18), a paradigmatic narrative of hospitality and not merely a pearl of literature in the Old Testament. Our objective is not so much a detailed comparison of the narrative in order to extract some kind of exegetical novelty but, by taking advantage of an extraordinary interpretative tradition, to reach a comprehensive reinterpretation of the text, situating it in the context of a Theology of Religions. We believe, in fact, that around the theme of hospitality we can weave a conceptual network that is at the basis of 'a pedagogy of interreligious dialogue'. However, there is no dialogue without the recognition of an otherness and personal uniqueness. This is all the more reason to appreciate the importance of the practice of hospitality which reorganizes in a new way our very understanding of individual identity. Only when we are welcomed

---

2. *Cfr* Ronchi E, Presentazione in *Lo straniero: nemico, ospite o profeta?* (Milano: San Paolo, 2006), 10.

3. C Di Sante, *L'io ospitale* (Fossano; Esperienze, 2001), 107.

can anything really begin: the human person experiences this unconsciously from the moment of conception and later, even more so, in being born and during the early years of life.

Hospitality is a precarious and fragile gift. From the beginning of the practice of this fundamental human virtue it becomes obvious that we cannot remain guests indefinitely. The condition of a guest, of being in transit, is a precondition for an expanded vision of those who give as well as those who receive hospitality. We hope that we ourselves will benefit by this contribution with a widening of the horizon of our gaze upon the world and all peoples.

From the outset, I would like to express my profound gratitude to Elena Bolognesi and Brigitta Bianchi who, with their patient and kindly gaze, have accompanied all the stages of the preparation of this writing, enabling with their suggestions to make it more accessible to those who will undertake this reading (Sisters Emmanuella, sister Mary Columba and, finally, Miss Venessa De Obaldia, for English manuscript).

Part One

Hospitality in the Traditions of the Three Abrahamic Religions

Introduction

It is not possible for a Christian to question the meaning of hospitality, or the sense of what it means to be a foreigner and a citizen, apart from the biblical reference of God's will for a 'land of welcome' and the dream of peaceful relations among creatures. This reference has a very vast horizon, equivalent to that which is defined as the 'Semitic world'.

In reality, we should speak in the plural because there is no single Semitic world or Semitic concept, although, drawing from its usage in the Bible, a much broader meaning has been adopted today. With the term 'Semitic' reference is made to a blend of people whose lineage, essentially linguistic (Arabic, Hebrew, Canaanite, Akkadian, and Aramaic), does not erase strong cultural differences and the existence of various cults, as noted in the genealogical account of Genesis 10.[1] Giovanni Garbini speaks of two successive levels of religiosity: one of an agricultural and sedentary type, beginning from the fourth century BCE, generally called 'Canaanite,' and a second expressive of a nomadic or a semi-nomadic culture, highly clannish in nature.[2]

---

1. There was probably a time when non-Semitic peoples were speaking Semitic languages among themselves, like the Philistines in Palestine. At one point, the idea of a proto-Semitic language had developed. However, it is difficult today to admit the existence of an original Semitic root that, as a result of successive migrations, would give rise to various Semitic peoples: the Akkadians in Mesopotamia, the Canaanites in Syria and Palestine (3000 BCE), the Amorites in Mesopotamia and Syria (2000 BCE), the Israelites and the Syrians in Palestine and Syria (1200 BCE), and finally the Arabs of Muhammad, who were the protagonists of the most important and recent Semitic immigrations.
2. *Cf* G Garbini, 'La religione della Siria antica', in G Castellani, editor *Storia delle Religioni*, II (Torino: UTET, 1971), 195–231.

Therefore, it is necessary to make some choices and we would like to concentrate our attention on a geographical area which is very confined: the region of Canaan, between Syria and Palestine, where each Semitic group had its own national or clannish god (according to forms of henotheism). It is not easy to determine the identity of the many peoples who occupied this region before the arrival of the Hebrew tribes. It was a question of populations that interchangeably lived apart and sometimes together, who were both natives and foreigners, and therefore in transit, always ready to depart. This mobility justifies in part a weak national self-consciousness and, more pointedly, a weak ethnic self-consciousness[3]. It is in this context that the history of the Patriarchs of Israel is situated. One can legitimately ask if the Book of Genesis can be used to reconstruct this account of the primordial Hebrew clan, whose nomadic life dates back to at least the second millennium BCE! The debate remains open and the speculations very divergent. Jacques Pirenne recalls that Genesis is the narrative of the history of Israel's earliest clans, translated in the form of personal stories. In them the Palestinian folklore would be well preserved and the state of the institutions well defined, to make them a reliable source for understanding the society of Israel during the nomadic era.[4]

---

3. Speaking strictly theologically, it would be interesting to compare this weak ethnic self-consciousness with the undeniable ethnocentric connotations in the Old Testament theology of election, not limited only to the post-exilic period. Certainly, this dimension always coexists with the theme of conversion understood as a possibility of the insertion of foreigners into the Chosen People.

4. J Pirenne, *La Société Hébraïque d'après la Bible* (Paris: Albin Michel, 1965), 11, FN 1. We will return to the question of the historicity of the lineage of the Patriarchs when we address the question of Abraham.

Hospitality in the Jewish Tradition

The Origins of the Chosen People

An ontological 'otherness'

By analysing the biblical references, most experts agree in situating the story of the Exus around the thirteenth century BCE. The patriarchal period would be placed, consequently, in the first part of the second millennium BCE. More precisely, it is during the era of Hammurabi, the best-known ruler of the first Babylonian dynasty and author of the famous Code bearing his name. Also situated during this period is the migration of groups, probably nomads, who would gradually occupy the region of present-day Syria and Palestine, from the country of Amur (west of the Semitic region), as witnessed by numerous cuneiform documents and archaeological excavations. This could be the historic cradle of the ancestors of Israel. It is an assumption which, however, entails problems still not completely solved, because how the achievements of the Patriarchs of Israel have been transmitted for about a thousand years before they were finally put in writing around

---

Box 1 The Other, The Stranger, The Immigrant: A Lexical Search

Among the fundamental terms of the Hebrew Bible in the definition of 'the stranger,' are firstly *zar*, which recurs most often in the Pentateuch and designates 'the other far away', sometimes one 'rejected' by society or community, like the leper. Here, it refers to a more cultural and spiritual sense: the *zar* is the one who is not a neighbor, the one who is not part of the family, a foreigner to the culture, that is to say, 'secular' or 'profane' (cf. Ex 29:33). In certain prophetic texts, the term *zârîm* seems to represent a foreigner in the ethnic and political sense: the Assyrians, the Babylonians, the Egyptians, and all others (cf. Jr 30:8; Ezk 7:21; 11:9). According to the latter sense, *zar* represents a hostile character: in the prophetic oracles, in fact, foreigners are often enemies and oppressors. Finally, there is a meaning with a greater moral connotation: for example, one can talk about 'foreignness / strangeness' as referring to adultery. This variety of meanings is well captured by the Greek terminology derived from LXX, which translates *zar* as *heteros, echtros, laos* and even once with *pornê*. The term *nokrî* has a mainly ethnic meaning, namely, 'a passing stranger' in the sense of the unknown (cf. Pr 5:20; 27:2.13), coming from abroad (Gn 17:12; Dt 17:15; 23:21; 1K 8:41), from a distant land (Dt 29:21), or not conformable. He is one with whom one has no family or tribal ties, (Gn 31:15), or again, one who has only accidental and temporary contact with the inhabitants of the village because he is a traveler or a merchant.

If he has the right to hospitality ("The sojourner has not lodged in the street; I have opened my doors to the wayfarer;" Jb 31:32), customary laws are not applicable to him and he may be subjected to certain discrimination. The book of Deuteronomy does not hesitate to mention that one can demand from these foreigners interest which is forbidden to be claimed from the Israelite (Dt 23:20). The Greek translates *nokrî* with *allogenes, allotrios, allophylos, idios, xenos*.

The *ghêr* is distinguished from nokrî and from zar because we are dealing here with an immigrant or a resident alien, not a native but someone who has integrated (a condition that applies also to the Levites, members of the priestly tribe, who do not have their own territory and whose protective laws resemble the *ghérîm* (cf. Dt 12:12; 14:29; 26:12). Abraham is a ghêr in Hebron (Gn 23:4), like Moses in Midian (Ex 2:22; 18:3). This term is used continuously in Deuteronomy and is also often associated with the widow and the orphan, those weak and without property, who are on the margins of society and at the mercy of those who possess substantial wealth. Unlike the previous terms, *ghêr* does not define an ethnic category because it can refer to an Israelite. The same term may apply to a group as well as to individuals. The Israelites were *ghérîm* in Egypt ("You shall not wrong a stranger or oppress him, for you were strangers in the land of Egypt;" Ex 22, 21). The LXX translates this term as *xenos, paroikos, proselutos*.

the ninth to eighth Century BCE[1] have yet to be explained. Certainly, writing did not exist or, in any case, was not accessible to nomads. For several centuries, therefore, the traditions were transmitted only orally, which allowed the preservation and transmission of memories but also the creation of multiple adjustments. The complexity of the story of the origins of Israel appears in all its amplitude. Before becoming a single people, as we are reminded by the narrative texts of the Old Testament, Israel was a patchwork of many various groups, a mixed multitude: 'The sons of Israel left Rameses for Succoth, about six hundred thousand on the march—all men—not counting their families. People of various sorts joined them in great numbers; there were flocks, too, and herds in immense droves' (Ex 12:37–38).[2] Evidently, non-Israelite elements integrated the chosen People[3] and the very diversified Hebrew genealogy testifies to this variety of origins. Other sources reinforce this hypothesis and at times call some groups with the surname of *ghérîm*, namely, exiled migrants and pilgrims who come from other tribes, cities or nations, without protections or privileges.[4] For this reason, Israel has always considered and will continue to consider its ancestors as nomads and migrants, defining itself as a foreigner: a definition that reveals a very

---

1. *Cf* M Quesnel-P Gruson, editor, *La Bible et sa culture. Ancien Testament,* I (Paris: Desclée de Brouwer, 2000), 85. We must remember that the historical methodology of Eastern antiquity does not correspond to that currently practiced in the West. We have inherited from the Greeks the concern to link events and to sort them in the sense of the importance and to highlight connections. The Eastern historian sometimes places the most insignificant facts on the same level as those most relevant and correlates disparate sources with often contradictory traditions (*cf* M-J Stève, *Sur les chemins de la Bible* (Paris: Athaud, Paris 1961), 17.
2. Bible quotations are taken from *The Jerusalem Bible* (New York: Doubleday & Company, 1966).
3. See also Jos 6:22–25 (the house of Rahab is preserved from the destruction of Jericho); Jg 1:22–26 (The people of Benjamin did not drive out the Jebusites who dwelt in Jerusalem; so the Jebusites have dwelt with the people of Benjamin to this day); Gen 38 (Judah, the fourth son of Jacob and Leah, married a Canaanite woman named Shua; he gave his eldest son to another Canaanite woman named Tamar). Or again, the great assembly at Shechem (Jos 24), which seems to allude to a multitude of different tribes, each with its own preferred deity. We could cite many more examples.
4. *Cf* I Cardellini, 'Stranieri ed "emigrati-residenti" in una sintesi di teologia storico-biblica', in *Rivista Biblica* XL (1992): 129–181. We will return to the question of terminology of the alien in the Bible and, in particular, in the Hebrew language.

profound theological meaning essential to the understanding of the history of the Chosen People.

The theme of the stranger is, in fact, profoundly biblical; not simply a concept positioned as something essential to Revelation, but a notion that accurately describes the path of the 'Saints of God': from Abraham, the migrant of Yahweh, to Christ himself, who had no place to lay his head. When St Paul helps us to deepen a believer's attitude towards life, he makes reference to the faith of Abraham, who 'set out, without knowing where he was going' (Heb 11:8). Breaking away from the violence of the world, as evidenced by the episode of the Tower of Babel, Abraham accepts being in this world as one 'cast out' and isolated. He allows himself to be seduced by the voice of God and leaves his country, his family, the house of his father, to become a pilgrim, a 'passing stranger' (*ghêr* and *tôšab*,[5] Gen 23:4). Departing without knowing where he would go, toward ever new and never definitive destinations, this migrant of God becomes the model of the believer. He enters into an uncertainty lived as a grace of receptivity to the newness of divine love. Abraham does not autonomously choose his own paths of existence in order to receive them from an "Other". He embarks on a journey to enter into communion of life with God; a geographical wandering that reveals the inner adventure promised to all humanity.[6] He thus assumes the responsibilities of an evolving experience.

Later, the epic story of Moses will set the slavery of Egypt in Jewish memory (a slavery that originated as hospitality from pharaoh granted to Jacob in the land of Goshen; *cf* Gen 47:1–12). The name of the first son of Moses will crystallize this episode: Gershom, meaning 'I am a stranger in a foreign land' (Ex 2:22), is based on the root *ghêr*.

---

5. See details on the following page.
6. It is no coincidence that all the places of passage of the Patriarch's caravan mentioned in the scriptures are classic stages of Semitic nomadism. Harran, for example, the first stage of his pilgrimage, was a crossroads of major Syro-Mesopotamian thoroughfares: on one side the road between Aleppo and Nineveh, on the other between Babylon and Anatolia. At the same time, this site was a center of pilgrimage because of its sanctuary dedicated to the moon god Sin. The moon was, in fact, the heavenly body that was dearest to a caravan that traveled preferably at night, to avoid the daytime heat and to qualify for a particular lighting that only a sojourn in the East allows one to fully appreciate.

But who is the stranger in the Old Testament according to the Talmudic tradition? In this research we cannot investigate in depth an etymological analysis of the 'vocabulary of foreignness.' The Hebrew language uses different words to describe it, reflecting the socio-political-religious historical shifts that denounce, in the end, the absence of specific terms to define hospitality. At the same time, the Hebrew nouns used to define 'guest' or 'pilgrim' ('*oreach*) are not frequently used in the Bible and never in the Pentateuch.[7] As Philippe Bornet underlines:

> It seems that the Hebrew Bible does not address the concept of a pilgrim received as a guest in any particular way. Hence, within the biblical corpus the notion of hospitality is, if not non-existent, at least not frequently mentioned, contrary to the practice of hospitality itself, whose various accounts would suggest otherwise.[8]

Returning to the patriarch Abraham, God had given him the key to interpret his wandering: 'I will give to you and to your descendants after you the land you are living in, the whole land of Canaan, to own in perpetuity, and I will be your God . . .' (Gen 17:8). Stated differently, the land of Canaan was promised to Abraham and his descendants, but God would remain the real owner. Israel, *ghêr* of God, is no other than a renter ('Land shall not be sold in perpetuity, for the land belongs to me, and to me you are only strangers and guests' Lev 25:23). This idea contains in principle the spiritual attitude that we find in the Psalms. The Israelite knows that he has no right before God and he wants only to be his guest ('Lord, who has the right to enter your tent, or to live on your holy mountain? The man whose way of life is blameless, who always does what is right, who speaks the truth from his heart, whose tongue is not used for slander' Ps 15 [v 14]:1–2). Israel recognises that he is a stranger in his own home, in transit like all his ancestors ('Yahweh, hear my prayer, listen to

---

7. A Even-Shoshan, in A New Concordance of the Bible (Grand Rapids: Baker, 1989) cites four occasions: Jg 19:17; 2 S 12:4; Jer 9:1; and 14:8.

8. P Bornet, 'Entre normes religieuses et impératifs éthiques', in A Montandon, editor, *Le livre de l'hospitalité*, (Paris: Bayard, 2004), 145. This quote, as are all those from non-Italian sources included in this volume, is our translation. For some more details on the lexical search to define the stranger in all its features, refer to the insert on the previous page.

my cry for help, do not stay deaf to my crying. I am your guest, and only for a time, a nomad like all my ancestors', Ps 39 [v 38]:12) and again: 'Exile though I am on earth, do not hide your commandments from me' Ps 119 [v 118]: 19). In more general terms, it corroborates the transitory nature of human life in this world and, therefore, is expressive of divine hospitality. Abraham himself, the first among all the ancestors of Israel, is actually without a plot of personal land and his territory will never be a possession, but solely a hope that involves a simple small 'anticipation:' the cave of Machpela ('opposite Mamre' according to tradition; Gen 25:9). There will always be a faith like that of Abraham's to believe that Israel would still have a future in his homeland! It is precisely from the small plot of Machpela that will develop into the territory of the future nation of God's people, whose heirs do not cease to be the prototype of the 'permanent migrant', in biblical history as well as post-biblically, in the Mediterranean basin first, then in Europe and eventually the entire world.

The elements we have just sketched give the story of Abraham a very original character when compared to that of the Ulysses, that other great pilgrim of ancient history. The great philosopher Emmanuel Levinas reminds us that, if Ulysses represents the archetype of the human vocation as an eternal return to one's origins, a reclaiming of one's 'authentic self' (as in fact, he will return to Ithaca, his homeland), Abraham, by contrast, offers a very different image of the human condition: his is that of a 'journey of no return.' It is here that we find the uniqueness of biblical faith. Jean-Louis Ska, a Belgian Jesuit and professor at the Biblical Institute in Rome, writes thus:

> The ideal of Israel, on this point, is quite different from that of Greece. In the great epic of the Odyssey, the ultimate goal of the hero is to return home and find again his wife and family. The ideal is, then, to return in a known world, to what rightfully belongs to the hero because he is the owner and the legitimate sovereign. He is again at 'home.' For Homer, the parable of existence is a long journey, filled with trials and difficulties, but the parable takes one back to the point of origin. He who comes back has a mature personality, rich in extensive experience, and eventually 'finds himself.' Again, the ideal of Socrates is 'know thyself,' according to the famous oracle of Delphi. In the Greek perspective, the ultimate aim of the human adventure is to 'return home' after a long exile.

If for the Greek the human vocation is that of a 'return' to one's authentic self, the Bible in general and the figure of Abraham in particular suggest a much different image of the human condition: that of a departure without return. The real life is beyond the known world and the price of an authentic existence is high because it entails the risk of losing everything without knowing what will be found at the end of the journey. Odysseus returns home and finds his father Laertes; Abraham abandons his father, departs definitely from him. Ulysses finds his son Telemachus; Abraham is asked to sacrifice his son. Ulysses returns to free the faithful Penelope from suitors who want to marry her; Abraham goes to an unknown destination with a sterile bride, who has not assured him offspring. The 'Odyssey' of Ulysses is contrasted with the 'Exus' of Abraham: 'I am Yahweh who brought you out of Ur of the Chaldeans to make you heir to this land' (Gen 15:7). Ulysses finds identity in the world of his 'own,' while Abraham goes to look for it 'elsewhere,' in the universe of the 'other'.[9]

Alongside this philosophical and theological reading, we can, however, talk about the real historical existence of Israel just at the beginning of the long and difficult process of stabilization of the nomadic tribes in the land of Canaan; because a people can only begin to write their history after putting down roots in a land. The very creation of the myth of a common ancestor responds to the need to find a single point of reference to compensate for so much diversity; as also to the need to justify an exclusive and common relationship to a God who will not fall short in the fulfilment of his promises.

Integration in a semi-nomadic context

As the biblical scholar Gian Luigi Prato recalls, history shows that to see oneself as a stranger can become a means of self-defence, a way of differentiating oneself from those with whom one lives. In other words, the concept of 'foreigner' is created, on the one hand, to define others, legitimizing one's own presence and rights in a given place and to avoid the paradoxical risk of being considered a stranger in one's own home. But, from another perspective, one can define

---

9. J-L Ska, *Abramo e i suoi ospiti. Il patriarca e i credenti nel Dio unico* (Bolonga: EDB), 18–19.

'foreigner' to express a kind of irreducibility of the other, which is a condition prior to the encounter with someone 'other than oneself' (in this case, the religious factor plays a key role in determining a diversity that is a unique expression of the relationship to God and its transference to a symbolic and cultural sphere). However, often one goes from theological-symbolic considerations to a geographic and ethnic characterization of diversity.[10] One can legitimately ask what the relationship is that develops between the consciousness of being a foreigner, expressed in terms of 'native foreignness' or 'original nomadism,' and what that nomadism actually implied in the Syria-Palestinian region of the second millennium BCE. Referring to this epoch, Gian Luigi Prato tells us, in sociology one talks about a 'dimorphic society,' that is to say of a society engaging at the same time (but at different times of the year) in agriculture and sheep farming. Nomadism is no longer the permanent displacement of a large multitude of migratory groups, but a much-reduced form of local and seasonal transhumance, which varies according to the geographical configuration of the pertinent regions.[11] In the case of nomadism, or rather the semi-nomadic pastoral peoples, these moves were made on foot or donkey, behind the flocks; therefore they were very limited and characterized by frequent stops. One could not walk long distances nor, indeed, go anywhere (since owned land did not exist), nor at any time (the seasons dictated the movements).[12] These relocations, relatively small, were, however,

---

10. *Cf* GL Prato, 'Straniero:verso una definizione analogica del concetto in riferimento al territorio siro-palestinese del TB-FI e all'Israele delle origini', in I Cardellini, editor, *Lo 'straniero nella Bibbia'*, Ricerche Storico Bibliche (Bolonga: EDB, 1-2 1996), 17–40 (39–40).

11. We have for example horizontal movements to grazing outside in winter transhumance in Mesopotamia or vertical displacements toward Anatolian summer pastures (*cf* GL Prato, 'Straniero:verso una definizione analogica', 36).

12. Ernest Vardiman describes a condition which could correspond to that experienced by the Patriarchs of Israel: 'The movements that a flock made in one year were about a dozen and could be grouped into two cycles. The winter flock would graze in the portion of the desert "property" (those areas traditionally attributed to a precise family, specifically with the family well, but there were no official property contracts), made fertile by rain. Then, in the summer the flock moved to "paid" pastures, to lands of stable farmers. Abraham, for example, had to ask for hospitality from Abimelech, king of Gerar. This meant that he remained on the fields of Gerar "as a guest" and that to have the right to pasture

occasions for contacts and, sometimes also, the crossing over of different groups.

Such a sociological picture explains, at least in part, the very complex origins of the people of Israel, witnessed in the Bible itself. For example, the prophet Ezekiel, personifying Jerusalem, after having condemned the abominations, presents their identity as follows: 'By origin and birth you belong to the land of Canaan. Your father was an Amorite and your mother a Hittite' (Ezk 16:3).

'Amorites' (sometimes 'Amorite') is a term that has multiple meanings, even in the Bible. In certain texts it represents a specific population of Canaan; in others it designates any pre-Israelite population. Originally, for the inhabitants of Mesopotamia it denotes a geographic term: the West.[13] The biblical texts then, among others, make mention of Indo-European peoples as the 'Hittites' (Gen 23:20), which put an end to the first Amorite dynasty of Babylon in the mid-sixteenth century BCE. Again, the Bible uses the term 'Hittite' to designate generically the non-Israelite population of the region of Syria and Palestine, yet the non-Israelite tribes of this region are of course much more numerous! Michel Du Buit, in his *Géographie de la Terre Sainte*, enumerates among foreign peoples: Canaanites, Philistines, Phoenicians, Arameans, Ammonites, Moabites, Edomites and Arabs.[14]

In essence, one cannot seriously consider the complexity of this framework if one forgets to mention the diversity of tribes that formed and structured Israel.

---

and watering had to deliver sheep and oxen to Abimelech (Gen 21: 23-27).' EE Vardiman, *Nomadi* (Milano: Rusconi, 1981), 43.

13. See H Cazelles, 'Les Patriarches entre the Mésopotamie et l'Egypte', in A Lemaire, editor, *Le Monde de la Bible* (Paris: Gallimard, Paris 19980, 423–431 (425–426). Guy Vanhoomissen recalls that, in the Bible, 'Canaanite' means all that Israel is not. The Canaanite is, in some ways, a 'negative:' the perfect reverse image of what Israel should be. This biblical Canaanite does not exist as such. We are at the level of representations, and the danger posed by the Canaanite is more threatening as an internal danger and not just an external temptation.

14. M Du Buit, *Géographie de la Terre Sainte* (Paris: Cerf, 1958¹), 137–146. We must not forget that the settlement of the Jews in the Promised Land was not the result of a systematic campaign. It happened in successive waves, at the hands of tribes or groups of tribes. The occupation of the plains, inhabited by civilized peoples and armies, among other things, was not possible.

16   *Strangers With God*

> There have been [Cazelles continues] several successive waves
> of migration that demolished Canaan. They transported tribes
> of peoples which were sometimes of the same blood but, at
> other times, were mixed through alliances and adoptions,
> prior to ultimately constituting a people (*'am*), an army
> (*qahal*) and a state monarchy.[15]

Historical studies, which are predicated on the basis of archaeological research and on a tradition of sufficiently rich texts, are essential to sketch a picture of the situation in the land of Canaan, the destination of the wanderings of the Chosen People after their Exus from Egypt. However, it is not with anthropological categories that one can evaluate the theological idea of a nomadic lifestyle expressive of a nostalgic desire to return to a society of pure origins; where one lives in the context of an austere desert, as opposed to an urban and sedentary culture always increasingly corrupt. It is the ideological reading of history which offers the qualities of regeneration and purification in a place as hostile in itself as the desert.

---

15. H Cazelles, 'Les Patriarches entre the Mésopotamie et l'Egypte', 429.

Biblical Foundations of Hospitality

Historical-Sociological Foundations

In the Torah, the references to Israel's own destiny and to the identity of its members remain essential to understanding the significance of laws relating to the stranger. To justify them they are theologically contextualized: they are attributed to the authority and grace of God (as in *The Book of the Covenant*); to the love of God as the foundation of the election (*Deuteronomy*); and to the holiness of the Creator present among his people (*The Sacerdotal Laws*). This theological nucleus is, however, constantly placed in relation with the experience and historical path of the Chosen People and, particularly, with their Exus from Egypt. In fact, the period of the settlement of the Hebrews in the land of Canaan is a crucial turning point in the creation of an Israelite identity and, subsequently, in the perception of the other, of the stranger: the members of the Chosen People are to behave toward those who are in a situation of Exus in the same way as God acted toward them when they were in the land of Pharaoh.[1]

"If a stranger lives with you in your land, do not molest him. You must count him as one of your own countrymen and love him as yourself—for you were once strangers yourself in Egypt" (Leev 19:34; *cf* also Ex 22:20). And again: 'Love the stranger then, for you were strangers in the land of Egypt' (Deut 10:19). In short, the historical motivation would seem, here, even more important than theological reasons to ratify the sacredness of solicitude toward a guest (and this

---

1. *Cf* F Crüsemann, 'La Torah face au nouveau nationalisme', in *Concilium*, 248 (1993): 119–134.

pertains in the same way to a refugee excluded from his tribe after a murder or other serious offense, as we shall see below).

This finding, however, is challenged by a more ideological narrative of the Exus from Egypt where the meaning of *ghérîm* (resident aliens) is changed to that of *'abadîm* (slaves). The semantic change involves a fundamental ambiguity. While in the book of Deuteronomy especially, Egypt is often equated with a 'house of slavery' in which Israel is *'ebed* (servant) and, therefore, treated as a slave and not as a resident alien (*ghêr* is the singular of *ghérîm*),[2] on the other hand it also speaks of *ghérîm* in order to define the status of the Hebrews in Egypt and to draw the theological foundations of humanitarian law in favor of the poor and afflicted who are to be welcomed in Land of Canaan.[3] This contrast between these interpretations is clearly seen in two passages of Deuteronomy. In Chapter 23, we are urged to respect the land of Egypt because Israel has lived there as a 'guest' or *ghêr* 'You are not to regard [. . .] the Egyptian as detestable, because you were a stranger [*ghêr*] in his land. The third generation of children born to these may be admitted to the assembly of Yahweh' (Deut 23:8b–9); but in chapter 4 of the book it is specified: 'but as for you, Yahweh has taken you, and brought you out from the furnace of iron, from Egypt, to be a people all his own, as you still are today' (Deut 4:20). According to Innocenzo Cardellini, these apparent contradictions cannot be understood without assuming a strong theological elaboration of historical memories, already previously transformed into epic meanings: the migration of Israel was not only the result of economic and social consequences, nor was the Exus simply the inevitable conclusion of obligations increasingly heavier in the land of Egypt. The experience of the Hebrew people in Egypt is conceived as a time of a moral rebound, of a real divine election.

This theological revision of historical elements provides an interpretation for the next stages of the history of Israel. But in the long period of wandering in the desert, sociological factors add to this dialectic because compliance with the obligations of hospitality is also a condition for survival in a society based on tribal and family solidarity. More precisely, this is a 'society of honor' where, because

---

2. There are innumerable Biblical references: Deut 5:6.15; 6:12; 7:8; 8:14; 13:11; 15:15; 16:12; 24:18; Ex 13:3. 14; 20:2; Jos 24:17; Jg 6:8; 2 Kgs 17:7; Jer 34:13; etc.

3. *Cf* I Cardellini, 'Stranieri ed "emigrati-residenti" in una sintesi di teologia storico-biblica', 135.

Biblical Foundations of Hospitality

there is no 'democratic policing', the proprietor can exercise revenge and assure protection within the area he claims to control. The tribe must be 'restrained so as to be mobile and strong to guarantee its security; autonomous groups of families who consider themselves descendants of a common ancestor whose name they hold. Its members consider themselves brothers, united by blood ties. They are, according to the Hebrew expression, the flesh and bones of one another (*cf* 2 S 19:13).'[4] A first level of this solidarity is expressed in the institution of the *gôël* that, as Roland De Vaux tells us, will survive Israel's special time of wandering to become a pillar of family institutions at the heart of clan culture. In fact, blood relationship— real or supposed (it could be extended to non-original individuals who are integrated in a given group)—creates a solidarity among all members of the tribe. This very strong feeling seems to persist long after the settlement in the Promised Land. The honor or dishonor of an individual member is transferred to the whole group. Thus, a curse is extended to the whole race and God punishes for the sins of the fathers their children unto the fourth generation (*cf* Ex 20:5). Conversely, just as a whole group is affected by the error of its leader (*cf* 2 Sam 21:1), the whole family is likewise honored for the merits of its valiant chief. The leader of the group, for his part, expresses solidarity, positively, in the duty to protect all the members of his community, be they trustworthy or oppressed. The practice of the *gôël*, a term whose root meaning is 'to redeem' or 'reclaim' but also 'to protect,' goes back to an Arab context. Once again Father de Vaux, who has for long studied this Semitic institution, specifies:

> 'The most serious obligation of the Israelite *gôël* is to assure blood vengeance [...] The blood of a relative must be avenged with the killing of the one responsible for the crime, or, in his absence, with the murder of another of his family. Within the tribe blood vengeance is not exacted but the guilty party is punished or excluded [...] This law is expressed with a savage violence in the song of Lamech: "I killed a man for wounding

---

4. JL Vesco, 'Les lois sociales du Livre de l'Alliance', in *Revue Thomiste*, LXVIII (1968): 241–264 (244).

20   *Strangers With God*

me, a boy for striking me. Sevenfold vengeance is taken for
Cain, but seventy-sevenfold for Lamech' (Gen 4:23–24).[5]

This duty, exercised by all the members of a tribe, was permitted in
order to establish the prestige of the tribal group; instead it threatened
to unleash a chain of continuous vengeance, even though the intention
was exactly the opposite: to curb the dangerous degeneration of a
private justice, in a society without centralized, impartial protection.[6]
The practice of the *gô'ēl*, over time, will be first limited to the family
(even though it was not always easy to define the legal boundaries
of a family) and then progressively replaced with preference to
compensations of an economic order.

Theological foundations

But there is also a solidarity that is expressed beyond the ties of blood,
a duty which is based, first of all, on the love of God and the need to
imitate Yahweh '[who is] never partial, never to be bribed. It is he
who sees justice done for the orphan and the widow, who loves the
stranger and gives him food and clothing' (Deut 10:17-18; *cf* also Ps
146 and 145:9). The poor, the immigrant, the widow and the orphan
are traditionally mentioned as the recipients of the duty of hospitality
which extends as well to the Levite and one who commits murder. We
remember that the Levites represent the priestly caste, the members
of the tribe of Levi that, from the beginning, were excluded from the
division of the promised Land, receiving as heritage only their service
to God ('Yahweh said to Aaron, "You shall have no inheritance in
their land, no portion of it among them shall be yours. It is I who
will be your portion and your inheritance among the sons of Israel"'
(Num 18:20).[7] A murderer (that is one who killed by accident, without

---

5. R De Vaux, *Les institutions de l'Ancien Testament*, I (Paris: Cerf, 1989[5]), 21.
    Lamech is a descendant of Cain condemned to life in the desert.
6. De Vaux points out, however, that in the institution of *gô'ēl* the rule of pure
    compensation ('a man for a man, a woman for a woman' as written in the Qu'ran)
    is reduced and a certain protection of someone against a blood vengeance
    mechanically and ruthlessly exercised is affirmed. That is why the book of
    Genesis reminds us that God placed on the forehead of Cain, the fratricide, a
    sign to protect him from the vengeance of the first comer (Gen:4:15).
7. As Anne-Cécile Pottier-Thoby states ('De la trahison à la rédemption', in A
    Montandon, *Le livre de l'hospitalité*, 118–143): 'To welcome a Levite under their

premeditation) could be received in a shrine city where hospitality had a sacred character. He could live there until the death of the high priest, to be protected against private revenge (the *gô'ēl* tradition illustrated above): 'The towns you hand over to the Levites will be the six cities of refuge, ceded by you as sanctuary for men who cause another's death' (Num 35:6). But this kind of asylum does not pertain to one who intentionally kills another: 'But should a man dare to kill his fellow by treacherous intent, you must take him even from my altar to be put to death' (Ex 21:14).

We return to the priority given to the welcome extended to foreigners and the weak: It has a theological motivation and not only natural or sociological reasons, although the evolution of social structures, as we discuss below, will impact these practices. The Law, above all as given in the Code of the Covenant (Ex 23:20–33) and in that of Holiness (Lev chapters 17–26), knows that, by requiring love for the *ghêr*, it is proposing a radical break with sociological laws, the economic or even political society of the time (and probably of all times). To love the stranger as well as the weak and to extend this provision to an enemy is a sign of the holiness of Israel (*qedûšâh*)[8] and of its special relationship with God. That God commands us to serve others without further explanation and without evident correction from the biblical data, transforms an act of justice into an act of religion. God maintains transcendence, the distance between Godself and humanity, forcing one who wants to have direct contact with God to go through the 'other'. The theme of a divine presence hidden and welcomed in the other, which continually returns in the history of religious traditions and the literature of antiquity, is first of all, then, the result of the irreducible distance between the divine and the human. This philosophical bracket, which we borrow from Levinas' reflection, allows us to emphasize the complementarity

---

roof seems to be a rare honor (Dt 12:19), at least according to what the story of Micah (in the book of Judges) seems to imply. Welcoming a wandering Levite, Micah convinced him to live with him and to become a priest of his house, hoping to attract divine graces (Jg 17: 13; 2 Kgs 4:10)', 128.

8. Paradoxically, the Hebrew root that is at the origin of this word—*qdš*—expresses the idea of diversity, of separation and election to a unique task. The Chosen People must be *qâdôš*, different from and even superior to other peoples, for the observance of the commandments (*mitsvôt*) makes their lives so different, sometimes separated from other peoples.

and undeniable correlation between individuality and belonging to a social plurality, a relationship that must be carefully considered because it has a special meaning in Israel's history, influencing— once more and among other things—his openness to the neighbor. De Fraine who, in *Adamo e la sua discendenza* combines a series of studies on the notion of 'corporate personality' in the Bible, speaks of the existence of a biblical personalism that 'proclaims the integrity of the individual person in front of the group, while admitting that this person can, in certain circumstances, represent the entire group'.[9] Stated differently, throughout all of its history, Israel retains a particularly strong consciousness of its social and religious cohesion, even though its oaths, its prayer, and its individual worship manifest a deep conviction of the irreplaceable value of the individual as a religious subject.

Welcoming the stranger in the Old Testament: between ethnocentrism and universalism

We have drawn attention to the concept of a collective Jewish identity that expressed itself in a religious bond or faith in Yahweh who convened the tribes of Israel around a common sanctuary on the occasion of great feasts. This identity, particularly strong in crisis, suffered deep transformations at the time of the installation of the Chosen People in the land of Canaan.

> The tribes are scattered in villages or towns. The rearing of flocks follows the culture of the land, which implies a division of territory for the purposes of inheritance. The unity of the social group is no longer built around ties of blood but around the soil. The population is fragmented and the fortune of each no longer depends on that of the group but on personal success in agriculture. The social system becomes hierarchical; inequality creeps in and a rural proletariat is born around wealthy landowners. The fraternal solidarity of the past is threatened. Changes in social structures require new legislation.[10]

---

9. J De Fraine, *Adamo e la sua discendenza: la concezione della personalità corporativa nella dialettica biblica dell'individuale e del collettivo* (Roma: Città Nuova, 1968), 17.

10. J-L Vesco, 'Les lois sociales du Livre de l'Alliance', 244–245.

This historic turning point imposes not only a codification in the form of legal written rules, as would seem natural, but it also represents a radical distinction between Judaic and biblical culture in comparison with the vision of other civilizations of the time. In fact, if in ancient societies the principle of solidarity remains linked to the concept of kinship where the stranger is, therefore, excluded a priori, the Jewish and biblical tradition imposes solidarity even with the latter! Such an attitude, legally codified in *The Book of the Covenant*,[11] is no longer justified by bonds of blood, but is explained by referring to the royal theology of the Ancient Orient according to which the king, by divine order, is called to take care of the rights of the weakest; among the latter are included foreigners who work as slaves and are placed under the care of a master who must ensure them food, housing and protection.[12] Innocenzo Cardellini remarks that every monarch, at the time of his election, enacts laws and decrees to assert his will to restore justice for the poor, following the mission that God has entrusted to him. But, in the Bible, the commitment to the poor is taken up by Yahweh as the true king of Israel: 'You must not molest the stranger or oppress him, for you lived as strangers in the land of Egypt [. . .] If you are harsh with them, they will surely cry out to me, and be sure I shall hear his cry' (Ex 22:20, 22).[13]

We have already referred to the historical and religious elements that, within the biblical tradition, became culturally and socially effective in reducing the ambivalence of the relationship to foreigners (we refer especially to the historical experience of the Exus and the resulting image of a God who saves). Nor do we forget theological categories

---

11. The term is used in Ex 24:7 and refers to the oldest collection of laws in Israel as we know it.

12. The Book of Deuteronomy extends the obligation of hospitality even to fugitive slaves: 'You must not allow a master to imprison a slave who has escaped from him and comes to you. He shall live with you, among you, wherever he pleases in any one of your towns he chooses; you are not to molest him' (23:16–17). Inspired by this principle, Paul urges Philemon to liberate his runaway slave Onesimus and receive him as if he were himself (Phm 10-17). Still on the subject of the rights of foreigners, including slaves, on the day of Shabbat (the Jewish rest) it should be granted to them as well: it would be inconsistent to ask of a foreigner works that a Jew cannot do (*cf* HH Cohn, *Human Rights in the Bible and Talmud* [Tel-Aviv: Mod Books, 1989], 49–50).

13. *Cf* I Cardellini, 'Prolegomenonalla XXXIII Settimana Biblica: Lo'Straniero'nella Bibbia. Aspetti storici, istituzionali e teologici', in *Ricerche Storico Biblica*, 14–15.

like those of the election and the covenant. In summary, inspired by the analysis of the biblical scholar Cardinal Gianfranco Ravasi, one could say that, if in the Old Testament the theme of an exclusive election of Israel would seem to prevail, in reality a correct hermeneutics of biblical data shows the fruitfulness of a dialectic between ethnocentrism and universalism, where the theme of the particular election of Israel does not eliminate a universal vision of salvation[14].

Let us now look at some of the stages in the evolution of Israel's relations with others in Judeo–biblical thought, as also of their perceptions of God, the 'Totally Other' (according to a definition of Karl Barth in his famous commentary on the Letter to the Romans). We will proceed thematically and not necessarily in chronological order.

Welcoming the stranger according to the legislation of Israel

It is good to dwell further on the social laws in the Code of the Covenant: a legal collection that concerns the period of transition between the entry into Canaan and the foundation of the monarchy in Israel, as found in the book of Exodus (chapters 20–24).[15] This period is symbolically placed under the authority of Moses who receives from God the 'Ten Commandments' as a fundamental document of the alliance concluded with the people liberated from slavery in Egypt, a people who have not yet been organised as a state and without a king or temple. Israel has probably borrowed from the tribes of Canaan certain legal customs, expressive therefore, of a common legislative heritage. Moreover, the Chosen People had to partially absorb the populations already installed in this region.

According to Father Vesco, the *Code of the Covenant* advances two seemingly antagonistic attitudes or dispositions toward foreigners or, more generically, toward the weak. On the one hand it proclaims the need for a radical break with the foreign populations in Canaan; on the other hand, the same Code of the Covenant, in its first part, calls for special attention with respect to the *ghérîm*. Or again, in the

---

14. *Cf* G Ravasi, 'Universalismo e particolarismo nell'Antico Testamento', in *Parola, Spirito e vita*, XXVII (1993): 11–24.
15. According to Roland de Vaux, it is the law of a society of shepherds and farmers, annexed, as is the Decalogue that precedes it, to the covenant of Sinai, but with provisions that can only apply to a population that is already settled. Also according to the research of the great Dominican scholar, the Code of the Covenant could date back to the installation in Canaan. It was still the law of a federation of tribes (*Cf* R De Vaux, *Les institutions de l'Ancien Testament*, 150ff).

second part, the same text is presented as a law received on Mount Sinai in anticipation of their occupancy of the Promised Land. This latter is an attitude of possessiveness that assumes the character of an irreducible confrontation:

> I shall be enemy to your enemies, foe to your foes. My angel will go before you and lead you to where the Amorites are and the Hittites, the Perizzites, the Canaanites, the Hivites, the Jebusites; I shall exterminate these. You must not bow down to their gods or worship them; you must not do as they do: you must destroy their gods utterly and smash their standing-stones. [. . .]. I shall send hornets in front of you to drive Hivite and Canaanite and Hittite from your presence. I shall not drive them out before you in a single year, or the land would become a desert where, to your cost, the wild beasts would multiply. [. . .]. Little by little I will drive them out before you until your numbers grow and you come into possession of the land (Ex 23:22a–24.28–30.32–33).

On the other hand, it is said:

> You must not molest the stranger or oppress him, for you lived as strangers in the land of Egypt [. . .] You must not oppress the stranger: you know how a stranger feels, for you lived as strangers in the land of Egypt [. . .] For six days you shall do your work, but stop on the seventh day, so that your ox and your donkey may rest and the son of your slave girl have a breathing space, and the stranger too (Ex 22:20 and 23:9.12).[16]

Without discounting the fact that one who has suffered oppression is easily tempted to reproduce the same behaviour when the opportunity presents itself, the sacredness of the foreigner remains, as we have already pointed out, a part of Israel's past and is intensified by religious motivation, a theological principle affirmed by the Lord himself: 'If he cries to me, I will listen, for I am full of pity' (Ex 22:26). The content of this social commandment comes from an ancient 'primary ethic'. If it represents, within a canonical logic, a counterweight to a justifiable fear in the face of a stranger and does not require, a priori, a religious and therefore superior justification, in

---

16. According to Guy Vanhoomissen, these three are only times the *ghérîm* (as foreign residents) are mentioned before the fall of Samaria (722 BCE) (*cf* G Vanhoomissen, *Dieu, son peuple et l'étranger* [Bruxelles: Lumen Vitae, 2000], 29).

the Code of the Covenant, however, it acquires a weight equal to that of other fundamental religious norms. In other words, the hospitality and goodwill accorded to foreigners and the weak are a part of Israel's relationship to God. So, even if one can detect continuity between the Covenantal Code and other oriental laws as to its formulation and its contents, the biblical legislation is based not solely on human reflection but on divine imperatives, on the demands and like actions of Yahweh himself. The social situation in Israel is complicated, however, as can be inferred from the very detailed analysis of Frank Crüsemann. He writes:

> Among the prophets of the eighth century there is still no great importance given to the question of foreigners. They are not yet placed among those peoples in need of restraint. However, with the insistent advance of Assyria and the end of the independence of many peoples and small states at the end of the eighth century BCE, a flood of refugees is unleashed. Specifically, the end of the Israelite Kingdom of the North in 722 BCE played its role and caused, for example in Jerusalem, a rapid growth of the city and the formation of districts comparable to slums. This created a new and serious problem of refugees for Israel, which will later be treated in Deuteronomy and in the Prophets but, prior to that and in a fundamental way, in the Code of the Covenant.[17]

The latter, namely, enshrines fundamental options, going from a simple safeguard of the weak to the positive commandment of fraternal solidarity:

> It denounces vehemently the process of pauperization by prohibiting lending at interest and regulating the right to a pledge. This comes to the help of the economically weak; protects the slaves; and dictates to those in charge a line of conduct.[18]

---

17. F Crüsemann, 'La Torah face au nouveau nationalisme', 122.

18. Vesco analyses in detail the elements that characterize this code, emphasizing in particular certain formerly unpublished provisions with respect to the laws of the time: The Code of Hammurabi does not stress the difference between the indigenous people and foreigners (in Babylon, an international trade center, it was most often the citizen who was in danger of falling victim to a rich stranger). Another detail: in ancient Mesopotamia interest on loans and usury were not considered to be subject to sanctions. By way of contrast, the Covenantal Code

How do we accommodate these two seemingly opposing attitudes? How do we reconcile a command of fraternal solidarity with a vision apparently exclusive of the other, a vision of irreducible separation? We have already tried to sketch a first theological response. In fact, the two attitudes are not in contradiction because they refer to two different levels: the break with foreigners is at an essentially religious level and aims to safeguard the exclusive relationship of Israel with Yahweh. When one speaks, however, of attention to the needs of the *ghêr*—who is not, it must be remembered, neither the pure and simple stranger nor the foreigner within one's own home but a local resident—one thinks of individuals who have no property of their own and work for pay, people who are not assured the protection of their interests in justice, who live outside of their tribe and, therefore, are lacking the advantages of the solidarity of their clan. Now, the obligation to treat the stranger with benevolence is not only a prefiguration of the golden rule (do unto others what you would have them do unto you) but appeals first of all to history,[19] and goes even further: 'Israel reenacts the history of salvation; it is created anew. Because he was once a guest and is so no longer, he must remember; and there is no better way to keep this memory alive except by, in turn, not oppressing the guest'.[20] We would be tempted to say that this interpretation of father Vesco is a bit too strong. In the great humanitarian concern of the People of God, can one really say that there is a new rendition of the history of salvation? Yes, to the extent that compliance with the social law becomes a sort of memorial of past history. The only true saving action remains that of Yahweh in respect to his People, who in turn express their faith by their own benevolent efforts to free others in need. According to Vesco the Code of the Covenant 'should be understood as the ensemble of clauses of the treaty of the alliance concluded between God and his people [. . .] The people are committed to practice them [social laws, ed.] in order

---

does not provide for any sanctions against unpaid debts whereas the Code of Hammurabi as well as Roman law stipulate imprisonment. There are many commentaries on the legislative body of the Old Testament. We have referred to the studies of Father Jean-Luc Vesco and Rinaldo Fabris but also cite Gianni Barbiero ('Lo straniero nel Codice dell'Alleanza e nel Codice di Santita tra separazione ed accoglienza', in I Cardellini, *Lo 'straniero' nella Bibbia*, 41–69).

19. 'Israel must remember his past experience so as not to inflict on others the harassment he once knew' (J-L Vesco, 'Les lois sociales du Livre de l'Alliance', 250).
20. Vesco, 'Les lois sociales du Livre de l'Alliance', 250.

28   *Strangers With God*

to remain faithful to the contracted alliance. If they are transgressed, the alliance is broken'.[21] In other words, since this alliance between the people and God is contracted in the first person, to break this contract would mean to rupture the relationship with God himself! Instead, Israel can please God and keep his relationship with God by freeing the slave and protecting the widow and the orphan.

The Book of Deuteronomy, in particular its legislative section (Dt 12-26), constitutes a real and proper code that regroups, according to a predefined order, small collections of laws of varying origin. It is these texts that probably served as a reference for the great legislative reform that took place around 622 BCE and included Samaria as well: 'the necromancers and wizards, the household gods and idols, and all the abominations to be seen in the land of Judah and in Jerusalem, all these were swept away by Josiah to give effect to the words of the Law written in the book found by Hilkiah the priest in the Temple of Yahweh' (2 Kgs 23:24). Now, according to the study of Vanhoomissen:

> The Code is not satisfied to resume the prohibition to exploit the stranger: more positively, it goes beyond the legal, cultic and social prescriptions that simultaneously concern the Levite, the stranger, the widow and the orphan. There are several measures—continues our author—(the third year tithe, the gleanings, the Sabbath, the days of celebration, etc) to offer aid to the socially vulnerable and to stimulate the consciences of the leaders and of the people: the tithing is to serve all those who are in need, including the alien: 'Then the Levite (since he has no share or inheritance with you), the stranger, the orphan and the widow who live in your towns may come and eat and have all they want. So shall the Yahweh your God bless you in all the work that your hands undertake' (Deut 14:29). The stranger is associated with the joy of the holidays in which he participates as do the widow and the orphan (Dt 16:11.14). The treatment of the employee must be the same for all, Israelite or 'a stranger who lives in your towns' (Deut 24:14).[22]

If the *Code of the Covenant* already exceeded the simply legal level of precepts in the founding of the commandments on the affirmation

---

21. Vesco, 'Les lois sociales du Livre de l'Alliance', 250.
22. G Vanhoomissen, *Dieu, son peuple et l'étranger*, 30–31.

of a compassionate God, the Code of Deuteronomy offers an equally unprecedented statement as the basis of its measures for the protection of foreigners: 'God loves the stranger' (Deut 10:18). Little given to abstraction, Israel often gives ideas an affective coloring: to know, for the Israelite, is already to love. When the notion of love penetrates the religious psychology of the biblical person, it is imbued with a rich and concrete human experience. At the same time, this raises many questions. Can God, who is so great, so pure, lower himself to love someone so small and insignificant, a sinner? And if God does so love mankind, how could a man or woman not respond to this love with love? What is the relationship between God's love and the return of love on the part of humanity? The various religions strive, each in its own way, to give an answer to these questions, often falling into one of two opposite extremes: relegate divine love to an inaccessible sphere to maintain the distance between God and mankind; or, by making God present, reduce God's love to mere human love. To this religious concern, the Bible answers with clarity: God has taken the initiative of a dialogue of love with humanity. That said, the statement 'God loves the stranger' remains surprising in the Old Testament, because it serves as a counterweight to the love of God for Israel: 'It was for love of you and to keep the oath he swore to your fathers that Yahweh brought you out with his mighty hand and redeemed you from the house of slavery, from the power of Pharaoh king of Egypt' (Deut 7:8). But, as Vanhoomissen points out, the verb 'to love,' with reference to God as its subject, is even more rare: There are only three occasions in the Old Testament, the one we have just mentioned; another that has as object the ancestors of the chosen people: 'Because he loved your fathers and chose their descendants after them, he brought you out of Egypt, openly showing his presence and his great power . . .' (Deut 4:37); and a third refers to Israel in general: 'Yahweh your God will be true to the covenant and the kindness he promised your fathers solemnly. He will love you and bless you and increase your numbers . . .' (Deut 7:12–13). But among the Israelites there lives also the foreigner, recipient of the same love of God. Then, the love of a God who takes the initiative becomes an exhortation to the children of Israel, so that they model their behavior on that of God. The invitation to love the alien remains even more unique. 'It is the only time in all of Deuteronomy in which Israel is exhorted to love someone other than God, or something other than his commandments'.[23] Vanhoomissen concludes: 'We note also that the only text that applies only to foreigners without associating them with other disadvantaged categories (widows and orphans), is the commandment to love them. The command takes on an even greater importance'.[24]

The legislative body of the Code of Holiness (Lev chapters 17–26), the third large collection of legislative texts of the Old Testament, belongs as a whole to the priestly legislation of the book of Leviticus, but its final composition is undoubtedly later, most likely after the exile in Babylon (597–538 BCE). Just as the Book of the Covenant, the Law of Holiness presents a dual attitude of separation (Lev chapters 18 and 20) and welcome (Lev 19) towards foreigners. Around the theme of the elective sanctity of Israel, it is based first of all on a radical opposition to the sin of idolatry (represented by all sorts of sexual sin): 'I am Yahweh your God. You must not behave as they do in Egypt where you once lived; you must not do as they do in Canaan where I am taking you. You must not follow their laws. You must follow my customs and keep my laws; by them you must lead your life' (Lev 18:2b–4a). Later there is a whole list of sexual taboos. Now, the assertion of the elective sanctity of Israel associated with sexual precepts explains the moral character of Israel's separation from the other nations: 'Be consecrated to me, because I, Yahweh, am holy and I will set you apart from all these peoples so that you may be mine' (Lev 20:26). As the prophet Ezekiel makes very clear, it is the covenant with Yahweh on which Israel bases its diversity and not for racial reasons. Moreover, the fundamental sin of Israel is precisely that they want to be like the other nations!

The *ghêr* who lives among the Israelites is likewise required to observe the commandment of an unconditional love for the stranger, even if he is an enemy, as an undeniable sign of the sanctity of the people. Basically, we could say that, if there are obvious reasons first of all to safeguard their identity and religious heritage that can justify Israel's tendency to separate themselves from all other peoples, there is still paradoxically the theological motivation that inspires the duty of hospitality and the generous and benevolent welcome of the stranger,

---

23. A Marx, 'Israël et l'accueil de l'étranger selon l'Ancien Testament', in *Le Supplément* 156 (1986): 5–14.

24. G Vanhoomissen, *Dieu, son peuple et l'étranger*, 31.

the poor and the weak. It highlights once again that the experience of Israel is a unique case in the heart of the civilization of the ancient Middle East. For the priestly tradition,[25] God, the Holy One of Israel, is present among his people who are called to imitate their God in every sphere of life—in fundamental ethical and legal issues, as well as in the sacred and cultic—as a witness of this presence. In other words, respect for the rights of the poor is one of the preconditions for effectively belonging to the community of 'freedmen' who can now count on the benevolent initiatives of their Lord.[26]

---

25. The Pentateuch is traditionally an amalgam of four documents, issuing from different times and places, all later than but attributed to Moses. There are, first of all, two works of fiction: the *Yahwistic* (J), which, from the creation story on, uses the divine name Yahweh which was revealed to Moses, and the *Elohistic* (E), which uses Elohim, the common name for God. The Yahwistic source was committed to writing in Judah in the ninth century, the Elohist in Israel a little later; after the fall of the Northern Kingdom, the two documents were combined (JE). After the time of Josiah, the *Deuteronomic* source (D) was added (JED). The *Priestly Code* (P), made up for the most part of laws, was joined to the existing compilation after the exile and served to weld and bind together (JEDP).

26. This vision is the basis of the Deuteronomic reform that, after the fall of the Northern Kingdom (721 BCE), was aimed at purifying faith in Yahweh and restoring observance of the law. It was characterized by a heightened concern for the protection of vulnerable groups and the socially disadvantaged.

The Major Stages of the History of the Old Testament: A Land Lost and Found

Exile in a foreign land: Preserving the identity of the Chosen People

At the beginning of the sixth century BCE, the people of Israel experienced a double deportation to Babylon. For over a century, Assyria and Babylon had been struggling for power in the Middle East. Towards the close of the century, however, in spite of its alliance with Egypt, the Assyrian Empire was coming to an end. In 605 BCE, Assyria was overthrown by Nebuchadnezzar in the decisive battle of Carchemish and Judah's king Jehoiakim was forced to acknowledge Babylonian sovereignty—that same sovereignty against which Egypt had earlier placed him on the throne. However, three years later Jehoiakim rejected this vassalage and the Babylonian armies reacted very quickly to quell the rebellion. In 597 BCE Jehoiakim's son surrendered to Nebuchadnezzar, on condition that Jerusalem, the capital of the kingdom, not be touched.

This was the occasion of the first partial deportation of the nobility, the clergy and the middle classes of the kingdom of Judah, along with the treasure of the Temple; but the majority of the people, the peasants and the city dwellers, remained on site.[1] The throne was

---

1. The Second Book of Kings describes very well the details of this first deportation (*cf* 2 Kgs 24:14–16). There are no allusions to massacres, the king is not killed or tortured but replaced and deportation is very selective: artisans used to design and build a great Babylonian military are, as is customary, assimilated into the army of the winner. Finally, there is no mention of a destruction of the city walls or the Temple or the royal palace, leaving one to think of a campaign not particularly violent or traumatic; it is, after all, barely mentioned in the Babylonian chronicles (for more details *cf* G Pettinato, *Babylonia* [Milano: Rusconi, Milano1988]).

given to a puppet king, Zedekiah (596–586 BCE), and settlers from Mesopotamia occupied the gaps created by the deportation of the elite. Gradually, these settlers mingled with the Israelite population which then lost its narrow national and religious cohesion as it merged with the newcomers.

> Yahweh, adopted by this hybrid population, lost his characteristic trait of being the one God and took his place among the pantheon of Asian deities, while the ancient kingdom of Israel gradually abandoned its national character. Only Jerusalem remained a true center of Judaism, where Jewish monotheism was preserved.[2]

In the winter of 588–587 BCE, in the nineteenth year of his reign, Nebuchadnezzar appeared once more at the gates of Jerusalem to quell yet another revolt, and after eighteen months of siege the capital of Judah capitulated. This time, the deportation of the people of Israel was all but complete as well as the looting of Jerusalem and the destruction of the Temple.[3] Out of the depths of the catastrophe questions are raised about its meaning. Of course, the interpretation given the prophets is primarily theological: the ruin of Judah is regarded as a punishment inflicted by Yahweh on his people for the sins of which they were guilty. Amos and Micah, already before the exile, placed the blame on social injustice, Hosea on lack of love, first Isaiah on pride. Jeremiah, who witnessed the drama, lamented the repeated infidelity of Israel against Yahweh. Not just were enemy

---

2. J Pirenne, *La Société Hébraïque d'après la Bible*, 183.
3. The biblical account recounts the tragedy in all its breadth, presenting the very harsh contours of military action (*cf* 2 Kgs 25:8b–12). The fate of the 'rebel king' is dramatically described by the prophet Jeremiah: 'The Chaldeans captured the king and took him to the king of Babylon at Riblah in the land of Hamath who passed sentence on him. He had the sons of Zedekiah slaughtered before his eyes; he also had all the leading men of Judah put to death at Riblah. He then cut out Zedekiah's eyes. Loading him with chains, the king of Babylon carried him off to Babylon where he kept him prisoner until his dying day' (Jer 52:9–11). The second book of Chronicles has the same allusion to uncontrolled massacres (*cf* 2 Chr 36:17). In fact, only those who openly denounced the rebellion against Babylon were spared and remained in the city; actually, they were only the poorest and weakest of the population, as recorded by Jeremiah: 'Nebuzaradan, commander of the guard, left some of the humbler people, who had nothing, in the land of Judah, at the same time giving them vineyards and fields' (Jer 39:10).

peoples rising up against the people of Yahweh, but Yahweh himself was exciting the ardor of these peoples against Israel. The prophets say this unambiguously. By using the term 'enemy' in announcing misfortune, they underscore the inescapable determination of Yahweh contrary to his will and the original plan for his Chosen People: 'Israel has rejected the good; the enemy will hunt him down (Hos 8:3). In the Old Testament, the term 'enemy' is not so much a moral judgment expressive of behavior, but a reference to the very special relationship that exists between Israel and her God. Everything—feelings, attitudes, or actions—of neighbouring peoples that does not match the original will of God and his promises to his people, becomes an act of enmity. In other words, Israel's enemies took command of the situation that because of Israel's infidelity disrupted the divine plan.[4]

Without a doubt, an evolution of religious thought also takes place in Israel. If the kingdom of Judah has fallen, Yahweh can no longer appear as its defender. The old idea of a national god is replaced by that of a god of morality that is not only the God of the Jews, but the God of all humankind, the judge of all nations. Nevertheless, alongside those who think to settle in the land of exile and forget the past,[5] are others who, stimulated by the preaching of the prophets, look with hope to a future restoration of the kingdom of Israel. The uprooting of the exile forces new thinking among the Israelites with reference to other peoples, resulting in two essentially opposing positions: on the one hand, a tendency to ethnocentric closure, as is recorded in the books of Ezra and Nehemiah, and on the other the opening of a new cultural horizon that goes beyond the limits of the people living in the land of Canaan.

Re-establishing identity in the post-exile

Upon their return from exile and the rebuilding of the community of returnees under the direction of the priest and scribe Ezra, all the

---

4. *Cf* J Schreiner, 'Nemici del popolo come punizione di Yahvé, in J Schreiner and R Kampling, *Il prossimo, lo straniero, il nemico* (Bolonga: EDB, 2020), 52–54.

5. We recall that the Jews in the land of exile generally knew extraordinary growth: they multiplied and increased their wealth, to the point that some of them refused to return to Israel in order not to abandon their fortunes (so Josephus attests in his *Antiquities of the Jews*).

social and cultural intransigence against the ancient populations of Canaan referred to in the Deuteronomic Code are renewed and strengthened.[6] Arriving in Jerusalem as the representative of the king of Persia, Ezra had been invested with the functions of high priest (Ez 10:8), to which he was entitled by birth, picking up the government of the country. He convened the Council of Chiefs and Elders, and on agreement with them, convened a meeting of all the men of Judah, Benjamin, and Jerusalem, the territories over which extended the authority of the Temple. This assembly was not that of the Israelite elders, but that of the 'community of returnees' alone (*cf* Ez 10:8), who from that moment enjoyed the right of citizenship. Participation in the meeting was required, on pain of confiscation of their property and exclusion from all meetings, that is, in effect, the loss of citizenship. Now, before all the assembly gathered on the Temple Mount, Ezra, to restore the status of the holiness of God's people, not only prohibits any marriage between a Jew and a foreign woman, but also proscribes the annulment of marriages already contracted in the past, through which the holy root had been profaned (Ez 10:10–11).[7] In actual fact, in the period after the exile, the miscegenation within the people of Israel was very strong, the result of a trend which had already begun before the deportation itself: 'The Israelites lived among the Canaanites and Hittites and Amorites, the Perizzites, Hivites and Jebusites; they married the daughters of these peoples, gave their own daughters in marriage to their sons, and served their gods' (Jg 3:5–6). Solomon had done the same thing at the end of his reign (931 BCE): not only had he married the daughter of Pharaoh,

---

6. *Cf* Deut 7:3–4: 'You must not marry with them [foreign nations]; you must not give a daughter of yours to a son of theirs, nor take a daughter of theirs for a son of yours, for this would turn away your son from following me to serving other gods and the anger of Yahweh would blaze out against you and soon destroy you', Deut 7:16: 'Devour, then, all these peoples whom Yahweh your God delivers over to you, show them no pity, do not serve their gods, for otherwise you would be ensnared.' We have already clarified the meaning of the term 'Canaanite', attributed generally to every foreigner outside the narrow circle of the Chosen People.

7. If, in the past there were many marriages with Babylonian women, the term 'foreign' now applies here in the same way to women who belong to the schismatic Samaritan kingdom. The Babylonian exile had, in fact, accentuated the divisions, already experienced earlier, between the tribe of Judah and the northern tribes, divisions that the position taken by rigorist Ezra now made virtually irreversible.

but his harem consisted of a large number of foreign women, of those peoples (Moabites, Ammonites, Edomites, Sidonians and Hittites) of whom Yahweh had said to the Israelites: 'You are not to go to them nor they to you, or they will surely sway your hearts to their own gods' (I Kgs 11:2).[8] Of course, the history of mixed marriages within the Chosen People is a clear sign of religious corruption or, more precisely, the prelude to an impending disaster with respect to true worship:

> When Solomon grew old his wives swayed his heart to other gods; and his heart was not wholly with Yahweh his God, as his father David's had been. Solomon became a follower of Astarte, the goddess of the Sidonians, and of Milcom, the Ammonite abomination. He did what was displeasing to Yahweh, and was not a wholehearted follower of Yahweh as his father David had been (1 Kgs 11:4–6).

In 445 BCE Nehemiah, a Jewish scribe, was appointed royal governor of Jerusalem to give the city, in agreement with the high priest Ezra, its new constitution. The organs of the city government were reorganized and Jerusalem, represented by the governor, remained subservient to the king of Persia. Nevertheless, the city had its own government, whose head was the hereditary high priest who acted as intermediary between the people and the Persian authorities. However, since the high priest was assisted primarily by the council of priests, the Levites, the state became clerical, and the only law was to Yahweh. The book of Nehemiah testifies that, in the establishment of this new state, the widespread rejection of the foreigner was expressed in two steps. The first concerned the penitential liturgy through which those who belonged to the descendants of Israel were distinguished from all the foreign peoples, because they confessed their sins and the sins of their fathers before God (Neh 9:2). The second was related to the removal of the grandson of the high priest Eliashib from priestly service because he defiled the priesthood by marrying the daughter of the governor of Samaria. 'And so I purged

---

8. The case of Solomon is hardly isolated in sacred history and similar examples can be multiplied: There is Moses who married an Ethiopian woman (Numb12:1), and Booz who took as wife the Moabite Ruth (Ruth 2:10). The mother of Solomon himself was married in first marriage, to a Hittite officer . . .

them of everything foreign; I drew up regulations for the priests and Levites defining each man's duty' (Neh 13:30). Certainly, this hardline approach did not levy a consensus within the Jewish community of Jerusalem because it went far beyond the rigors of the *Deuteronomic Code* in the sense of a definitive separation that ignored the lesson of Egypt: 'You are not to regard the Edomite as detestable, for he is your brother; nor the Egyptian, because you were a stranger in his land' (Deut 23:8). Originally, the referral meant the cleansing of all foreign elements and not persons of mixed blood. Even so, we do not forget, for example, that all contacts with the Samaritans did not cease[9]! The author of the book of Ezra is concerned to report the existence of a minority opposed to the intransigent policy of the high priest, as we see on the occasion of the proclamation of the prohibition of mixed marriages: 'Only Jonathan son of Asahel and Jahzeiah son Tikva, supported by Meshullam and Shabbethai the Levite, were opposed to this procedure' (Ez 10:15).

Sometimes, the oscillation between good will and hostility towards strangers responded only to questions of interest: possibly for economic reasons or it may have been linked to proselytism. Such is the case of the great prayer of Solomon at the time of the consecration of the Temple of Jerusalem, mentioned twice: in the first book of Kings (8:41–43) and in the second book of Chronicles. The latter rendition would, however, in the eyes of commentators today, be a text inspired by Deuteronomy and a post-exilic redaction. Turning to Yahweh, the third king of Judah put it this way:

> And the foreigner too, not belonging to your people Israel, if he comes from a distant country for the sake of your name and of your mighty hand and outstretched arm, if he comes and prays in this Temple, hear from heaven where your home is, and grant all the foreigner asks, so that all the peoples of the earth may come to know your name and, like your people Israel, revere you and know that your name is given to the Temple I have built (2 Chr 6: 32–33).

---

9. The Second Book of Chronicles refers to two incidents, the first in which the Jews gave up fighting the Samaritans (*cf* 2 Chr 11:3–4) and, on the other side, where the Samaritans treat a large number of Jewish prisoners of war in a fraternal and compassionate manner (*cf* 2 Chr 28:11, 4–15).

The prophetic literature: opening an eschatological perspective toward foreigners

The question of the identity of the visitor who is received will always remain on the margin of the texts as they relate to his reception; and the ambiguity between understanding the biblical texts themselves and some of the more restrictive positions among the Talmudic commentaries, especially medieval, will never be fully dissipated. The early prophets themselves, Elijah and Elisha, following the example of their father Abraham (even his universal opening is questioned in some Talmudic texts, a problem to which we will return in the next chapter), were not prejudiced against non-Israelites,[10] nor were the authors of the historical books. The opposite is true of the prophetic literature of the exilic and post-exilic periods which renewed the tension between welcoming the stranger and hostility toward him; this especially since the return from exile does not coincide with the restoration of the kingdom of Judah, but with a whole succession of foreign domination over the people of Israel (Persians, Greeks, Syrians, Egyptians, Romans). It would take too long to analyze in detail the many significant prophetic passages, but we can select a small sampling before regrouping, in a schematic way, some examples related to the rejection of foreigners.

The stranger is condemned mainly as a persecutor and enemy of Israel even though, as such, he is the unknowing instrument of the punishment of God because the Chosen People have been unfaithful, as we have already seen. The short book of Obadiah contains a prophetic malediction against Edom, who was guilty of having cooperated with the Babylonians at Judah's expense and of taking advantage of the destruction of Jerusalem in 587 BCE to invade southern Judah. All foreigners are associated with the curse of Edom:

> For the slaughter, for the violence done to your brother Jacob, shame will cover you and you will vanish forever. On the day you stood by as strangers carried off his riches, as barbarians passed through his gate and cast lots for Jerusalem, you behaved like the rest of them. Do not gloat over your brother on the day of his misfortune (Ob 9b–12a).

---

10. The story of Elijah accepting hospitality from a foreign widow outside the borders of Israel is well known (1 Kgs 17:8–19). Elisha in his turn heals the foreigner Naaman, army commander of the king of Aram, of his leprosy (2 Kgs 5:1–19).

Jeremiah presents a similar oracle foreshadowing the fate of Edom: 'Edom will become a desolation; every passer-by will be appalled at it, and whistle in amazement at such a calamity. As at the overthrow of Sodom and Gomorrah and their neighboring towns, no one will live there anymore, Yahweh proclaims, no one will make their home there ever again' (Jer 49:17–18). The fifth Lamentation, called *The Prayer of Jeremiah*, begs, in face of the destruction of Jerusalem, the mercy of Yahweh to his legacy passed into foreign hands, 'Yahweh, remember what has happened to us; look on us and see our degradation. Our inheritance has passed to aliens, our homes to barbarians' (Lam 5:1–2). The segregation of the community after the exile becomes, in the interpretation of some of the prophets, the eschatological anticipation of the exclusive election of the People which will not grant entrance to the Canaanites. The prophet Zechariah says: 'And every cooking pot in Jerusalem and in Judah shall become sacred to Yahweh Sabaoth; all who want to offer sacrifice will come and help themselves from them for their cooking; there will be no more traders in the Temple of Yahweh Sabaoth, when that day comes' (14:21); the *Vulgate*, the *Targum*, and the Greek version *Aquila* improperly mistranslate 'trader' as 'Canaanite'. The prophet Joel recalls in a more general way: 'You will learn then that I am Yahweh your God, dwelling in Zion, my holy mountain. Jerusalem will be a holy place, no alien will ever pass through it again' (4:17). Even Ezekiel, after having criticized the Jews for introducing foreigners into the Temple, prophesies that in the future, 'The Lord Yahweh says this: No alien, uncircumcised in heart and body, is to enter my sanctuary, none of those aliens living among the Israelites' (44:9).[11]

We can probably see in these statements the last tremors of the ideology of *hérem* (literally 'separate,' a sacred separation), typical of the theology of Deuteronomy, which reflects a double concern, both religious and nationalist. 'It is necessary that the "holy" people be preserved from all contamination, from the risk of being compromised by the influence of a pagan environment'.[12]

---

11. This statement is not inconsistent with the fact that the same prophet Ezekiel later became the cantor of the universalism of the heavenly Jerusalem, where all the people on earth who have recognized the one God will be gathered.

12. G Vanhoomissen, *Dieu, son peuple et l'étranger*, 37–38. According to several midrash (Rabbinic Bible commentaries which have as their purpose to clarify legal points of the sacred text and to lavish a moral teaching), the presence of a non-Jewish traveller among the Chosen People often poses serious problems. If he does not know anything about the law (written or oral) and especially if he is not able to say the blessing, he risks being dismissed or, at the very least, he plays the fool, and his attitude insults his Jewish host.

By refusing to accept the alien, a transition is made first of all to the eschatological perspective of the post-exilic prophets and is based, in this specific case, to a much older tradition that announces the admission of foreigners to Judaism as long as they adapt to the obligations of the Covenant: above all, circumcision, which is like the guarantee of incorporation.

> Only circumcision can make the stranger a 'citizen;' this inscription in the flesh counts as a signature or contract of hospitality and the rules that determine it. Nevertheless, even an uncircumcised alien remains subjected to the obligation of the Sabbath (Ex 20:10) and the observance of the rites of the Day of Atonement (Lv 16:29). The circumcised children of foreigners are to be welcomed to the same securities as the children of Israel. And God honors all prayers. This tradition abrogates the previous rules of Deuteronomic exclusion . . .[13]

Among the examples of this new attitude towards the stranger is the extraordinary portrait of the restoration of the new messianic people, sketched by the prophet Ezekiel (end of the fourth century BCE), where the entry of foreigners with full rights is expected among the Chosen People:

> You shall share out this land among yourselves, between the tribes of Israel. You are to divide it into inheritances for yourselves and the aliens settled among you who have begotten children with you, since you are to treat them as citizens of Israel. They are to draw lots with you for their inheritance, with the tribes of Israel. You must give the alien his inheritance in the tribe in which he is living—it is the Lord Yahweh who speaks (47:21–23).

Another example, a little later, is that of Third Isaiah, who writes explicitly in the fifth century BCE: 'Let no foreigner who has attached himself to Yahweh say, "Yahweh will surely exclude me from his people." [. . .] Foreigners who have attached themselves to Yahweh to serve him and to love his name and be his servants—all who observe the sabbath, not profaning it, and cling to my covenant—these I will bring to my holy mountain. I will make them joyful in my house of

---

13. A-C Pottier-Thoby, 'De la trahison à la rédemption', 129.

prayer. Their holocausts and their sacrifices will be accepted on my altar, for my house shall be called a house of prayer for all peoples' (56:3a, 6-7).

We need delve further into these Biblical citations to really understand the meaning given to the term 'foreigner.' Does it mean simply the foreigner now living in the land of Israel (*gêr*)? Or does it refer as well to a foreigner in the ethnic sense of the term (*nôkrî*) or in the sense of the 'unknown' (*zar*)? We prefer the first solution because Third Isaiah does not concern itself with a social context: it limits itself, preferably, to religious relations. The same author also speaks of foreigners as collaborators with the Jews, helping them rebuild the walls of the Holy City (Isa 60:10a) or discharging material tasks (Isa 61:5).[14]

Finally, in the eschatological perspective, Proto Zechariah (a lesser known author than the two previous writers in the late sixth century BCE) includes foreigners among those who have the right of access to the Temple (8:20-22), referring to the Oracle of Isaiah 2:1-5 which foreshadows the eschatological procession of all the peoples of the earth to the heavenly Jerusalem. It is, as we say, a broadening of perspectives beyond the exclusivity of the rigorous Deuteronomic tradition, but always within the dream of a 'spontaneous proselytism' to which some passages of the best-known prophets belong concerning specifically those on pilgrimage to the heavenly Jerusalem[15].

Alongside this analysis of the religious and theological relationship between Israel and foreigners, it must be emphasized that the

---

14. King David himself anticipates this prophetic tradition by putting all the foreign residents in the service of the construction of the temple (1Chr 22:2).

15. This beginning of universalism announces the New Testament notion of *prosélytos* (literally a Gentile convert to Judaism who accepts circumcision). These *goyîm* embrace Judaism by way of strict laws—specifically that of circumcision. 'Alas for you, scribes and Pharisees, you hypocrites! You who travel over sea and land to make a single proselyte and when you have him you make him twice as fit for hell as you are" (Matt 23:15). Foreign converts and proselytes are distinguished from mere sympathizers of the Jewish cause, prosaically called the 'God-fearing,' as the centurion Cornelius in Caesarea (Ac 10:2), or the purple-dye trader Lydia of Philippi (Acts 16:14), whom Peter and Paul have respectively visited. The categories of pagans and foreigners disappear with Paul. In the redemption won by the blood of the Crucified, '[they] are no longer aliens or foreign visitors: [they] are citizens like all the saints, and part of God's household' (Ep 2:19). For a discussion of these issues refer to J Sievers, 'Lo status socio-religioso dei proseliti e dei timorati di Dio', in I Cardellini, editor, *Lo straniero nella Bibbia*, 183-196.

prophets from Amos to Jeremiah and continuing through Ezekiel, speaking in the name of Yahweh, defend the rights especially of the most vulnerable–among whom are foreigners as well as orphans and widows—while denouncing the social crimes and political arrogance of nations. Respect for the rights of the weakest, regardless of their ethnic or religious origin, is a sign of conversion and the basis for a widening of the horizons of salvation and a more universal vision of the one God: the final overcoming of the idea of a national or clannish God, the demise of which had begun at the time of the exile in Babylon.

This eschatological opening onto a new universal perspective constitutes, in fact, one of the guidelines of the theology of the post-exilic prophets. It also means a return to the past in which the first books of the Old Testament originate—especially those of Genesis and Exodus. There is a need for a reinterpretation of the founding myths of the universe and humanity, within which to relocate the vocation and the experience of the Chosen People.

The myths of origins

The faith of the people of Israel in God the creator of the universe and of all humankind is the basis for a radical renewal of the vision of the other, the stranger. To the extent that Israel relates the love of God to the work of creation, thus far does she find the theological reason that drives her to advance the vision of the other and not only in a benevolent opening towards him. In the light of creation, in fact, Israel came to understand more clearly that all humanity, without distinction, has the same dignity. The biblical person has a sense of the greatness and beauty of every human being and considers each as a masterpiece shaped by the divine hands (*cf* Ps 8). On the other hand, the biblical person is also aware that human dignity lies not in beauty or in the complexity of one's being or intelligence but in the fact that God is mindful of them and takes care of them. It is the love of God which gives man his dignity: 'Ah, what is man that you should spare a thought for him, the son of man that you should care for him? Yet you have made him little less than a god, you have crowned him with glory and splendor . . .' (Ps 8:4–5). That is why on the one hand, humankind is supported by a feeling of deep trust, and on the other is aware of its fragile and pitiable condition. If the dignity of every person is founded and fortified in the remembrance of God, this divine evaluation cannot be imposed upon human history; on the contrary, history seems to have taken an altogether different assessment of humanity. In reality, the simple fact of being a creature consolidates the rights and dignity of being human, and not citizenship or other types of belonging. And human dignity is free, a gift even before becoming a law.[16] We return, therefore, to the 'universal man' (*hâ-âdâm*) that precedes every ethnicity, of clan or of religion, traditionally considered as the only context for identifying a person. Even members of the Chosen People must, before all else, recognise the figure, glorious and sinful, to whom all humanity relates: 'God created man in the image of himself, in the image of God he created him, male and female he created them' (Gen 1:27). They are male and female in Adam and not only because they are Jews. This is, evidently, a theological reading even before it being anthropological (according to this perspective, the secular debate between monogenesis and polygenesis has no meaning). It also includes a direct reference to original sin (Gen 3).

In all the milestones in the history of Origins, we find that it is God the Creator who takes the initiative in a unique and personal rapport with *âdâm*. This rapport, however, flounders due to the latter: a rupture which also affects human relationships, which now become violent and dramatic, culminating in a symbolic representation of the first murder in history. In chapter 4 of Genesis we likely find the first biblical evidence of 'foreignness:' diversity is synonymous with non-belonging to a race or a clan, a biological or sociological unit. The tragic cry of Cain at the beginning of human history describes implicitly the original plight of the stranger: 'I must [. . .] be a fugitive and wanderer over the earth. Why, whoever comes across me will kill me' (Gen 4:14). Cain, driven from the face of God because of his murder, himself becomes a fragile casualty of broken human relationships because everyone is born of the one Creator. It is this same God who takes the initiative to stop, on the day of the murder, the dynamism of violence: 'Yahweh put a mark on Cain, to prevent whoever might come across him from striking him down' (Gen 4:15b). The stranger, the creature banned, no longer that he might kill, but as

---

16. *Cf* B Maggioni, 'Lo straniero nell'Antico e nel Nuovo Testamento', in *Per la convivenza tra i popoli oltre il razzismo e l'intolleranza* (Milano: Vita e Pensiero, 1993), 34–36.

one accepted and protected by God.[17] This is much more than simply a bridle placed on human passion, always so ready to return evil for evil, to unlimited revenge. God is gradually revealed as the only legitimate avenger of injustice.[18] The Law of Holiness will proscribe the human desire for revenge at its source: 'You must not bear hatred for your brother in your heart [. . .] You must not exact vengeance, nor must you bear a grudge against the children of your people. You must love your neighbour as yourself' (Lev 19:17–18). This duty of forgiveness is racially limited and will tend to widen universally only with the *Wisdom Books*: 'He who exacts vengeance will experience the vengeance of the Lord, Who keeps strict account of sin. Forgive your neighbour the hurt he does you, and when you pray, your sins will be forgiven' (Sir 28:1–2).[19] This mythic expression of universalization

---

17. *Cf* J Daniélou, 'Pour une théologie de l'hospitalité', in *La Vie Spirituelle*, 367 (1951): 340. God is the ultimate judge who probes the mind and heart and rewards each one according to his deeds. Even more precisely, the Lord speaking to Israel says: 'Do not be afraid (. . .) I will help you—it is Yahweh who speaks—the Holy One of Israel is your redeemer' (Isa 41:14). To redeem or ransom is an action that in the Jewish tradition is made use of in a compromised situation. The redemption itself, whether it is a liberation from an alien power or of a person in slavery or concerning ownership of land, lies within the competence of the family—specifically within the competency of the closest relative of the one who suffers the wrong. This closest relative is called the *gōél,* the redeemer. God says of himself that he is the *gōél* for Israel. God is its closest relative, we might say, Israel's older brother, father, mother or spouse; in any case the closest relative who not only cares about the fate of Israel, but it is engaged with a pact to exercise this office of redemption.

18. "In biblical language revenge designates primarily a re-establishment of justice, a victory over evil. If vengeance is always forbidden for hatred of the evildoer, it remains a duty to avenge a maliGened right. However, the exercise of this duty has evolved throughout history: removed from the individual, it was given to the community. Above all, God is revealed gradually as the only legitimate avenger of justice" (A. Darrieutort and X Léon-Dufour, voce 'Vendetta', in X Léon-Dufour, editor, *Dizionario di Teologia Biblica*, (Casale Monferrato: Marietti, 1971), 1347–1350 (1347).

19. The interpretation of the term 'neighbour' in the Old Testament context remains a subject of debate. However, it is undeniable that the Bible demands love for the stranger: 'If a stranger lives with you in your land, do not molest him. You must count him as one of your own countrymen and love him as yourself—for you were once strangers yourselves in Egypt' (Lev 19: 33–34a). That said, according to rabbinic interpretation, love of neighbor cannot be extended to idolaters, in the sense that idolatry is one of the major sins.

and the true theological root of biblical solidarity is a common participation in the same covenant (*berit*)[20] with the one God. The theme of the covenant appears very early in the Old Testament, but prior to its being applied to God's dealings with humankind, it pertains to the social and legal experiences that bind people together with agreements and contracts involving the—typically mutual— rights and duties of each.[21] The covenant with Yahweh is obviously not a pact between equals: it is God's free and sovereign choice, the revelation of God's intimate being; God's promises. The act of creation, just barely mentioned, is actually the first cosmic alliance. It will not, however, be really celebrated until after the flood when a twofold pledge of the contracting parties will ratify the pact. God's promise: 'I establish my Covenant with you: no thing of flesh shall be swept away again by the waters of the flood. There shall be no flood to destroy the earth again' (Gen 9:11), corresponds to Noah's promise to spill no more blood, to not unleash the unending chain of revenge (Gen 9:6). The Covenant with Noah, signified by the rainbow and extending to the whole of Creation, is effected, first of all, in the saving of a small fraction of persons ('Yahweh said to Noah, "Go aboard the ark, you and all your household, for you alone among this generation do I see as a good man in my judgment"' Gen 7:1). That is why, even though earlier in time, this story represents, in its late drafting, a universal mythic reinterpretation of the covenant at Sinai. It represents a model of universal brotherhood that progressively widens its path in the Jewish sensibility and becomes the basis for the possibility of a universal solidarity, only fully comprehended in the Christian understanding of Christ's message. A purely fundamentalist reading of the Old Testament, which disregards historical data and the existence of a progression in biblical revelation, would lead us to

---

20. The translation of the Hebrew word *berit* is very controversial. Some, disputing the interpretation 'alliance,' include the sense of an 'obligation' of one of the parties involved. It is undeniable that this term has known many applications in Hebrew as well (oath, promise, commitment, treaty . . .) but all seem to express the partial elements that do not capture the totality of the meaning of this term. The best English translation appears to be 'covenant.'

21. There are many examples: the pact between Isaac and Abimelech (Gen 26:28), between Joshua and the Gibeonites (Jos 9:8, 11), the pact of friendship between Jonathan and David (1 Sir 18:3), or even the pact between King Solomon and Hiram of Tyre (1 Kgs 5:26).

believe there is a contradiction between this universal proposition and the doctrine of election, apparently ethnocentric and exclusivist. Yet in reality, the election of Israel, according to Gianfranco Ravasi, cannot be interpreted only in terms of an eschatological perspective: the election of Israel is the result of a momentous decision of God in view of the final good of all nations. It is the exaltation of diversity within a substantial unity: all nations descend from Noah and the blessing is given to him: 'God blessed Noah and his sons, saying to him, "Be fruitful, multiply and fill the earth"' (Gen 9:1). Every human destiny is unique, the same for all nations, universal; a richness exalted in the biblical page, the 'Table of Peoples', the tenth chapter of the book of Genesis. This text, which belongs to the priestly tradition, organizes the peoples descended from Noah's sons in the form of a genealogical tree, by historical and geographic relationships rather than by racial affinity. The intention of the author is certainly theological: his aim is to illustrate the fulfilment of the divine blessing given to Noah. 'These were the tribes of Noah's sons, according to their descendants and their nations. From these came the dispersal of the nations over the earth, after the flood' (Gen 10:32). This dispersion was made according to the language of each nation and concretized in each specific region. 'From these [Noah's sons] came the dispersal to the islands of the nations . . . according to their countries and each of their languages, according to their tribes and their nations' (Gen10:5). The God of the covenant, continually breaking that uniformity which expresses a false unity, so scatters the peoples on earth; but this dispersion, which bespeaks a real diversity among nations, does not cancel the principle of unity. The manifold family tree has at its head a single father Noah, father of all humankind after the flood (as Adam was for humanity prior to the flood). This 'monogenism' in religious terms is the affirmation of a fundamental fraternity among the human family and of a common birth-right in God who created humankind in God's own image (Gen 1:26 and 5:1).

In any case, the narrative that follows that of the 'Table of Peoples', is the myth of the 'tower of Babel' (Gen 11:1–9) in the Yahwist tradition; it speaks quite differently. We are confronted with a permanent conflict between two aspects, however complementary, of the history of a world in which mingle the steadfast commitment of God and human malice: this latter does not recognise the one fatherhood of God and, because of this, harms interpersonal relationships as well. There is a pining for a less exacting relationship with the Creator, for an illusory autonomy of creation. The tower is a corporate construction of a place where each person loses his own name in favour of a collective partnership; a place where language no longer serves as a light to demonstrate differences and where the 'we' is no longer an alliance of the many 'I' who, although individually speak a different language, still participate in a single fraternity, the corollary of a single and recognized divine fatherhood. "'So they are a single people with a single language", said Yahweh. "This is but the start of their undertakings. [. . .] Let us go down and confuse their language on the spot so that they can no longer understand one another'" (Gen 11:6-7). The relationship between races and different lineages remains problematic and is to be avoided where there is no absolute reference to the one God, the Creator, because only in God does diversity retain an orientation to communion. It is only at the table of hospitality prepared by God for all the nations of the earth that a richness of diversity can be experienced.

The saga of the Patriarchs

The saga of the Patriarchs would seem to reintroduce in the biblical reflection an important element of exclusivity, a retreat into partisanship. But a more careful reading of the texts reveals a continuity with the universal message, which will be theologically confirmed especially in reading the New Testament ('in Christ Jesus the blessing of Abraham might include the pagans . . .' Gal 3:14).[22] Far from being a restriction, this concentration of the promise made at one time to a single descendant of Noah, Abraham, is the condition of a true universalism defined according to the plan of God. In fact, if the calling of Abraham, described in Genesis 12, is the root of the theology of the election of Israel as a unique and lowly people, chosen from dozens of other nations, the blessing (*brk*) establishing a permanence of the Patriarch in his house is paradoxically, intended

---

22. Paul's Letter to the Romans is, on this issue, without equal: 'Not all those who descend from Israel are Israel; not all the descendants of Abraham are his true children. Remember: *It is through Isaac that your name will be carried on,* which means that it is not physical descent that decides who are the children of God; it is only the children of the promise who will count as the true descendants' (9:6b–8).

from the outset for other families or nations of the earth.[23] In essence, the blessing of Yahweh is never an individual privilege given to Abraham: the Patriarch's vocation is to be a father and his glory is in his progeny. According to the priestly tradition, the name change (Abram becomes Abraham) attests to this approach, because the new name is interpreted as the 'father of a multitude of nations' (Gen 17:5). Again, the expression might be considered as limited to the heart of the Chosen People, but the fate of Abraham seems however to have wider repercussions from the moment he takes on the task of interceding for foreign cities condemned by God to punishment (Gen 18:16-33). The interpretation given in the Jewish tradition about the oracle of Genesis 22:18 will also have a universal connotation:

> Abraham was the great ancestor of many nations, there was no one like him in glory. [. . .] This is why God promised by oath to bless the nations in his seed, to multiply as the dust of the earth, and to exalt his seed as the stars, and to give them an inheritance from one to another sea, from the River to the ends of the earth (Sir 4:19, 21).

Abraham's life, and in particular his vocation, develops under the sign of the free initiative of God and in a universal sense. God chose Abraham from a family that observed a foreign cult ('Yahweh the God of Israel says this, "In ancient times your ancestors lived beyond the River—such was Terah, the father of Abraham and Nahor—they served other gods" Jos 24:2); and was made to leave his homeland to be led him along the path to an unknown country ('It was by faith that Abraham obeyed the call to *set out* for a country that was the inheritance given to him and his descendants, and that *he set out* without knowing where he was going', Heb 11:8). The

---

23. This idea returns continually in several biblical passages: 'All the tribes of the earth shall bless themselves by you' (Gen 12:3b) is a formula—substituting sometimes 'clan' or 'nation'—which refers to Gen 18:18; 22:18; 26:4; 28:14. The root of the blessing (*brk*), according to Cardinal Ravasi, is used both in a reflexive sense (the nations shall be blessed in Abraham, that is, you will say to one another: 'May you be blessed as was Abraham') that will be stated in a passive sense (as in the translation of the Septuagint and the reinterpretation of the New Testament: 'in Abraham will all the nations of the earth be blessed'). In both cases, however, there is an indissoluble connection with the election of the nations of Israel (*cf* G Ravasi, 'Universalismo e particolarismo nell'Antico Testamento', 15).

Patriarch embodies, in his own history, the 'original nomadism' of the Chosen People, the sense of which goes beyond a mere geographical significance. The divine pedagogy that unfolds in the period of the Patriarchs is the origin of a kind of progressive destabilization of identity, because God plays a central role in becoming the ultimate source of identity, God, the unknowable and irreducible to any human thought and any attempt to fix an image. We see the presence of resistance, the sign of a slow and often painful conversion, in the uncompromising attitude of the Patriarch who refuses to allow his son to take a wife from the daughters of Canaan (this legacy bears the influence of a Deuteronomist ideology then at its height; *cf* Ne 10:31).[24] Returning to the earlier question of the choice of Israel above all the other nations, it is paradoxically because of its apparent absence of any special qualities, of the insignificance and fragility of the people of Abraham, that we can understand the uniqueness of his call.

> If Yahweh set his heart on you and chose you, it was not because you outnumbered other peoples: you were the least of all peoples. It was for love of you and to keep the oath he swore to your fathers that Yahweh brought you out with his mighty hand and redeemed you from the house of slavery, from the power of Pharaoh king of Egypt (Dt 7:7–8).

The heart of the election and the privilege of Israel must be sought in the relationship between the impoverishment of the people and the bountiful love of God. Israel is a people set apart, not because of its race but because of its ancestors who were loved by God, wandering, suffering ancestors, who were finally freed from slavery by God's own intervention. The tiny nation of Israel becomes the living symbol of God's love for the poor and lowly.[25] The 'original nomadism' mentioned above is still strongly sociological-geographic and will be more sharply understood by the concept of 'Exus', a more theological

---

24. As recounted in the book of Genesis, Abraham, before he died, sent one of his servants to look for a wife for his son Isaac after having made him swear by oath: "I would have you swear by Yahweh, God of heaven and God of earth, that you will not choose a wife for my son from the daughters of the Canaanites among whom I live. Instead, go to my own land and my own kinsfolk to choose a wife for my son Isaac" (Gen 24:3-4).

25. *Cf* P Bovati, 'Lo Straniero nella Bibbia', in *La Rivista del Clero Italiano*, LXXXIII (2002): 405–418; 484–503 (410).

term, or better, more biblical, which introduces the second major stage in the period of the Patriarchs. The Exus is the climax of the election of Israel. The election, as a gift of divine grace, implies a freedom which expresses itself by an absence of clear geographical references. In fact, if the whole biblical tradition infers an alliance of the Jewish people with a land called 'Canaan' (so named by those who lived there previously), this people is even more distinguished by an eternal yearning for a 'promised land' (the expression of a more radical search for the origins of their identity progressively recognized as a gift). This longing is particularly manifest during their exile in the land of Egypt, in their deportation to Babylon or in the modern condition of a permanent diaspora. Essentially, as Pietro Bovati recalls, the relationship with the land, despite being at the heart of the divine promises, seems neither decisive nor essential for the establishment of Israel. Israel remains an alien to all other peoples, in every situation in which it is found.[26] Now, the recollection of having been a stranger in the land of Egypt and the subsequent journey of escape, takes on a defining value for the Chosen People; it forms part of the first article of Israelite faith: 'I am Yahweh your God who brought you out of the land of Egypt, out of the house of slavery' (Deut 5:6). This is much more than just a divinely benevolent glance toward the condition of the people. 'God spoke to Israel in a vision at night, "Do not be afraid of going down to Egypt, for I will make you a great nation there. I myself will go down to Egypt with you. I myself will bring you back again"' (Gen 46:3–4a). The rabbis have always interpreted these verses literally: it is God in person who accompanies the people in exile. Hence, the birth of a new concept, that of the Divine Presence in exile ('*Shekhinta begaluta*'). Just as the Hebrews suffer humiliation in *galut* (exile, slavery), so God also 'suffers' a kind of diminution with the exiled people. This reveals a surprisingly new face of God: theologically, God is present as the one who hears the cry of people in a foreign land, even though this cry is not directly addressed to God: 'I have seen the miserable state of my people in Egypt. I have heard their appeal to be free of their slave-drivers. Yes, I am well aware of their sufferings. I mean to deliver them out of the hands of the Egyptians and bring them up out of that land to a land rich and broad, a land where milk and honey and honey flow . . .' (Ex 3:7–8).

---

26. Bovati, 'Lo Straniero nella Bibbia', 414–415.

Therefore, we must return again to the figure of Abraham, because it is through the experience of the patriarch that Israel discovered its vocation as a 'guest of God', one received by God. So the book of Deuteronomy does not limit itself to recalling for the Chosen People their experience of suffering and deliverance in Egypt; it further underscores the constant attitude of a God who 'sees justice done for the orphan and the widow, who loves the stranger and gives him food and clothing' (Deut 10:18). Israel is thus led to rediscover the meaning of hospitality thanks to the memory, direct or indirect, of having been foreigners themselves: 'If a stranger lives with you in your land, do not molest him. You must count him as one of your own countrymen and love him as yourself—for you were once strangers yourselves in the land of Egypt' (Lev 19:34); and, even more, because of the kindness and hospitality of Yahweh towards you.[27] The author of historical books shares this view, putting in the mouth of King David the following prayer: 'At this time, our God, we give you glory, we praise the splendour of your name [. . .] All comes from you; from your own hand we have given them to you. For we are strangers before you, settlers only, as all our ancestors were' (1 Chr 29:13, 14–15).

The Hellenistic period: Culture shock and the bias toward xenophobia

As we have seen in both the historical and prophetic literature as well as in the wisdom literature and the later compositions that form the midrashic corpus,[28] there is a tension between the acceptance and rejection of foreigners. We limit ourselves to two general types of consideration in a review of the Book of Ecclesiasticus or Sirach, which alter what has just been said. First of all, the author of this book expresses a lack of trust in the stranger; his very diversity causes a modification of customs and, very often, disrupts interpersonal relationships: 'Bring a stranger home with you and he will start trouble, and estrange you from your own family' (Sri 11:34). From an initial call for caution in welcoming the other, he goes on to clearly advise against hospitality

---

27. The New Testament, by the Word of Christ himself, will bring Old Testament theology to its peak by speaking of love of neighbour, non-exclusive of sinners, pagans, even enemies, on the model of the love of the Father (*cf* Matt 5:43–48).
28. These are books generally considered post-exilic (after 538 BCE) and contain a kind of wisdom-teaching; more precisely, the Books of Ruth, Tobit, Judith, Esther and Jonah.

because, among other things, according to the wisdom of Ben Sirach, hospitality places the needy at a disadvantage: it is much better to be satisfied with little while maintaining independence than to become as a parasite and suffer the risk of bad treatment from the host who, in any case, will act toward the person received as to a stranger: 'It is a miserable life, going from house to house; wherever you stay, not daring to open your mouth; you are a stranger, you know the taste of humiliation [. . .] It is hard for a cultured man to hear himself begrudged hospitality and treated like an undischarged debtor' (Sir 29:24, 28). These are considerations of common sense, but they seem to deny one of the sacred duties of ancient Israel! In fact, the Book of Ecclesiasticus marks the beginning of the era of Hellenistic influence in the social and religious spheres; peacefully yet profoundly the new theocratic structures of post-exilic Jewish society and customs are overturned. A preliminary observation of John Deiana is illuminating. The quote in full is as follows:

> The stranger, for the most part Greek, who for whatever reason is living in Palestine in the Hellenistic period, is not one who asks for help or protection. Rather he is the bearer of a dominant culture and occupies a pre-eminent social position, bound as it were, to the structure of the central government (for example, soldiers, tax collectors, merchants, artisans). In practice they are the real masters while the natives become as foreigners! Usually it is the stranger who, like it or not, yields to the local culture; in the case of the Greeks, however, they are the ones who, by their presence, transform the local culture and impose their own.[29]

The persuasions of the priestly caste and the wealthier social strata, willing to compromise with their new masters, create deep divisions within the Jewish world. In fact, these Jewish 'collaborators' believed in the possibility of a reconciliation with Hellenism, while retaining the autonomy of their value system and cultural and religious vision of life. The *Sibylline Oracles*, Jewish compositions of this period that correlate the Sibyl as a new prophet in a number of texts that promote the Jewish religion among the Gentiles, are an example of this attempt

---

29. G Deiana, 'Lo straniero nel periodo qumranico', in I Cardellini, editor, *Lo 'straniero' nella Bibbia*, 174. These considerations as applied to the Greeks seem to be valid for the Romans as well.

at encounter between two very different worlds. Yet there is another whole current of Jews who, because of their austere Jewish faith, will not lend themselves to accommodation nor accept ambiguity. These Jews faithful to the tradition will not be the only ones to dissociate themselves from the increasingly dominant class (*cf* their rebellion under the Seleucids). They will be joined by separatist groups and sometimes openly take refuge in isolated places, in order to live a strict observance of the faith of the Fathers;[30] or organise themselves into increasingly radical opposition movements, if not to say violent and xenophobic, which will end in the revolt of the Maccabees. From an initial cultural hostility will evolve an open hostility towards all people.

Without claiming to deal in these pages with the complex issue of the Hellenization of Jewish society,[31] we cannot fail to evoke the factors that brought about this interior trend toward xenophobia. Among the great changes brought by the Greeks, John Deiana cites language, introduced in Palestine since the third century BC, especially in the administrative sector, but the greater shock is the definition of a new religious mentality. In the Hellenistic culture, every local deity was considered an expression of a universal entity; thus, every believer, worshiping his or her own god, rendered worship to this universal and common entity. Yahweh, whose name was not to be pronounced by the Jews, was soon identified with Olympian Zeus; pagan sacrifices were increasingly offered in the Temple of Jerusalem.[32] The new generations of high Jewish society were growing up with a mentality that understood nothing of what Ezra had advanced. Men such as these, called to occupy the key posts of Palestinian secular society, were to ask the Seleucids to turn Jerusalem into a Greek *polis*.

---

30. This is the case of the very well-known Essenes or, more precisely, the members of the community of Qumran, near the Dead Sea. They emphasized the geographical isolation of the desert as a permanent place of residence, not merely a temporary refuge.

31. *Cf* WD Davies and L Finkelstein, ediors, *The Cambridge History of Judaism*, II (Cambridge: Cambridge University Press, 1999), 657–716, which has an immense bibliography of studies on this topic.

32. As Deiana recounts: 'It must be supposed that the Greeks did not intend to sacrifice victims to Yahweh but to their own gods. This phenomenon, already codified in Lev 22:24 became so prominent that in the Herodian Temple a courtyard was reserved exclusively for the use of the Gentiles' (176). A little later, under Antiochus IV Epiphanes, the cult of the Temple itself was reformed according to the Hellenized function of society. If the Temple remained dedicated to Yahweh, the supreme god, the latter could be venerated under the most universally known form: that of Zeus precisely, the supreme god according to the Greeks.

The possibility of a reconciliation between Hellenism and Judaism became then, for many Israelites, absolutely impractical. The disciples of Ezra chose loyalty to Judaism and formed a coalition against the Hellenists, looking, at first, to manage the commercial traffic in the Holy City (in particular the trade of unclean animals) and to reinforce traditional Jewish religious values. These intransigent Jews made little distinction between different categories of foreigners, whether fugitives, pilgrims, immigrants or refugees of any kind. They came to an agreement only with those unconditionally open to the Torah. Foreigners who accept the Torah were called 'followers'[33] and were integrated into the very heart of the Jewish community; all others were considered impure and therefore, increasingly excluded from social life. The lack of patience in waiting for the end of this new exile, however, soon led to a confrontation far more violent and to the actual extermination of enemies. The books of Joel, Job, Esther and Judith could already foresee the imminent desire of vengeance. The Psalms celebrating revenge against the children of Babylon were resumed and increasingly amplified.

Yet the bias toward violent confrontation is best situated in the epic of the Two Books of Maccabees. In 1 Maccabees we see a Jerusalem that has been refashioned into a Greek *polis* and the backlash of traditional Judaism against the process of Hellenization: 'The citizens of Jerusalem fled because of them, she became a dwelling place of strangers; estranged from her own offspring, her children forsook her. Her sanctuary became as deserted as a wilderness, her feasts were turned into mourning, her sabbaths into a mockery, her honour into reproach' (1 Mac 1:38–39. There seems to be no room for a welcome of the stranger because his very presence eclipses the obligation to receive him[34]. In the realization of defending their traditional cultural

---

33. *Cf* note 15, 57.
34. The rich literature found at Qumran confirms this very strict vision of foreign pagans and the almost obsessive leitmotiv of the destruction of pagan peoples. In the 'Temple Scroll', one of the oldest, dating back to the foundation of this sect, there is no hesitation to talk about the dangers of the alien with whom the true Israelite must not maintain relations, not even social (*cf* I Cardellini, 'Stranieri ed "emigrati-residenti" in una sintesi di teologia storico-biblica', 156–157). This posture of total rejection of the Gentiles will translate to a profoundly Manichean theological vision: The Qumran community was made up of 'children of light;' all others were 'children of darkness', and to be hated out of obedience to an explicit command of the rule of the community itself (*cf* G Deiana, 'Lo straniero nel periodo qumranico', 180).

and religious values, the Maccabees did not, however, hesitate to enter into alliances, sometimes quite questionable, with foreigners such as the pagan Romans (*cf* 1 Mac 8) or Spartans. In his letter to the king of Sparta, Jonathan, the high priest of Jerusalem, even dares to evoke a common descent from Abraham to the two peoples, speaking of the Spartans and the Jews as brothers (*cf* 1 Mac 12:20). Similar contradictions regarding the attitude of these fundamentalists against foreigners are frequent in the accounts of the Maccabees, according to the political axiom: the enemy of my enemy is my friend[35].

Finally, in the Hellenistic age great importance is accorded the issue of election, advanced especially by the Essenes of Qumran, at the expense of a universalist opening which seemed to be in ascendency at the time of the return from exile in Babylon (ca 539 BCE). The Holy People, who long considered themselves the light of the nations, have by now closed themselves off in a strict observance of the Torah and Jewish customs, in reaction to the laws and practices of the pagan peoples. At best, there is an attempt at tolerance of the other, but nothing that could considered a truly equal treatment in respect of another's legitimate diversity. To better understand this aspect, we must reflect on the translation for the term gêr/gérîm by *prosélytos* in the LXX version.

If we limit it to its purely religious and cultural understanding— which lies at the heart of the Chosen People—it marks de facto the definitive alteration of resident alien status. Many non-canonical Palestinian texts maintain not only a strong anti-foreign vision generally, but also a decisive movement toward self-righteousness and a conviction of the inability of the non-Israelite to understand the Torah and thereby attain the resurrection of the just. As stated, the stranger, especially when he is not in need but instead bears a culture that wields hegemony, may be the cause of a profound upheaval in which it is installed; and all the more when that culture introduces a partnership with its economic and political power.

---

35. Outside of such an assertion, for example, it would be difficult to explain how Jonathan, leader of the revolt against the Seleucids after the death of Judas Maccabeus, was able to accept the position of high priest conferred by the Seleucid king Alexander: not only was the latter not authorized to bestow such a charge; but Jonathan himself was not even born in a priestly family (*cf* 1 Mac 10:15–21, 61–62).

In fact, the history of the Old Testament as we have retraced it, presents an intersection of economic, social, cultural and religious elements which necessarily complicate the attitude towards foreigners: attitudes that may vary and sometimes take on contradictory characteristics. On one hand, we will celebrate the Lord who unfailingly protects the stranger (*cf* Ps 146 / 145:7, 9); on the other, in the same literary collection, the victory of a God who breaks the resistance of enemy peoples as if they were clay pots (*cf* Ps 2:8–9). Evidently, neither a process of assimilation nor the opposite of a rejection will completely eliminate the fear of the unknown regarded as a threat in the social, cultural and, above all, religious spheres.

Nevertheless, remaining always within the biblical tradition, there are religious and symbolic elements that can reduce the ambivalence of the relationship with the stranger. In the first place, we have evoked the image of a creator God who established the obligation of peoples to live and encounter one another in diversity; and, secondly, there is the experience of the God of Exus and in exile, in solidarity with the homeless and the oppressed. The task of broadening universally the translation of God the Creator's actions into human ethical requirements will be entrusted to the prophets and the wisdom literature. In accord with nomadic culture, the Temple of the Lord is considered symbolically as a tent under which the righteous man will not be just passing through, but will become a permanent tenant who enjoys constant protection.

Hospitality According to Rabbinic Literature

A religious duty

To understand the rich tradition of Jewish hospitality, we cannot limit ourselves to the Bible: we must go beyond Israel's biblical narrative to its tragic end, the destruction of Jerusalem and its Temple, corresponding with the Jewish War. The radical rejection of a foreigner epitomized by the Maccabees' revolt does not represent a total extinction of hospitality toward the pious and observant Israelite. At the core of Judaism, hospitality remains a moral institution that rabbis will continue to judge as more important than the gift of divine presence itself! This observation is intimately tied to a theological consideration: in the Jewish understanding, biblical revelation is, first of all, ethics. That is, it is not in the order of revelation by which we understand 'who God is', but in the order of an act in which we discover what 'God does for us'. Within this context, a knowledge relationship such as that between *res cogitans* and *res extensa*, a subject that knows and its object, is not applicable, but, precisely, an encounter that unfolds through the sequel of a story.[1] This is why some rabbis go so

---

1. This first manifestation of God as irreducible otherness, despite being extreme, characterises the whole story of the Exus and, in particular, the famous revelation of God's name: 'Then Moses said to God, "I am to go, then, to the sons of Israel and say to them, "The God of your fathers has sent me to you." But if they ask me what his name is, what am I to tell them?" And God said to Moses, "I Am who I am. This," he added, "is what you must say to the sons of Israel: "I Am has sent me to you"' (Ex 3:13–14). Beyond any attempt at philosophical and metaphysical interpretation of this mysterious self-definition of God (God as fullness of being), the commentators suggest we read the text in the light of the verses above, where, as we have said, God appears in his 'being for us': 'I Am who I Am' becomes the 'I am he who will always be attentive to the cry of humanity.'

far as to consider the practice of hospitality more important than the welcome reserved for the Shekinah (the place of the presence of the Glory of God).[2] The great mistake of the Sodomites was precisely the transgression of this law (*cf* Gen 19). In rabbinic literature, hospitality is viewed primarily as a *mitzvah*, that is, a religious duty essentially linked to charity. When the Bible speaks of charity, the corresponding Hebrew word is *tsedaqah*, which, however, also means 'righteousness, virtue and equity,' and shares the same root—*tsedeq*—with the word 'justice'. The Hebrew etymology stresses therefore more the idea of a moral and legal duty than a simple burst of compassion. Thus, it is the law itself which compels us to come to the aid of the poor, the stranger, the widow, and the orphan. The law always specifies in detail the conditions of this duty to help from which no one is excused, not even those who lack substantial means. No one can pretend to serve God without beginning to serve, first of all, his neighbour. Beginning with ancient Judaism, love of neighbour and love of strangers have not been vague sentiments, but sentiments that entail precise behaviour. To love your neighbour means to pay your employee a just wage, to lay aside a part of the harvest for the disposal of the hungry, not to use a separate weight or measure when practicing justice toward the powerful and another for the poor, or to tarnish yourself with extortion or theft against your neighbour.[3]

---

2. Rabbi Judah said in the name of Rabbi (one of the first Babylonian spiritual leaders who lived around 250 CE): 'Hospitality is more important than the acceptance of the *Shekinah*, as it is Written: "My lord", [Abraham] said, "I beg you, if I find favour with you, kindly do not pass your servant by" (Gen 18:3); R Eleazar said: 'You see, the divine essence is not like human nature and will not tolerate that a young man can say to an older brother: "Wait till I come back", when it is written about the Holy One, blessed be He: "Lord, if I find favour . . ."' (from the Babylonian Talmud, *Shabbat* 126b, quoted by P Bornet, 'Entre normes et religieuses impératifs éthiques', 151). To understand this quote we must realize that, in the rabbinical interpretation of the text of Genesis 18, Abraham, before receiving his guests, was held in the same divine presence and that he had dismissed the latter before going to the meeting with the mysterious pilgrims (a detail that confers incomparable value to hospitality).

3. *Cf* C Chalier, 'équité et bonté', in O Gandon, editor *La Charité. L'amour au risque de sa perversion* (Paris: Autrement, Paris 1993), 20–24. In summary, we may speak of two ways of exercising charity: classical charity is the offering of alms (especially financial aid) to the poor. Another expression of charity is personal service. This form is of higher value because it involves personal commitment and is included within the exercise of hospitality. According to the *Trattato dei*

'*Tsedaqah*', which in several rabbinic texts is translated as 'reception of travellers', is an act whose scope extends beyond simple goodness and, from a religious point of view, deserves remuneration. Usually considered as models of hospitality and *Haggadah*,[4] several stories are told of Abraham and Job in this regard: the doors of their homes (or tents) were open on all four sides to allow foreigners to find easy entry regardless of where they were coming from. In fact, as Rabbi Yosé b Yohanan of Jerusalem explains, the gathering place of *Pirqé Avot*, 'a large open house' (in the sense of the four corners) makes it easier for the poor coming from different regions to not go around in circles to find the entrance and, at the same time, it expresses symbolically an unconditional welcome.[5]

It is said that Job always had in his house forty tables set for strangers and twelve tables set for widows! This is a symbolic illustration of the extraordinary means available to the 'just one tried by God' who will, nonetheless, be rewarded in the end for his unswerving faith well above his wealth. However, again, according to the interpretation of *Pirqé Avot*, Job was punished because he was less sensitive than Abraham about hospitality towards strangers. He always remained inside his home, whereas Abraham positioned himself at the entrance of his tent to invite people passing by and would often spontaneously

---

Padri o *Pirqé Avot* (a collection of judgments of the Sages of Israel that followed the biblical prophets of the time) and that figure in the fourth section of the *Mishna*, (that is the oral law in all its aspects), this active charity represents one of the three pillars that hold up the world, together with the Torah and service in the Temple. Another biblical tradition, however, taken from the Babylonian Talmud, founds the world solely on charitable generosity, from which all other duties inevitably flow. (*cf* Talmud di Babilonia, *Shabbat* 127a, commented on by P Bornet, 'Entre normes religieuses et impératifs éthiques', 147). For a more detailed analysis of Charity in Jewish doctrine and practice, we refer to the study of E Gugenheim, 'La carità', in *L'ebraismo nella vita quotidiana* (Fierenze: Giuntina, 2007), 169–173.

4. Literally 'narrative, the story', is an anthology of liturgical texts from different cultures and epochs; but, more particularly, it is the text used for the domestic celebration of *Pessah* (Passover) and the volume that contains this ritual.

5. 'Yosé son of Yohanan of Jerusalem says that the house should be open widely, and that the poor be [in your home] as members of your own family' (*Pirqé Avot*, I, 5, in E Smilévitch, *Leçon des Pères du monde* [Paris: Verdier, 1983], 25.)

head towards them.[6] As Philippe Bornet underlines, hospitality plays a major role at the heart of a 'theology of retribution:'

> It is because Job did not give hospitality with the same zeal of Abraham that all the misfortunes we know have fallen on him; *ergo*—in the prescriptive aspect of the text—it is good that the Jew who respects the scriptures and recognises the authority of rabbinic literature, applies himself as much as possible to the gift of hospitality[7].

The encouragement of hospitality and the insistence on its central role in the *mitzvot* or Jewish religious imperatives, are renewed continuously in rabbinic literature and not only in the moral treatises. The problem is determining what to do when this practice enters into a conflict with other religious duties of the complex system of Jewish rules. A typical case is the arrival of guests on the day of the *Shabbat* which pertains to the entire household, the servants, the strangers who live under the family roof, and even the animals ('The seventh day is a sabbath for Yahweh your God. You shall do no work that day, neither you nor your son nor your daughter nor your servants, men or women, nor your animals nor the stranger who lives with you' (Ex 20:10). Even in this case, decrees the *Mishna*, hospitality can justify an exception to the law, always within certain limits and, therefore,

---

6. "When misfortune struck Job, he cried out to the Holy One, blessed be He: Master of the world, have I not fed the hungry and given drink to the thirsty, in other words: 'Have I taken my bread alone, not giving a share to the orphan [. . .]?' (*cf* Job 31:17). And did I not dress the naked, according to the verse: 'as he felt the warmth of the fleece from my lambs?' (*cf* Job 31:20). [. . .] The Holy One, blessed be He, however, said to Job, you have not yet reached the half to the extent of Abraham: You were sitting inside your house and travellers came to you. You gave bread to those who had the habit of eating bread. You gave meat to those who had the habit of eating meat; and you gave wine to those who had the habit of drinking wine. But Abraham did not act in this way. He left his home and went in search of the pilgrims, and when he found them took them to his house. Here, to those who did not have the habit of eating bread, he gave bread; to those who did not have the habit of eating meat, he gave meat; and to those who did not have the habit of drinking wine, he gave wine' (*cf Pirqé Avot de Rabbi Nathan*—A, VII, in E Smilévitch, *Leçon des Pères du monde*, 121).

7. P Bornet, 'Entre religieuses normes et impératifs éthiques', 148

without questioning it as Law.[8] But what is even more interesting to emphasize, is that hospitality as *mitzvah* can also replace other religious duties and replace the office of daily prayer, especially when it is lavished on a wise man:

> The ruling of Rabbi Yosé son of Hanina in the name of Rabbi Eliezer son of Jacob: anyone who receives a disciple of a Rabbi (in other versions it says 'disciple of a wise man') into his house, sharing with him his possessions, is counted in Scripture as if he had offered the perpetual burnt offering (literally *tamid*, which corresponds concretely to the daily holocaust offered by the priests every morning and every afternoon in the Temple; cf Ex 29:38–42; 30:7–8; Num 28:3–8).[9]

Philippe Bornet underlines this text by placing it at the heart of the development of Jewish religious practices at the time of the second destruction of the Temple in Jerusalem, when the domestic space replaces the sacred space and the tables where meals are served resemble the altar of the Temple where they proceeded to make offerings [. . .] Hospitality is therefore a stop-gap measure—obviously one of many—of certain commandments that became impractical following the destruction of the Second Temple.[10]

---

8. An important example of the Babylonian Talmud (which we shall refer to as TB) compares the act of hospitality with 'making room:' 'It is allowed to evacuate up to four or five baskets of straw or of agricultural products to make room for guests in case of the unavailability of the house of studies, but not the entire warehouse . . .' (TB, Shabbat 126b, quoted by P Bornet, 'Entre normes et religieuses impératifs éthiques', 149) . It is therefore allowed to evacuate a certain amount of space but not an immeasurable amount as that of an entire store. As for the reference to the house of studies, it is indeed a place of meeting of the wise and the students of the sacred Law.

9. TB, *Berakhot* 10b, in J Bonsirven, *Textes rabbiniques des deux premiers siècles chrétiens* (Rome: Pontificio Istituto Biblico, 1992). The Treaty of the Talmud speaking of the same *Sukka* (literally 'tent' or 'hut', in relation to the great celebration of Autumn) draws a parallel between the exercise of almsgiving and works of charity that progressively take the upper hand: This [almsgiving] is done with money, while charity first touches the body; almsgiving is practiced towards the living poor; works of charity are practiced towards the poor and the rich, living and deceased' (TB, *Sukka* 49b, in Bonsirven J, 249).

10. P Bornet, 'Entre normes religieuses et impératifs éthiques', 148.

A confessional hospitality

We have focused so far on the study of issues tied to the multiplicity of meanings of hospitality more than to the study of the practice of hospitality. It is a choice forced in part because it is not easy to reconstruct the evolution of these practices from a historical point of view.

Hospitality in the Jewish world, as we have been given to analyse it in more recent writings, seems to correspond very closely to a literary description historically established and will present in fact, strong scriptural foundations. As Philippe Bornet recalls, as early as the third century CE the synagogue probably included rooms adjacent to the main building designed to accommodate traveling Jews[11]. In this case, there exists the possibility of a real risk of incorporating the traveller, the pilgrim or simply the alien into the practices of the Jewish community. The welcomed person is in fact obliged to recite the *kiddush* (the blessing pronounced on the occasion of a meal or even at the beginning of the Sabbath) in the synagogue, according to the intention of the travellers who will remain and consume the meal.

As for practices of hospitality, public places of welcome based on the Greek model have been built since the end of the fourth century in competition with Christians but also and primarily to assist the weaker members in the community. Much later, in the Middle Ages, the *Sefer Hasidim* (Book of the Pious)[12] declared punishable by excommunication *(herem)* Jews who refused to contribute to donations flowing to charitable institutions.

> Although in this city there are the poor who are not able to earn a living, even a very mediocre one, it is established, under pain of excommunication, that everyone will have to give a share corresponding to his means [. . .] But if the nobles come to be aware of someone who is really poor, they are not to force them to pay, and will discreetly return to them what they had already given.[13]

---

11. P Bornet, 'Entre normes religieuses et impératifs éthiques', 160. There is no explicit mention of receiving non-Jews or pilgrims who have no intention of joining Jewish religious practice.

12. This is mainly due to the Ashkenazi movement flourishing between 1150 and 1250 CE in Speyer, Worms and Mainz, and especially to the work of Yehoudah hê-'Hassid, d 1217. It is an exceptional source regarding the relations between Jews and Christians in the Middle Ages, as also an expression of a current 'piety:' a sharp fall from the uncompromising practice of daily Jewish traditions.

13. *Sefer Hasidim*, 857, quoted by P Bornet, 'Entre normes et religieuses impératifs éthiques', 161.

The reference to the poor seems to be limited to the circle of the Jewish community, but it is already possible to note the importance given to charity and the means deployed to preserve social justice. However, this is a sphere of an institutionalized hospitality that does not directly affect our research and is, of course, only one aspect of the practice of hospitality.

The ritual of hospitality in the Jewish world

To conclude our journey of hospitality in the Jewish world, an itinerary essential to also understand the welcome in the heart of Christian culture, we evoke the milestones of a ritual that has been codified over the centuries.

If rabbinical requirements regulate general questions relative to hospitality, we will explore the details of its organization only marginally. As a general rule, the Talmud insists on the duty of hospitality and makes it clear that the latter cannot be limited to a meal or the distribution of food, but that it consists also of protection given by the host and in the deployment of a standard code of interaction between the one who welcomes and the one who is welcomed. We have to remember that the foreigner looks for hospitality, first of all, from among the people close to him, from someone who belongs, at least vaguely, to his family,[14] or, even, from a Jewish believer if he himself is an Israelite. In the absence of such conditions, sometimes, even after dark, one could still continue the journey so as not to be forced to ask for hospitality from complete strangers (Jg 19:12).

---

14. We have already recalled the story of Abraham's old servant who was sent to find a wife for Isaac from among the daughters of his kin (*cf* note 72, page 57 in reference to Gen 24:3–4). When the servant noticed Rebecca and found his mission to have been fulfilled by the Lord God, he prayed thus: 'Blessed be Yahweh, God of my master Abraham, for he has not stopped showing kindness and goodness to my master. Yahweh has guided my steps to the house of my master's brother' (Gen 24:27). Even more significant is the passage in the book of Tobit, where the elderly father, looking for a guide to escort his son in Media, meets the angel Raphael and tries to reassure himself about his knowledge of the way. The angel's answer is reassuring: 'I know all the ways by heart, and I have stayed with Gabael, one of our kinsmen' (Tb 5:6). The Jerusalem Bible continues the explanation: 'It usually takes two days to get from Ecbatana to Rages; Rages lies in the mountains, and Ecbatana is in the middle of the plain.'

66 *Strangers With God*

The rituals of hospitality described in biblical accounts follow precise codes that we can appropriate in some aspects, even if they are not always delineated in a systematic way: the preliminaries of the welcome, the crossing of the threshold, the ablutions, the meal and exchange of gifts (elements already present in other cultures). Among the initial characteristics of welcome we find recurrent modes of behavior, such as the host who sees the stranger from afar and runs to meet him (Gen 18:2; 19:1; 24:29; 43:16; Jg 19:3; 19:17). To go to meet or precede a traveller is a sign of great esteem.[15] Prostration, on the other hand, holds several meanings in Scripture.

> [Prostration] may be a sign of holy fear before the light of divinity; it may be a collective (Numb 14:5) or an individual (Nb 16:4) gesture. It may indicate supplication (Matt 15:25) or gratitude (Lk 17:16). On either side of the encounter, the *proskinesi* regards the guest in two ways: Solomon, receiving his mother Bathsheba, 'rose to meet her and bowed before her; he then sat down on his throne; a seat was brought for the mother of the king, and she sat down at his right hand' (1 K 2:19). This deference and gesture of respect for his mother (and the eminent position she occupies), expresses in this case the honour due in welcoming a guest of honour. [. . .] Such gestures may also emanate from those who receive hospitality. Joseph, now an official of Pharaoh, receives the visit of his brothers eager to buy grain in anticipation of the approaching famine. They who had previously sold him into slavery now fearfully 'bowed down before him, their faces touching the ground' (Gen 42:6). The hospitality is shadowed behind the terror of a power by which their fate is determined.[16]

---

15. When Jethro went to visit Moses in the desert, Moses, the biblical text tells us, 'went out to meet his father-in-law and bowing low before him he kissed him; and when each had inquired of the other's health, they went into the tent' (Ex 18:7).
16. A-C Pottier-Thoby, 'De la trahison à la rédemption', 130–131. This attitude is even more clearly expressed when Ruth the Moabite, having been allowed by Booz access to his land and authorised by him to gather the ears of corn behind the reapers, 'fell on her face [before him], bowing to the ground' (Ruth 2:10) . We find other examples in Gen 25:27 and 33:3. Returning to the gesture of prostration, we analyze in detail the story of Mamre (Gen 18:1-8) and the attitude of the patriarch Abraham. For a detailed study on the significance of the prostration, between its practice and sociological meanings and liturgical ritual, we refer to two articles of Roberto Tottoli that, while aimed primarily at

The stranger is very often a pilgrim of passage who asks for hospitality. This request is not always expressed explicitly but through attitudes free of any gestures. The story of the Levite of Ephraim who had taken as his concubine a woman from Bethlehem of Judah and followed her trail after her disappearance is significant. During the journey back to his hometown, he falls victim to the inhospitality of the Benjaminites. This is how the book of Judges describes the scene: 'The Levite sat down in the middle of the public square, but no one offered to take them into his house for the night' (Jg 19:15). A foreigner, who sits in the central square of a city at sunset, manifests implicitly, simply by his position, the intention to stop (because he seated himself) and ask for hospitality (he is outdoors, in middle of a beautiful piazza). He does not speak and does not ask for anything explicitly because, on the one hand, his attitude is eloquent, and on the other, he does not yet know if he can establish friendly relations in that unknown environment. The reply of the people of Gibeah is also eloquent in its silence: not to invite a stranger means not only to not meddle in his affairs, but it is also a real and proper rejection! They do not want to know anything about him because he is an Ephraimite (although a Levite) and they are Benjaminites. An old man, also from the mountains of Ephraim but now residing in Gibeah, turning toward him, recognises him as worthy of welcome, simply for the sake of welcoming someone.

In several stories of welcome, the guest received is identified with an angel or a messenger of God, if not with Yahweh himself (Gen 18:1–16; 19:1–23; Jg 13:16); sometimes the visitor simply represents another more prestigious character (Gen 24:34).

The host who welcomes the pilgrim with his generosity ensures his welfare; but very often the passing stranger also gives joy to those who welcome him. In the story already discussed, that of the meeting between Tobit and the angel Raphael, the latter responds to the greeting of the landlord: 'and the other answered, wishing him happiness' (Tob 5:10). The greeting is crucial because it demonstrates respect and kindness and, at the same time, represents a first contact which may be an opportunity to ensure the health of one's host (Ex 18:7). Like the formulas of a blessing, a greeting is part of the ritual that

---

prostration in the context of Islamic prayer, do not fail to analyze its biblical and pre-biblical origins (*cf* R Tottoli, 'Muslim attitudes towards prostration (sujūd)', in *Studia Islamica,* 88 (1998): 5–34 e in *Le Muséon,* 111/3, 4 (1998): 405–426).

each of the two protagonists of hospitality play and assumes almost a character of supplication or even of deep gratitude by the welcoming host, 'My lord, I beg you, if I find favour with you, kindly do not pass your servant by' (Gen 18:3). In the deferential words of the patriarch Abraham to the unknown pilgrims who pass by his tent, one senses the sacred character of the hospitable gesture that ennobles the one who makes it, even before it represents a blessing for those who receive it. The visitor, or more generally the one who is welcomed, is a gift from God himself (a theme we have already discussed in the course of our study): Tobit advances towards Sarah, his future daughter-in-law, praising God in joy and exclaiming 'Welcome, daughter! Blessed be your God for sending you to us, my daughter. Blessings on your father, blessings on my son Tobias, blessings on yourself, my daughter. Welcome now to your own house in joyfulness and in blessedness. Come in, my daughter' (Tob 11:17). This biblical passage emphasizes the joyful side of hospitality, which is also one of its main characteristics, as recalls the treatise *Pirqé Avot*: 'Shammai says: make your [study of] Torah a fixed reference, speak little and act much, and welcome every one making a good impression.'[17] 'Making a good impression' or 'making the best' is, in fact, the expression of a joyful attitude, because he who gives with sadness is as if he had given nothing, as the rabbinical commentaries note.

If the greeting frames the act of hospitality, the leave-taking is based on the same model, and the absence of a greeting (not to mention the insult) constitutes an unforgivable shortcoming. Sent by the Seleucid king Demetrius to repress the revolt of the Maccabees, General Nicanor is guilty of this transgression: 'After these events Nicanor went up to Mount Zion. Some of the priests came out from the Holy Place with some elders, to welcome him peacefully and to show him the holocaust that was being offered for the king. But he mocked them and laughed in their faces, defiled them [according to a Jewish tradition, by spitting towards the Temple] and used insolent language, swearing in his rage' (1 Mac 7:33–34).[18] Nicanor, shortly

---

17. *Pirqé Avot*, I, 15, 26.

18. Nicanor was general of the Syrian army waging war in Judea; by deception, he tried to complete the project of the destruction of Jerusalem by mocking, among other things, the rules of hospitality, because he was introduced earlier as a friend and with a peaceful attitude: 'He came to Judas [Judas and his brothers] and they greeted each other peaceably enough; however, the enemy had made preparations to abduct Judas. When Judas became aware of Nicanor's treacherous purpose in coming to see him, he took fright and refused any further meeting' (1 Mac 7:29–30).

after launching an attack on Adasa, meets his death and his remains are displayed on the walls of Zion. Failure to observe the rules of hospitality or, more simply, inhospitality, as we have already pointed out, brings with it serious consequences with repercussions on the theology of retribution, both communal and individual. Further, hospitality given or refused, according to Talmudic commentaries, brings with it consequences that go beyond the limits of this world, reaching even into an eschatological future.[19]

Places of accorded hospitality

We have mentioned crossing the threshold among the rites of hospitable gestures. 'The place of this frontier—explains Pottier-Thoby—was regarded as the abode of the spirits. This is the meaning of the tradition of leaping over the threshold, as it is explained after the ark of God fell into the hands of the Philistines. These placed the ark in the temple of their main deity (the god Dagon).'[20] As explained in the first book of Samuel, the holiness of the ark had disturbing effects on the statue of the god Dagon which fell to the ground on its face before the ark of Yahweh, with its head and hands lying severed on the threshold of the temple. 'This is why the priests of Dagon and indeed all who enter Dagon's temple do not step on the threshold of Dagon in Ashdod to the present day' (1 Sam 5:5). This custom (which was probably transferred, in some cases, even to the threshold of private homes) is violently condemned by the prophet Zephaniah: 'I mean to punish all those who are near the throne [literally 'those who ascend the step' (here probably the dais of the throne)], those who fill the palace of their lord with violence and deceit' (Zep 1:9). With these words, the prophet stigmatizes the degeneration of the idolatrous practices of the Holy City, guilty of being seduced by foreign cults and practices (Ez 23:41; Isa 65:13). The threshold in the Bible also indicates the area for the inscription of the Law ('Listen, Israel: Yahweh our God is the one Yahweh. You shall love Yahweh your God with all your heart, with all your soul, with all your strength. Let these words I urge on you today be written on your heart . . . You shall fasten them on your hand as a sign and on your forehead as a circlet;

---

19. *Cf TB Shabbat* 127a o ancora *TB Berakhot* 54b.
20. A-C Pottier-Thoby, 'De la trahison à la rédemption', 133.

you shall write them on the doorposts of your house and on your gates' (Deut 6:4–5; 8–9); that is, the boundary between the inside and the outside of the house which protects access. Basically, to enter a home means to accept hospitality under the eyes of God: a rendition in the Semitic context of *philoxenia* that turns into *teofilia*, already strongly present in the Greek context.

Between the first blessing that accompanies the crossing of the threshold of the tent or home and the meal, the apex of the act of hospitality, the custom reported in the scriptures and Talmudic commentaries required that one offer water for the ritual ablution. Examples of this are innumerable (Gen 18:4; 19:2; 24:32; 43:24): it is for the guest to get rid of the dust that covers his feet, which is an impurity. In the evangelical recommendation, 'If anyone does not welcome you or listen to what you have to say, as you walk out of the house or town shake the dust from your feet' (Matt 10:14), we capture the value of a highly symbolic gesture that can become a judgment of impiety. Conversely, when hospitality is accorded, it establishes brotherhood and removes any sense of hostility (represented by the dust of paths travelled in constant danger of attack when one is not protected). However, in the case of a rejected welcome, judgment is merciless: 'On the day of Judgment it will not go as hard with the land of Sodom and Gomorra as with that town' (Matt 10:15) because the comparison with Sodom (whose crime was precisely the transgression of the holy rules of hospitality) reveals the importance of the welcome reserved for a stranger. But beyond purification and ablution, water—especially well water—is one of the focal points in the biblical world that make possible the existence of a human society (after all, following the ablutions, among the first concerns of the host is quenching the thirst of a guest). The wells are meeting places, like tents of nomads in perpetual transhumance, around which are created 'a microcosm of human society, with its individual cravings and needs to measure toward others its generosity or selfishness'.[21] The wells become venues of a particular type of hospitality: that between a man and a woman, especially in the Hebrew Bible. Three texts depict the natural background of the evangelical encounter of Jesus with a woman of Samaria: We have Gen 24:12–14, which revolves around

---

21. Fr John di Taizé, *Alla sorgente. Gesù e la Samaritana* (Paova: Edizioni Messaggero, Padova 2011), 14.

Abraham's attempt to procure a bride for his son Isaac; Genesis 29:1–14 where, in a reversal of roles, Jacob offers water to an unknown woman, Rachel, who will become his bride;[22] and in Ex 2:15–22 Moses comes to the aid of the priest Reuel's seven daughters at the well of Midian. All three Old Testament stories of encounters at a well culminate with a wedding; hospitality results in a marriage covenant, a gift, without doubt, the most ambivalent of all the gifts of hospitality because it can also intervene in the context of the transgression of hospitality itself. On the one hand, it seems that the sacred duty of welcome has a value larger than the honor or even the existence of a woman or a bride; on the other, the linkage between sexuality and hospitality seems consistent with a certain ambiguity.

> So–Pottier-Thoby reminds us–to possess his wife, David does not hesitate to break the rules of hospitality with regard to one of his officers, Uriah, a foreigner (a Hittite) living under his roof (2 Sam 12:4). Reversing the situation in a kind of sexual blackmail against an invited guest, the hostess, the wife of Potiphar, Pharaoh's captain of the guard, proposes the hospitality of her body to Joseph in her marital home [. . .] In either case, the lure fails; for Joseph, her lack of hospitality brings him disgrace and punishment, from which, nevertheless, he emerges more or less victorious (Gen 39:7; 41:36).[23]

But, leaving aside sexual extremes, the sharing of a meal is undoubtedly the pinnacle of the act of hospitality.

> If the tablets of the Covenant were the sign of God's hospitality toward the Chosen People as they journeyed to the Promised Land (Ex 31:18); and if the oblations offered on the altar of the Temple ensured the exclusive hospitality of Israel's heart toward the one God; then on the contrary, the royal table of antiquity did *not* represent the height of human hospitality. For one who more or less served the interests of the prince, to be admitted to his table was an honor [. . .] In oriental courts, young foreigners, born to subjected peoples, were educated and served from the king's table: such was the case of the young Daniel (Dn 1:5).[24]

---

22. In both cases, it is very significant that the initiative is taken to refresh the thirsty person, even before his or her identity is known.
23. A-C Pottier-Thoby, 'De la trahison à la rédemption', 143.
24. A-C Pottier-Thoby, 'De la trahison à la rédemption', 139.

The host must balance the joyful welcome to which we have alluded with a desire to put his guest at ease. To do this, the host places himself at the service of his guests, emphasizing his desire to satisfy them in everything, without, however, overwhelming them with insistent attention.[25] Of course, the person to whom hospitality is offered is free to accept or decline the invitation, but he must not on his own initiative bring another guest or cause harm to those who receive him (for example, by giving away food reserved for the children and servants of the host). On the contrary, the guest received must leave some food on the plate to show that the meal that had been reserved for him was enough. The servants can benefit from the leftover food afterwards, except for when the host explicitly invites the guest to finish the portion that had been offered.[26]

In the Middle Ages, and more particularly after the Crusades, hospitality became increasingly a necessity and not just a gratuitous act or a sign of extravagance. Poor beggars or traveling students were received in public hospices. Early on, a voucher was also established that allowed pilgrims to receive food and lodging, a custom still present today in the form of public housing. Of course, every abuse and all forms of parasitism (which may relate to the host as well as to the guest), brought with it unpleasant consequences, especially when a man considered to be wise was responsible for the transgression:

> A *talmid hakham* [a wise man or, literally, 'a disciple of the wise;' ed.] who allows himself to be invited to innumerable banquets, will eventually cause the ruin of his home, make his wife a widow, his children orphans, and will eventually forget his knowledge and stir up numerous criticisms in his regard, etc.[27]

The progressive institutionalization of charity transforms the sacred duty into an act of justice, allowing those who are in need regain their dignity and become able once again to provide independently for their own needs. However, we must fear the possibility of hospitality becoming routine when it limits itself to safeguarding the fulfillment

---

25. *Cf* Aa.Vv, 'Hospitality', in *The Jewish Encyclopedia* (London and New York: Funk and Waqualls Company, 1904), 480–481.
26. *Cf* Aa.Vv, 'Hospitality', 480–481.
27. *TB Pessahim*, 49a, cited by P Bornet, 'Entre normes religieuses et impératifs éthiques', 158.

of an outward rite, separating the container from the content; that is, removing the gesture from its profound meaning and from the spiritual foundation that ought to animate it. It is here that one must be loyal to the biblical roots of the act of hospitality, that is, to the divine reference as the first component of Jewish morality, reference to which is added the memory of a concrete experience: the historical journey of the chosen people continually welcomed by their God.

Conclusion

A study of the statute and profound significance of 'the foreigner' in the Old Testament and then, a fortiori, in later Jewish perception, places us before experiences and biblical definitions that seem contradictory or, at least, hardly reconcilable. They are theological reflections of a complex story which blends economic, social, cultural, and religious elements. Nevertheless, one cannot but see that the underlying reasons that give coherence and unity to biblical legislation on the rights of foreigners and on which the duty of hospitality is founded, come from a religious experience that constitutes the foundation of Israel's belief, and not from natural or sociological reasons, or from those based on political calculation. It remains, however, a paradox, not to speak of a real contradiction, in the Jewish vision of the foreigner and the posture taken towards him. On the one hand, the Psalmist will sing the biblical text that celebrates the Lord who establishes the Kingdom which remains true because Yahweh 'gives justice to those denied it, gives food to the hungry. [. . .] Yahweh protects the stranger . . .' (Ps 146:7; 9). On the other hand, again the psalms celebrate the victory of God over foreign peoples at the hands of a king who will break them with an iron scepter and shatter them like potter's ware (*cf* Ps 2:8–9). We have here the testimony of a very articulate perception of foreigners, sometimes seen as a threat, and sometimes in a social, cultural, and, above all, religious, context. But the response does not only determine a process of assimilation aimed at reducing, if not eliminating, fearful differences; nor does it try to exorcise the fear of the other through an opposite more or less destructive process of rejection.[28] As Rinaldo Fabris reminds us:

---

28. *Cf* R Fabris, 'Lo straniero nell'Antico Testamento', in *Servitium*, 25 (1991): 29–39. As Bruno Maggioni recalls, rightly, it is very curious that obedience to the commandments of God alone has never been able to solve the obvious tension

There are within the biblical tradition some religious elements which, beneath the cultural and social contours, effectively diffuse the ambivalence of the relationship with a stranger. The first element of great symbolic efficacy is the image of God the Creator who founded the right of peoples to meet and live in their own diversity. The second great fertile principle in biblical history is the experience of the Exodus and the corresponding image of God in solidarity with the oppressed and abused, and therefore defender and guarantor of the rights of the poor, the orphan, the widow and the stranger. This image of God as Creator and Saviour is the basis of biblical 'righteousness' as a network of relationships that promote the life and dignity of every human person. In fact, the action of God as Creator informs the experience of gratuitousness and God's intervention as Redeemer remains the standard of our own care for one another.[29]

We shall see later how, in Christ, this new image of God will reach its peak in solidarity, as well as the need for Christians to be open to the needs of their less fortunate brethren, who have now become members of the one and only family of God.

---

between different positions towards foreigners. For the love of God they fought the pagans to defend the purity of their religious affiliation; in the name of that same love of God, they welcomed and protected the foreign migrant in Israel, and still for the sake of God, they tried to assimilate and integrate them, at least in part, into the heart of the Chosen People itself. Obviously, everything depends on the idea that what we do is for God and for the love of God (*cf* B Maggioni, 'Lo straniero nell'Antico e nel Nuovo Testamento', 31–34).

29. B Maggioni, 'Lo straniero nell'Antico e nel Nuovo Testamento', 39

Hospitality in the Arab World

We began our research on the value of hospitality chronologically, looking first to the culture and history of the Jewish people. Now however, since the Arab world is obviously more in continuity geographically and culturally with the Jewish context, we depart from chronology for a more logical approach. We begin here our examination of the Islamic tradition, before resuming with the New Testament and the Christian tradition.

Welcome in the Middle East

The Middle East: defining a geographical and cultural area

The concept of 'Semitism,' which we used at the commencement of this journey, is not alone in creating questions of scientific merit. We are confronted here with a second term much discussed and debated: that of the "Middle East.[1]" It originated at the heart of the strategic interests of the European powers in the early twentieth century and was developed principally during the two world wars. In 1942, as designated by the British War Office, the Middle East was comprised of Iran, the Arabian Peninsula, Turkey, Egypt, Libya, Sudan and the Horn of Africa (Eritrea, Ethiopia, Djibouti and Somalia).[2] Today, anthropologists and cultural geographers refer to the Middle East as that region of the world which extends from the Anatolian Peninsula in the North to the Horn of Africa in the South and from Mauritania in the West to the Indus River (the eastern border of Pakistan) in the East.[3] This amalgamation of countries is justified both historically and geographically. Indeed, this corresponds, in broad strokes, to those territories that were, in successive eras, three great Muslim empires: The Umayyad Empire (661–750); the Abbasid Empire (750–1258) and the Ottoman Empire (1281–1922). Mauritania was included in this area as part of the Maghreb[4] and Sudan as an integral part of

---

1. The Middle East is an expression of Anglo-Saxon origin which became prevalent in the West during the early years of the twentieth century.
2. *Cf* P Beaumont, GH Blake, JM Wagstaff, *The Middle East. A Geographical Study*, cited by U Fabietti, *Culture in bilico*, (Milano: Mondadori, 2002), 2.
3. U Fabietti, *Culture in bilico*, 2.
4. Literally means 'sunset.' Geographers coined this term in the eighth century (during the time of the Arab-Islamic conquests of the west and Mediterranean

Egypt. Alongside the historical and geographical criteria, there are more strictly cultural considerations: for example, two-thirds of the population of Pakistan is related by language, culture and social organization to the community of the Iranian world.

From these more general considerations and for the purpose of our research, we have adopted the term 'Middle East' to avoid speaking about the Arab-Muslim world *tout court*. Not all Arabs are Muslim; nor are all the peoples or countries of this geographical area only Arabs or Muslims. Thus, we bypass a double contradiction easily challenged.[5]

A commonly held representation of the Middle East alludes to a kind of 'tribal' society. A tribal society will confer a great importance on interpersonal agreements between groups and individuals, in order to determine the legal rules to be developed, only much later, in constitutional or written law. It is surprising to note that there is greater stability and statistically fewer conflicts in the forms of social solidarity than in family relationships. Nonetheless, many anthropologists make no distinction between family relationships and those established among individuals not related by kinship.

Certainly, to draw conclusions about hospitality in the Arab world, limiting ourselves specifically to Bedouin tribes in a Middle Eastern context might seem quite arbitrary and not sufficiently representative. The practices of the pre-Islamic Arab Bedouin tribes

---

coast of Africa) because it is situated in the westernmost part of the Arab countries. Only later as the Muslims began to stress their absolute opposition to Christianity and clashed with Europe as 'barbarians' and 'infidels', were the formulas *dar al-harb* ('land of war'—those areas not yet conquered by Islam) and *dar al-islam* ('abode of Islam') created to include the much larger territories of the Middle East today.

5. We return here to the idea, already mentioned, of a 'primordial Semitic substratum' preexisting Islam. It is a concept introduced by the Orientalists of the eighteenth century who considered Islam as an intolerant and oppressive religion. In the nineteenth century, Auguste Renan (1823–1892) will assign to the Arabs of the desert or to the Bedouins the role of representing a 'proto-Semitic culture'. In a course taught at the Collège de France (1888–1889) on a topic comparing the patriarchal legends of the Jews and the Arabs, Renan maintained that Islam has had little influence on the type of life led by the nomadic Arabs, and that the better part of their social practices predated Islamization and were common to the Semitic world (cf. U. Fabietti, *Culture in bilico*, 11). These statements reflect a rather negative view of Islam and even a tendency to assert the autonomy of anthropology over that of religion.

represent a particular case within a world much more extensive and diversified. We analyse this setting, however, because it reflects a human, social and cultural ambient most likely to be very close to that of the patriarch Abraham and his clan and so, by extension, to the natural cradle of the Chosen People's beginnings[6].

Antonin Jaussen: hospitality in a Bedouin context

Without neglecting obvious parallels with the customs of the inhabitants of the Negev, Father Antonin Jaussen, whose research concerned the nomadic and semi-sedentary peoples of Moab, emphasized in speaking of good deeds among the Arabs: 'Never will an Arab eat a piece of bread, either on the road or in a tent, without inviting all his companions or any stranger present, to take part in his meal.'[7] The great Dominican ethnologist organized in two separate chapters all that concerns hospitality in an Arab context: one chapter deals more particularly with the ritual of welcome and the meal, lingering on the characteristics of the accommodations and the food; the second chapter examines hospitality when bestowed as an act of protection of a foreign traveller or to a Bedouin hunted by the terrible blood vengeance. The author, in carrying out his task, describes the relationships within the family, clan or tribe with particular care, gradually casting light on the roles the different actors play in their social life: from the Bedouin *sheikh* (the head or elder) of the tribe to the women of the *harem*. Blind spots remain, most likely because these relationships are not fixed or definitely established. Nevertheless, Antonin Jaussen discovers among the Bedouins all the sociological types that are represented in the Bible: a family reduced to its limits up to and including the tribe if not the entire people; no unifying characteristics apart from the same worship and reference to the one eponymous ancestor. The discretion and modesty of the researcher, conscious of intruding into a very complex world, are present throughout the whole of his study.

---

6. We will refer to two studies in particular: the renowned *Coutumes des Arabes au pays de Moab* (Paris Victor Lecoffre, 1908) of Father Antonin Jaussen, Dominican; and *Sons of Ismael. A Study of the Egyptian Bedouin* (London: Routledge, 1935) of the Scottish geographer GW Murray who lived just under twentyfive years in the Egyptian desert.

7. A Jaussen, *Coutumes des Arabes au pays de Moab*, 78.

Entering into a relationship with an Arab seems, at first glance, a very simple undertaking. The welcome beneath the tent is always in conformity to the ancient traditions of hospitality so often described by travellers. But the consumption of once-in-a-lifetime roasted mutton, an indulgence in fresh, savory butter from a large wooden container, and sweet camel's or sheep's milk offers only a minute corner of this bizarre existence; the true forms, the actual outlines, will always remain in the shadows; the intimate feelings will never be manifested; the constitution of the family, the functioning of the tribe and, more importantly, the Arab's religious aspirations, will almost entirely escape the visitor's gaze who, introduced to that part of the tent reserved for guests, cannot penetrate the inner sanctuary where the Bedouin's life unfolds. To gather information, one must be resigned to spending long hours, virtually silent, squatting on a carpet in a 'house' of animal hide that just barely protects from the sun; must answer questions both curious and prying; and must deflect the suspicion aroused simply because one is not of Arabic blood. One will be constrained to accept the Bedouin manner of handling the food, always insufficient for a European, and overcome a repugnance for plunging one's hands into a common plate and drinking water that seems not too clear from a jug that holds enough for about fifteen or so invited guests. Evening comes. With the greatest care, the host prepares a bed for the stranger: one or two carpets lying on the ground; a camel saddle to act as a pillow, a blanket that one accepts with some apprehension: it augurs well for a happy and peaceful night.[8]

We continue with some particularly interesting details of this description, beginning with the place that sets the scene for the meeting and ritual of hospitality: the tent.

The *sheikh's* tent: The heart of the ritual of hospitality

The tent derives its importance neither from its dimensions nor from the elegance of its material. Constructed of goatskin stretched over wooden stakes, there is not, in most cases, any pretense of magnificence or luxury. This tent, in appearance so fragile, is however protected by a strict law, the violation of which can have serious consequences.

---

8. Jaussen, *Coutumes des Arabes au pays de Moab,* 2–3.

> Anyone entering beneath this coarse bit of cloth, whether he comes as guest or friend or by any other title, commits himself thereby to respect the dwelling and all its inhabitants. If it should happen that, during a conversation, two strangers or even two Arabs of the tribe in question, quarrel to the point of hurling insults or coming to blows, the householder is bound to subdue the uprising and to make amends for the outrage committed against his tent.[9]

The 'right of the tent' (or the Law of the tent, *haqq al-baīt*) is so stringent as to require, even for small violations, a reparation sometimes enormous, because the tent is owned by a Bedouin and, consequently, shares his dignity and honour. The nomad considers the tent as a part of himself and defends its honour as if it were his own personal ug enough to represent him in this charge. This defense extends beyond other persons to include livestock as well as all their possessions. George Murray, in his study of the Egyptian Bedouins, tells us that, conversely, the tent also protects its owner because no one will ever kill someone inside a tent; in fact, to avoid such a risk the Bedouins generally leave their weapons outside. Murray questions the origin of this inviolability of the tent and his answer is quite impressive: he draws a link between the sacredness of the tent and the protection lent by a woman when matriarchy still had some importance. In the pre-Islamic Arabic tradition, a refugee was under protection when a woman covered him with her cloak. One can imagine a symbolic continuity between a man's possession of a *harīm*[10] and his possession of a tent: the latter represents a new mantle of protection. It varies in shape and, above all, by its size: that of the chief of the tribe is the largest of the entire camp. In pre-Islamic times, it was the center of the camp, often at an elevated position, protected by dogs, sometimes surrounded by a circle of small fires

---

9. Jaussen, *Coutumes des Arabes au pays de Moab*, 200. The author specifies further that there are two ways the conflict can resolved: it can be brought before a judge or it can be settled amicably.

10. This term can mean at the same time 'sacred' or 'hearth.' It shares the same root as the word *haram*, 'forbidden,' in the religious sense of the word, designating properly the sacred precincts of Mecca and Medina, the two holiest cities of Islam par excellence. By extension, *harīm* is the sacred place of the hearth where the women live and which cannot be accessed except by the host's invitation. It can also serve as a hiding place to shield a man pursued for blood vengeance.

and often of a different color than the others.[11] In the Islamic era, with the transition to stable housing units, the center of the village was gradually set aside for the mosque, alongside which is found, most often, the dwelling of its representative caliph.[12] However, even in this new context, the *sheikh*'s dwelling stands out from among the other houses of the village because of its location which is a bit distant from the rest and near the great caravan routes, making him accessible to travellers. He can therefore, enhance his reputation and extend his influence by welcoming all foreigners with kindness and concern.[13] The reputation of the *sheikh* and consequently of the whole tribe depends very much on the generosity of the welcome (it is not unusual for tribal leaders to sacrifice all their goods to fulfill the obligations of hospitality) and must be completed with gifts made to the chief lieutenants as well and to the leaders of neighboring tribes, as well as distributing aid to the poor: allotting a camel to this one, a sheep to another, to show himself a father to all.[14]

---

11. *Cf* B Scarcia Amoretti, *Un altro Medioevo. Il quotidiano nell'Islam* (Roma-Bari: Laterza 2001), 28.
12. This shift from a private home, usually that of the tribal chief, to the house of prayer is already foreshadowed by the meanings of a common Semitic root term for 'dwelling:' for the nomad the reference is to a 'tent;' 'house' is reserved for a more permanent abode (made of stone, wood or brick) and circumscribed in a determined place. The radical term is *baīt* or *beīt*. In Arabic, *al-Baīt*, applies to Mecca, the holy place par excellence. Besides this literal meaning, *baīt* is used in a figurative sense to refer to one's ancestors. The noun *beyt* is still used by the Arabs to speak about their parents while they continue to live together with them. Among the nomads it is rare to hear the term used in the sense of 'house,' although the term is not unknown, both with the meaning of an encampment or inhabited place and in the sense of a private home.
13. Father Jaussen reports that an individual *sheikh* might come, in a single day, to give hospitality to sixty or eighty people; in this case it would not be unusual to slaughter three or four rams on the same day (A. Jaussen, *Coutumes des Arabes au pays de Moab,* 130).
14. If the *sheikh* is accompanied while visiting a city or entering a bazaar, he is morally obligated to buy for his traveling companions the same objects that he procures for himself (*cf* Jaussen, *Coutumes des Arabes au pays de Moa*b, 130). In short, there is no *sheikh* without a substantial personal fortune that allows him to fulfill these charges and especially to practice hospitality. The *sheikh*'s wealth is fuelled largely by three sources: his land, his livestock and by raids (Jaussen, *Coutumes des Arabes au pays de Moa*b, 136). It is the sheikh's duty also to inquire about the condition of the desert and that of neighbouring tribes, about conflicts breaking out and raids in progress. In a word, the *sheikh* is expected to know

Welcome in the Middle East

There are other details that underline the importance of the tent of welcome. The traveller or pilgrim must arrive at the back of the tent and not pass the main entrance in order to avoid embarrassing the women or lacking in respect for the men. (If the path leads to the entrance of the tent, etiquette suggests that a slight detour be taken, a detail that seems curiously at odds with the principle that the tent be open on all four sides as an indication of unconditional hospitality). The new arrival can then enter the tent from the right of the entrance, the other side generally reserved for the women and family[15]. Only after the visitor has been settled on the carpet do the customary greetings begin, several times repeated. Antoine Jaussen tells of three types of greeting in practice among the Bedouins. The simplest, common to all the East, consists in a wish for peace, *salām,* by those who meet: 'Peace',[16] says the nobler to his inferior. 'Peace upon you', replies the latter. In place of this formula we sometimes hear another: *gawwak,* 'that God (understood Allah) may strengthen you'. 'There is no mention of any gesture of either head or hand; having uttered these words, each continues quietly on his way'.[17] The second type of greeting is used especially in an encounter between friends, or when a Bedouin, arriving from the desert, is among a group of his neighboring tribe. After the greeting of peace, he extends his hand to all those present and returns it to his heart, asking the question: '*Kaīfa anta,* how are you?' After this first manifestation of mutual joy on meeting again, he sits on the carpet and again receives peace, a friendly *salām,* by all those present, to which the guest responds: *Allah iusallimak* (God keep you in peace).

---

everything necessary to inform his course of action, because he has to ensure not only the good order of his tribe but also effect good external relations with the neighbouring tribes.

15. This provision is not always respected. Commonly, that part of the tent reserved for the family is called *harīm,* while a separated space for guests to eat, sleep and entertain, is the *siq.* A cloth curtain, usually very rich, called *sahah,* serves to separate the two areas mentioned above. Murray notes that, on special occasions, the entire tent can be provisionally opened up to welcome guests (*cf* Murray, *Sons of Ismael. A Study of the Egyptian Bedouin,* 81).

16. There is of course also the extended form *al-salamu alaykum* which can be translated as 'peace be upon you'.

17. Jaussen, *Coutumes des Arabes au pays de Moab,* 280.

> The most solemn formula of greeting is used in meeting friends or an esteemed Bedouin: an embrace three times, touching forehead to forehead, and a kiss on the cheek as a sign of affection.[18]

This wealth of details, this multiplicity of ways to address the other in greeting, highlights the importance, quite unknown to Westerners, of establishing a good contact and, above all, of creating a climate of mutual trust between the host and the guest in the desert.

> An Arab who offers no peace is considered an enemy, and will be treated as such. If he passes near a camp without extending any sign of friendship, he will immediately be regarded with suspicion and sometimes constrained by force to explain his behaviour.[19]

In some tribes, each of the Arabs present, in turn, offers peace to the new arrival who is then obliged to respond to each one. A fire is lighted and a hot drink prepared as a sign of hospitality, which will be offered at least twice (all present are encouraged to partake, usually drinking from the same cup). The visitor will wait patiently for the meal to follow but will not ask explicitly for it, even if he is very hungry. The very fact of being seated in the tent is already a sufficient indication of the visitor's desire and the householder's duty in this matter. In like manner, it would be a serious dishonour to the master of the tent to leave just before the meal is served, even if it were to answer another call. For his part, a nomad who receives a foreigner has the obligation to stay with him the entire time of his stay, refusing any other invitations or commitments. That being said, if the stay in the camp is prolonged, the guest is not permitted to visit other tents or accept their food. Once more, a visit to the tent of the *sheikh* is a sign of respect indispensable to the heart of an established protocol.

The hospitality meal and its service

The ministrations toward guests for the meal are not necessarily the same as that of their reception and the first exchange of greetings. Concerning the food, meat is not a staple among nomads, chiefly

---

18. Jaussen, *Coutumes des Arabes au pays de Moab*, 280.

19. We will return later to the relationship between the formula of greeting and belief.

Welcome in the Middle East   85

because of its high cost and the difficulty of preservation after slaughter. Unquestioningly absent among the poor, meat is not served very often even by rich and wealthy Bedouins. Even so, it is good to give a few more details on the rite of sacrificing the ram of hospitality. Once again, we rely on the impressive study of Father Jaussen.

> The victim—says our author—must be sacrificed in honor of the guest who arrives; it is for him that the blood is spilled;[20] and it is by the shedding of blood that the guest's dignity is enhanced. If after a first immolation and the meat already roasting on the fire, a second guest, more important than the first or of the same rank, is at the threshold of the tent, the householder must slaughter a new victim, spill the blood of another sheep. Even if the first had been sufficient for the meal, the arrival of a new guest is to be honored with a new outpouring of blood. It is the *dabīhat ad-Daīf* [sacrificial victim for the guest] that pays honor and 'binds us together,' the Arabs say, because, before the immolation of the victim, the guest is still free to leave the tent in which he was received; once the ram is killed, he no longer can; he is bound [. . .] The *dabīhat* (victim) is entirely for the guest, even if he is alone or accompanied by only one person. A sheep or goat is laid before him on a large flat copper plate brought in by the servants [. . .] The *dabīhat* served at noon cannot be offered again in the evening. Meat is not to be kept within the tent; once the guest had been satisfied, what is left over must be given to the poor, always very numerous in the camp (but first, and very often, to the women and children waiting for the remains to eat).[21] It is not even permitted to serve guests any of the meat that had been reserved: It is necessary to offer sacrifice, the *dabīhat* is intended.[22]

---

20. This account makes us realize that the slaughter is made in a *halal* manner; that is, that the animal was slaughtered and its blood left to run out entirely.

21. It would be wholly improper for the traveller to ask to take along any part of the sacrificed animal for the rest of his journey.

22. Jaussen, *Coutumes des Arabes au pays de Moab*, 349–350. Father Jaussen reminds us that the Arabic word *dabīhaeh* properly means 'female animal,' such as sheep, goat, camel . . . (338). Now, the slaughter is characterized by an outpouring of blood and not only by its use, and this in itself takes on an almost ritual significance. But again Antoine Jaussen insists, 'we should not give a religious meaning to all the sacrifices, on which, moreover, I do not want to pass judgment [. . .] It is not my intention, by sometimes translating *dabīhaeh* as "sacrifice", to

Thanks to this description, it is easy to realize why the presence of meat is very rare for the nomads of the desert. A whole ram, even for a single guest, necessarily manifests a lavishness that is no longer a simple expression of what is humanly possible but symbolises an almost divine generosity.

In fact, the staples in a normal Bedouin diet are barley, corn, wheat, rice, lentils, and dates. Often the traveller will be satisfied with a plate of ground wheat, sun-dried and then cooked with butter (much more available than fresh milk and easier to maintain) or oil,[23] except perhaps under the *sheikh's* tent where a particular abundance may be enjoyed. Bread and water are virtually the only two foods in most of the tents (the bread in particular is already a luxury and many people in the desert will go for months without tasting it, living instead on milk and dates.[24]. Whatever may be prepared is offered to the guests on a plate of wood or copper. Despite a long tradition of well-kept ablutions, Jaussen notes that the Arabs are very limited in its usage, generally washing their right hands, the hand that will be dipped into the dish, with a little water poured from a servant. The diners, squatting around the great dish resting on the ground, after having tucked up their sleeve, usually very long, and after pronouncing the invocation 'in the name of Allah very merciful,' dip their right hand into the flat dish all together.[25] Eating is so important that nothing is to be spoken during the meal. The *sheikh* rarely eats with the guests; he will limit himself to joining the others after some delay and urging

---

make it a ritual act, invested with all the conditions of a true Semitic sacrifice; it will be good to see in my use of this term simply a way to avoid repeating the word "immolation" too often' (338–339). By these clarifications, Father Jaussen advises us not to attribute a sacrificial meaning, in the religious sense of the term, to the immolation of an animal for a meal in the context of Bedouin hospitality, too hastily.

23. Murray calls this dish *burghul,* distinguishing it from ground wheat simply prepared with water like rice or lentils, often with butter, and called *jereisha* o *ğarišeh* (Murray, *Sons of Ismael. A Study of the Egyptian Bedouin,* 86).

24. There are several kinds of milk. In Bedouin culture, milk, as well as salt and water, loses much of its value by being bought and sold: trade in these foods is essentially considered disrespectful because of their sacredness.

25. Jaussen notes, however, that 'despite the fact that the Arabs attack their food with a certain greediness, they know how to restrain themselves before a visitor and demonstrate some courtesy before him' (Jaussen, *Coutumes des Arabes au pays de Moab,* 129). In short, ordinarily a guest is the first to bring his hand to his mouth.

them to eat heartily. Very often, he will bring a pot of melted butter to pour over the meat which has usually already been amply buttered. It is a sign of generosity and a way to honor the guest.[26] When the first diner rises, he responds to the *sheikh* who had invited him to take more, 'I have had enough thanks to Allah'. It is inappropriate, in fact, to finish everything on the plate; as already mentioned, a little is left for the poor of the tribe who are waiting, always wordlessly, for what remains. Even the ablutions after the meal are rare; usually the guests will wipe their hands on the tent flap set aside for this use.[27]. To a guest of repute, be he an Arab or a foreigner, a bit of water may be taken to wash his hands and rinse his mouth.[28] Once the meal is finished, normally the position taken at the time of welcome is resumed, to sip a cup of coffee or tea,[29] and thus complete the feast.

Hospitality is an honour shared with the entire tribe

Long conversations begin only when the meal is ended and after a sacred bond of trust and respect has been established, because it is precisely in the sharing of food that defines the privileged relationship between the host who offers welcome and the guest who receives it. The Bedouin in encountering an enemy will refuse to eat with him or offer him food, even outside his tent. Conversely, once a relationship has been created, one can venture the most intimate questions and sleep beneath the shelter of the same tent without fear of theft or abuse.

---

26. Father Jaussen notes that the *sheikh* may even place his own hand in the dish to choose the most tender pieces of meat and place them before his guest (Jaussen, *Coutumes des Arabes au pays de Moab*, 129).

27. Called the *raffah*, the 'outer border' (Jaussen, *Coutumes des Arabes au pays de Moab*, 74).

28. This custom, in some circles, is considered a sign of decadence. This is evident from the ironic observations of an old Bedouin as recalled by Father Jaussen: 'Soon our Arabs will be demanding forks and spoons! At one time, we ate good butter with both hands and then wiped our fingers on our beard; we had no towels, but we were the stronger in war, the bravest in the raids, and sometimes killed sheep to feed the poor' (Jaussen, *Coutumes des Arabes au pays de Moab*, 81–82, footnote 2).

29. What was said concerning the *dabīheh*, or the 'sacrificial victim for the guest', can be applied by analogy to the presentation of coffee in the desert; offering a cup of good black coffee is the first act of hospitality beneath the tent. It could happen that the coffee maker is full, but when a guest arrives custom demands that new coffee is made (Jaussen, *Coutumes des Arabes au pays de Moab*, 350).

We have already seen that the nomad's bed is very simple: a carpet placed on the ground as a mattress and a blanket to protect against the cold of the desert nights. Yet the care and the quality of reception are always directly proportional to the importance of the visitors. In most cases, the leaders and all the more important members of a tribe have a *madafah*, that is, a space reserved for guests. Each will dispense liberality at will. But in many encampments a specified place for guests is reserved (as is the custom in settled areas as well and not merely in a nomadic context); this will be a tent or a house under the charge of the whole tribe. In this case, by unanimous agreement within the clan, each in turn will have the responsibility of receiving guests and feeding them, as well as looking after their animals of transport.[30] If the family that has the duty of hospitality is not present or is unable to fulfill it, the *sheikh* himself is to find a substitute. When an important guest, having been received by the *sheikh,* is about to leave, it will often be the *sheikh* himself who brings the horse or camel for him to mount.

Jaussen has questioned whether the ritual of welcome might be extended to include the role of women if the chief should be absent. In this instance a woman may bring in the wooden plate (she is normally in charge of procuring the meal, even in the house of the *sheikh* when, because of the large number of guests, a superintendent is assigned the task of preparing and distributing the food), the fire, the coffee and the grain, with the necessary implements in the preparation of a simple meal. She withdraws discretely only after arranging everything before the guest. There are other circumstances, quite exceptional, in which a woman, especially of high social rank, is not afraid to converse with the stranger. When, however, a woman presents herself to the meeting, she is introduced as the well-established wife of the *sheikh* in the *marhamharīm,* that portion of the tent or dwelling reserved, in fact, for the women.

---

30. Again Father Jaussen testifies: 'On arriving at a camp it is sometimes heard, "Who is hosting the guests today?" and immediately another will answer, "I do" and hurry to prepare what is necessary. At other times the nomads will bicker among themselves in claiming the honour of receiving the guests in their own home' (Jaussen, *Coutumes des Arabes au pays de Moab,* 83).

Violations against the rule of hospitality

The *bawq* and the transgression of honor

A guest is entitled to the protection of the one who receives him into his tent but, in turn is obligated to conform to certain rules, especially loyalty, eschewing any betrayal. A guest who takes advantage of his unconditional welcome by committing a theft or any other wrongdoing would be subjected to contempt and the harshest of reprisals; essentially, he would deserve no compassion. The most serious infringements to the sacred rules of hospitality on the part of the perpetrator give rise to *bawq*. In Arabic literature this term signifies 'a disgrace,' 'a disaster,' 'an evil,' or even 'a lie'—but this etymology does not convey the meaning of *bawq*. Father Jaussen explains that the master of the tent, the victim of this terrible act, would cut a piece of black cloth from the tent itself with his sword and place it atop a stick or spear. Thus begins a pilgrimage to the nearby camps, signaling, with this kind of mournful flag, the wrong done to him as a welcoming host. Once a *bawq* is implicated, the *sheikhs* of the other tribes have the right to receive the guilty party or, conversely, to banish him from their own camps. The unfortunate man is anathematized, thoroughly dishonoured and loses every right to a gratuitous welcome. This is a radical poverty for a nomad because even if he were to be stripped of his entire belongings inside his own tent, there could be no recourse to have them returned to him. Further, if later on he himself were to welcome a guest and be harmed by him, he could not in turn seek vindication because, being a man disgraced before all the people of the desert, it was acknowledged as a risk to offer asylum.

It is perhaps appropriate to offer some clarification on this point. One must realize that the desert nomad has a very strong sense of honor and is willing to endure any hardship in defence against anything that could defame him: a betrayal, going back on his given word, refusing hospitality. This is what Father Jaussen calls 'saving face';[1] one's 'face' is an expression of the inviolability of one's honour.[2] To maintain one's face, one will often make use of a person of considerable influence and repute, asking the support of a powerful protector or, in any case, one stronger than his oppressor. When a dispute arises within a clan or tribe, it is not unusual for the injured party to appeal to a *sheikh* of another powerful tribe, appointing him not only to resolve the conflict but also to decide the compensation claimed by the victim.

The *dakhalah* or right of asylum

The above mentioned 'saving face' is not to be confused with the 'right of asylum' (or entrance) or *dakhalah*, which is of particular interest in this study of hospitality. The *dakhīl*[3] is an Arabic term that the dictionary translates as 'interior' or even 'intimate.' The Arabic language lends the sense of 'a guest whom one has an obligation to protect' and includes an element of 'foreignness,' of 'stranger' or 'passing traveler.' This second group of meanings, vaguer and indeterminate, seems to have less following among the nomads. Actually, the Bedouins favor the first sense of the term that refers to the institution of the right of protection to any applicant, even in cases particularly delicate. The *dakhalah* combines, in fact, elements of the institution of hospitality with those of the right to asylum, the latter customary throughout the Semitic world and certainly pre-Islamic.[4]

Father Jaussen describes how a 'seeker of asylum' enters the tent of another stronger than he, whom he regards as his protector, and takes refuge in his strength in order to obtain justice, if he is oppressed; or

---

1. The French 'le droit du visage' used by Father Jaussen in the original is usually rendered 'saving face' in English.
2. One speaks of 'saving face' even in the context of military expeditions, allowing the conquered party a certain 'honor' in the terms of surrender.
3. These translations are taken from the Encyclopedia of Islam (*Encyclopédie de l'Islam*, XIII (Paris-Leiden-New York: Brill, 1960–2009).
4. *Cf* Lecerf, "Dakhïl", in *Encyclopédie de l'Islam*, II, 02.

to reach safety if he is in imminent danger.[5] This is a second meaning of *dakhalah*: the '*dakhalah* of law', which is to restore justice against oppression in every case except that which concerns a murderer being pursued for justice. In this instance, we speak instead of the '*dakhalah* of blood:' this is invoked when a Bedouin kills another nomad and is in search of protection against the fury of his avengers. We remember that when a murder has been committed, the relatives of the victim have the right of revenge for three days following the act, killing the murderer himself or another within his family, or even destroying his possessions. It is therefore of vital importance that they be *dakhīl* (protected) by someone powerful enough. This latter, once chosen, is constrained to effectively defend his *dakhīl*. The sacredness of this practice is demonstrated in this extreme case; but it is legally possible and attested to in practice, for a *dakhīl* to seek refuge in commonplace disputes and against any imminent danger. Even in these ordinary circumstances the possible victim has the right to *dakhalah*. The protector, if he requires assistance from his own *dakhīl* (because it affects him personally or another member of his clan), must postpone the solution of the dispute until later.[6] It remains important to stress that the immunity granted to a Bedouin who seeks asylum beneath another's tent and is thus protected from the fearful blood revenge, continues even outside the tent of hospitality by virtue of sharing bread and salt; this is the existential message established by the 'law of salt'. This is why, when a Bedouin questions a stranger about where he comes from, he is often more interested in learning about his eventual protector than about him personally.

Finally, we recall a very delicate situation concerning the legal application of the law of *dakhalah*: It could happen that a Bedouin, fleeing the wrath of his enemy, is killed some distance from the tent in which he sought refuge. The legal question is as follows: Must

---

5. *Cf* Jaussen, *Coutumes des Arabes au pays de Moab*, 208.
6. There is an exception to this rule in the serious situation of murder. If the *dakhīl* were previously guilty of the murder of a member of the clan to which he was fleeing, even though his application for protection was accepted by the clan leader, the latter could not be held responsible if his *dakhīl* were to be killed by a relative of his first victim. The reason is simple: the *dakhīl* had not requested protection against this first danger, but for another reason. The 'law of blood' could therefore be legitimately implemented (*Cf* Jaussen, *Coutumes des Arabes au pays de Moab*, 211–212).

the victim be considered as a *dakhīl* of someone who was not able, however, to welcome him, or as a victim of the desert and bad luck? According to Father Jaussen, the Islamic literature is lost in casuistry without reaching a clear and definitive conclusion.

These possible infractions against the rules of hospitality that we have reviewed in passing are very difficult to understand in our culture, but it is good to remember that, beyond the case studies, gratuity is the fundamental characteristic of Bedouin hospitality. There is no cost for the *sheikh's* hospitality; not only is it unimaginable and even reprehensible to think of paying him for this service, but his intervention often suspends the implementation of procedures that we would consider absolutely normal, for example, bringing a criminal offense to justice. The specific issue is in the point of reference because the societies in which the *dakhalah* is located are based, in great measure, on 'private' relationships. There are no supra-personal social and political structures as we have here in Western States. In this context, the danger of 'all against all,' the unending chain of vengeance, must be neutralized or, more simply, attempts made to reduce the widespread feeling of insecurity before the structural instability of the living conditions of the nomads in the desert or steppe. In this milieu, the hospitality accorded by the *sheikh* or lesser official is equivalent to exercising a genuine right over the life and death of the defenceless claimant! A highly generous act, which cannot but increase the prestige of the clan leader himself, as well as his family and the entire group he represents. This is, after all, the only and the most sought-after reward.

Hospitality in the vocabulary of the Qur'an

The *ijāra*: an extension of divine protection

We have considered the general features of the practice of hospitality within a determined geographical and cultural area of the Middle East but with no specific reference to any religious affiliation. We now take up the Islamic perspective. It cannot be denied that the cultural concepts and social practices of the Middle East pre-existed Islam but this does not deter Islam from influencing and deeply characterizing the entire culture of these peoples and not only their faith. If the institution of the right of protection to all who request it is well attested in every Semite epoch; and granting that there are limits to the theme of hospitality; it remains surprising to note that there is no incorporation of it into Islamic law. Nevertheless, there is no denying that hospitality (*ikram ad-daīf*), though not religiously codified, is considered a true duty from which no one, rich or poor, can escape. This is because with the arrival of Islam, the qualifying factor of a guest, usually understood in any case as transient, a passer-by, is found to be considerably reinforced. Many verses of the Prophet *Hadith*[1] and certain Qur'anic comments are devoted to the praise of the practice of hospitality, together with that of other acts of kindness.

---

1. The term means 'story,' or 'narrative' but it has a much greater significance because it constitutes the so-called Sunna, the second source of Islamic law (*shari'a*) following the Qur'an itself. The ensemble of *Hadith* is the narrative (i.e., oral) tradition of reference to Muhammad and, in time, included some of his companions or followers (among whom were the most authoritative Muslims of generations later than that of the Prophet); it acquires the force of law, especially when there is no explicit Qur'anic passage of command or prohibition.

Essentially, the fundamental notion underlying the practice of hospitality in Islam is *ijāra* (protection or neighborliness), a term which in Arabic refers to *jār*, the person protected and, more rarely, the one who protects. *jār* corresponds to the Hebrew *ghêr*, which we have already extensively analyzed. Both *jār* and *ghêr* assume a socio-religious significance, bringing protection in the human sphere into harmony with the divine: because the real protector is God and no one can give protection contrary to God's will.

> In whose hand is the dominion of all things, and He protects and cannot be protected from, if you happen to know? They will say, 'To God' (Qr xxiii, 88–89).[2]

> No one can protect me from God, and I will not find any refuge except with Him (Qr lxxii).

This sacralisation of the concept of protection leads very easily to link protection and conversion to Islam or, more precisely, protection becomes almost a pre-condition to the desired conversion. Converts become *jīrān* (protected) by God, under His *dhimma*. Actually, this last term designates a kind of 'agreement renewable for a determined time with which the Muslim community grants hospitality-protection to members of other revealed religions, provided they acknowledge the sovereignty of Islam'.[3] Hence, the specific reference is not to converts as such but to members of the 'Religions of the Book'.

Clearly, the treatment of non-Muslims in Islam is based on the conditions of conquest and not only on imitation of the paradigmatic example of the Prophet's hospitality. Again, the complex study of the differing doctrinal positions of Islam before the 'Religions of the Book' would take us too far afield from the subject of our research. We must not forget, however, that *dhimma* is not just about the comportment of Muslims towards non-Muslims on the level of institutional and social life; it corresponds, in its legal sense, on the one hand, to those elements that make an individual a subject of law; and secondly, it is the foundation of the notion of obligation that binds the debtor (the one conquered or the subject) to the creditor (the Muslim who conquers).[4]

---

2. References in English to the Qur'an are found on-line at http://blog.clearquran.com/
3. Taken from 'Dhimma', *Encyclopédie de l'Islam*, II, 234–238.
4. For further information on this issue, refer to C Chehata, under 'Dhimma (juridique)' in *Encyclopédie de l'Islam*, II, 238.

Returning to the subject of our research, the same tradition of hospitality as practiced among the pre-Islamic Bedouins is found in the Islamic context as well: anyone, even one who does not belong to a tribal group by blood relationship, even a non-Muslim, is able to seek protection by asking for it of a person or tribe sufficiently powerful to secure it. However, the really remarkable fact is that to be protected from the risks associated with one's faith, one must first be admitted to the 'House of Islam' (*dār al-Islām*), where the faith and peace of Islam reign.

> And if anyone of the polytheists asks you for protection, give him protection so that he may hear the Word of God; then escort him to his place of safety. That is because they are a people who do not know (Qr IX, 6).[5]

The Arabic language and the vocabulary of the Qur'an have a term that corresponds to the Greek *xenos* (stranger, enemy, guest): *daīf* literally means 'to change course,' 'to decline' (as the sun), or 'to deviate' (as an arrow); but the root of the verb also means 'to leave' (the path) and 'to stop to visit someone'; which gives substantial form to the word 'guest'—minus the ambivalence found in many languages (Italian and English, for example) which can also mean 'the host' or 'the one who welcomes.' Of course, 'the one who leaves the path' can also refer to an idolater who abandons the path of perdition to come to the safety of true faith in Allah (this is possibly the sense of the Qur'anic verse just quoted). We return to the image of God as protector or more exactly *walī*. In Arabic literature, this term comes from the root *w-l-y* which means 'neighbour', 'partner', 'friend', or even 'one who manages the affairs of another'. It is not, in general, a term that applies directly to God; but in many ways the *walī* directly benefits from the qualities of the one who befriends him, that is, of God himself, and therefore enjoys God's authority, virtue, power and particular attributes.[6] That is why, in the Qur'an, Allah is also called the *walī* of believers, or "He

---

5. In this Qur'anic passage, the term 'polytheists' (or idolaters) refers to any non-Muslim and in particular, those who worship any god other than the One God. This disapprobation includes Christians as well because of their faith in the Triune God. Notwithstanding, the reception of 'polytheists' remains a point of honor for Muslims.

6. *Cf* B Radke, in 'Walī. Exposé général', in *Encyclopédie de l'Islam*, XI, 120–123.

who protects and assists those who believe.[7] It is also forbidden in the Qur'an for Muslims to look for protectors (*awliya*) among Christians: 'O you who believe! Do not befriend those who take your religion in mockery and as a sport, be they from among those who were given the Scripture before you, or the disbelievers. And obey God, if you are believers' (Qr V, 57).

In these references essential to the Qur'anic vocabulary of welcome, it seems evident that the term 'protection' is preferred over that of 'hospitality.' Thus, protection becomes the pattern of relations between individuals within a society traditionally very hierarchical, although this strict organisational grouping is losing much of its force today.

Charity as an ethical requirement of faith

In Islamic thought, the idea of a communal submission to a single unifying principle is much more important than that of a collective responsibility towards others, be he a brother of the same clan or an unknown pilgrim . . . On the other hand, the *umma* (the people, the community, with particular reference to all Muslims world-wide), is the model in the theocratic and socio-political order that transcends tribalism and the interpersonal relationships that characterize the life of the Bedouin nomads. It all but points to a common faith that goes beyond the limits of kinship and clan. Now, God, as leader and guide of the *umma*, becomes the protector of all those who gain admission. If the concept of divine protection is favored over that of human hospitality, analogically, in the Islamic context, the preference is to speak in terms of 'proximity' rather than 'communion', developing the idea of a God who is nearer (*aqrab*) to us than one's own jugular vein ('We created the human being, and We know what his soul whispers to him. We are nearer to him than his jugular vein'; Qr L, 16). From the sketching of this theological background, we understand that it is the absolute sovereignty of God that is the foundation of every human attitude towards one's fellows. Every act of charity, every gift, every attention given to the needy originates from an ethical requirement

---

7. 'God is the Lord of those who believe; He brings them out of darkness and into light. As for those who disbelieve, their lords are the evil ones; they bring them out of light and into darkness-these are the inmates of the Fire, in which they will abide forever' (Qr II, 257).

Hospitality in the vocabulary of the Qur'an

of faith rather than from the sacred nature of the act itself. We return here to a consideration of the relationship between hospitality and charity, already taken up in the Jewish context, and which we will try to clarify even further when we come to the chapter on the Christian world.

In a Muslim context, the purely material action of the believer to the benefit of one's neighbor seems to be much more in agreement with the characteristics of charity than with an attitude of hospitality.

The definition of a person of charity in the Qur'an (Qr XC) seems to confirm this impression. The description is of one who walks the path of good, freeing the captive (Qr XC, 13), feeding the exhausted orphan or the ragged poor in time of famine.[8] The act of feeding the needy has such a value that it becomes a privileged way of expiation of sins.[9] The perspective of the Qur'an on the sharing of wealth and individual resources is rooted in several fundamental beliefs of Islamic theology, which refer to the absolute continuity between spiritual and material endeavours in the attitude of the believer; there is no separation between an act of faith and faith in action. This aspect is summed up perfectly in the description of the nature, the aims and operation of the Muslim community:

> You are the best community [*milla*] that ever emerged for humanity: you advocate what is moral, and forbid what is immoral, and believe in God (Qr III, 110a).

---

8. Here is the complete extract of these verses of the Quran: 'And what will explain to you what the ascent is? [that is, the path of good, editor] The freeing of a slave. Or the feeding on a day of hunger. An orphan near of kin. Or a destitute in the dust' (Qr XC, 12–16).

9. Works of charity are often mentioned in the Qur'an in connection with prayer, the other essential element of Islamic practice, that cannot be dissociated from the fundamental act of faith: 'And attend to your prayers, and practice regular charity [*zakāt*], and kneel [*rak'a*] with those who kneel' (Qr II, 43). Jacques Berque, in his renowned French translation of the Qur'an, adopts the term 'purification' in place of *zakāt* (legal alms): 'Accomplissez la prière, acquittez la *purification*, inclinez-vous avec ceux qui s'inclinent.' This translation seems to more faithfully preserve the etymological sense of the practice, at least until an institutional and fiscal meaning prevailed. The word *zakāt*, in fact, comes from an Arabic root that means 'pure being'; thus the origin of other terms such as 'integrity', 'honesty' and even 'justification'. The Qur'an goes so far as to say that prayer and works of charity can take the place of the recitation of the sacred text when there is lack of time (*Cf* Qr LXXIII, 20).

98   *Strangers With God*

These goals are valid also for those who, among the believers of the Religions of the Book, can be considered as just even if they are not officially Muslims:

> They believe in God and the Last Day, and advocate righteousness and forbid evil, and are quick to do good deeds. These are among the righteous (Qr III, 114).

As Fazlur Rahman, a Pakistani Muslim philosopher (1919–1988), pointed out in his investigation of the ethical foundations of the Qur'an: 'Islam points necessarily (and not merely implicitly or marginally) to the creation of a world order in which its imperatives and principles are so embodied that the whole earth will be purified.'[10] It is in this perspective that human beings, endowed by God with different skills and resources, are required, according to the Qur'an, to foster social solidarity in justice and generosity ("God commands justice, and goodness, and generosity towards relatives . . . Qr XVI, 90). God regards those who spend their resources to support others as especially virtuous (Qr LVII, 18) and condemns those who amass riches (Qr III, 180). These considerations are prerequisite to the institutions of *zakāt* and *sadaka*. Since these subjects are not of vital interest to us in this research, we note only that *zakāt* imposes an obligation on Muslims to pay a certain percentage (proportionate to personal property) for the benefit of the poor and other predetermined social categories; while the *sadaka* commonly designates free and voluntary alms.[11]

We should note that the legal structure that organizes and frames charity in the Muslim context represents a step further away from the character of the free and spontaneous generosity of the Bedouin environment of hospitality.[12] Beginning from the ninth century,

---

10. F Rahman, 'Some Key Ethical Concepts of the Qur'ān', cited in A Nanji, in 'Almsgiving', in JD McAuliffe. editor, *Encyclopaedia of the Qur'ān*, VI (Leiden: Brill, 2002–2006), I, 64.

11. To find more about these two practices, we recommend A Zysow, 'Zakāt', in *Encyclopédie de l'Islam*, XI, 2005, 441–457; and Weir-Zysow, 'Sadaka', in *Encyclopédie de l'Islam*, VIII, 1995, 729–736. Both contributions have a rich bibliography.

12. 'Muslim ethics, despite the deep asceticism it displays, is also encumbered by a formal character that ignores Bedouin society. The conjoining of the secular to the religious has, in effect, led to an accentuation of the attention given to

Muslim jurists have sought to develop rules and statutes that give concrete form to the Qur'anic prescriptions concerning alms and the distribution of resources. They try to justify this legal codification by referring it retrospectively to the practices of the Prophet and his first companions.[13] According to tradition, the Prophet Muhammad had already determined that even non-Muslims could benefit from charitable aid; and these should then, in their turn, be encouraged to establish foundations to help their needy. In short, every Islamic teaching that concerns the works of charity is a reflection of a vision and a very rigid organization of society and the interpersonal relationships that actuate it. The presence of the poor, the weak and the needy undermine all this because they are considered a wound inflicted on the work of God's creation, which must quickly be cured and returned to its original perfection. This endeavour is also an occasion for gaining spiritual merit.

---

the ceremonial dimension of social exchanges' (*cf* L Ibrahi-Ouali, 'L'hospitalité comme une oasis au milieu du désert', in Montandon, editor, *Le livre de l'hospitalité*, 168).

13. In contrast, Sufism (mystical Islam) places greater emphasis on the spirituality of almsgiving.

A witness of Muslim hospitality: The *Kitāb ādāb al-akl* of Al-Ghazali

Practical instructions for the benefit of ordinary people

To conclude this portion of our study of hospitality in the Arab world, it is of particular—and unusual—interest to briefly examine Volume XI of Al-Ghazali's well known treatise *Ihyā' 'ulūm al-dīn* (The Revival of Religious Sciences), entitled *Kitāb ādāb al-akl* (Good Table Manners[1]) It is certainly this author's most important work, in its amplitude (four volumes) and its content. It is divided into four parts, dealing respectively with the *'ibādāt* (practices of worship), *'ādāt* (social customs), *muhlikāt* (vices or errors that could lead to perdition) and *munjiyāt* (virtues or qualities that bring to salvation). Each of these sections is comprised of ten books.

> The *Ihyā'* is a comprehensive guide for the use of pious Muslims on all aspects of religious life: worship and devotional practices, comportment in daily life, purification of the heart and progress in the way of mysticism.[2]

---

1. Al-Ghazali (1058–1111) was an eminent theologian, jurist, philosopher, mystic and religious reformer. He was born and died in Tūs, in Kuhrāsān, Central Asia, but spent most of his life in Baghdad where he taught for forty years (before discontinuing teaching and his career as jurist and theologian, probably because of a nervous illness); but continued to study philosophy and to write. As for his writings, although he wrote much, some of the works that have been attributed to him are definitely not his. He lived for a time in Damascus, where he spent some time in Jerusalem and Hebron, before leaving for Mecca and Medina. When he returned to his native city, he lived as a poor Sufi, often in solitude, passing his time in meditation and other spiritual exercises. It was at that time that he composed the *Ihyā' 'ulūm al-dīn*.

2. Montgomery, 'Al-Ghazali' in *Encyclopédie de l'Islam*, II, 1977, 1065.

The book, 'Good Table Manners', is the first of ten parts of *'ādāt* or social customs, the second major section of the *Ihyā'*. Ghazali examines the rules of daily conduct, including those relating to sexuality and marriage, how to earn a living, the distinction between the lawful and the unlawful, between friendship and simple camaraderie and, again, the conduct of one on a journey. The *Kitāb ādāb al-akl* is not the only book of *Ihyā'* to treat the subject of food. In the tenth book of the same section, Al-Ghazali regards the comportment of the Prophet himself as a safe model for the believer to follow, even at table; in the third part of the *Ihyā* he speaks of the threat of deadly risks, including in first place an immoderate craving for food, before every other vice of the flesh, because greed is the basis of all other forms of wrongdoing. Now, a quick overview of his works will undoubtedly reveal the book 'Good Table Manners' as among the simplest. It appears to be just a practical and detailed guide of behavior for the use of ordinary people.[3] The author devotes a good part of his writing to the duty of hospitality underlining the merits that are acquired in its practice before Allah. Al-Ghazali is particularly rich in anecdotes that illustrate the radicalism of this generosity that must be manifested firstly towards people who are nearest.[4] The Prophet himself shows that

---

3. In the original introduction to his work, Ghazali writes: 'God created food to help man to obey and to do good deeds. The end of man is to meet Allah. The means to achieve it are knowledge and work which can only be accomplished when the body is healthy; hence the need for food. Man must therefore observe certain rules of conduct' (*cf* Al-Ghazali, *Ih'ya 'ouloûm ed-dîn ou Vivification des sciences de la foi*, translation and note by G-H Bousquet [Paris: Publications de l'Institut d'études orientales-Faculté de lettres d'Alger, 1955], 109). On the pages that follow are found rules with which one must comply before coming to the table: ascertain that the food is lawful, make the ablutions, correctly arrange the dishes before the diners, assume the right attitude to food when bringing it up to the mouth (do not take a new bite before having swallowed the previous one, use your right hand to eat, do not blow on food to cool it, do not use bread to wipe your hands . . .). There is a set of precepts that implicitly attests the need to primarily regulate collective cuisine (but Ghazali does not forget, first of all, to introduce rules of conduct that must be followed by those who eat alone); which involve, for this reason, a need to comply with different sensitivities (VIII–IX).

4. Johnson-Davies in the introduction to his translation of the *Kitāb ādāb al-akl* reports without giving the source, a *hadith* (a saying of the Prophet) concerning 'A'isha (the daughter of Abu Bakr, the first of the four caliphs, and the favorite bride of the Prophet himself) which states that, well aware of his duties towards his neighbour, he wonders who should have the priority of his concern. The response of the Messenger of God enjoins him to begin with those persons who

A *witness of Muslim hospitality: The Kitāb ādāb al-akl of Al-Ghazali*   103

everyone, regardless of their status, can be hospitable. A well-known *hadith* reported by al-Bukhārī,[5] recalls that food for two persons is actually enough for three; and that food for three is sufficient for four. In short, hospitality consists not so much in prodigality towards a small number of people but rather in the welcoming of the greatest possible number of persons gathered around a prepared table. Ghazali records that the Prophet himself had the custom of leaving his tent in search of someone to invite. Arabic literature abounds in texts where the welcoming host will endure every kind of sacrifice to protect the life of a passing guest.[6] The latter is *baraka* (blessing) as well as the meal that is eaten together. Moreover, another *hadith* recalls that 'a house where guests do not enter will not be frequented by angels',[7] the same angels who do not cease to invoke God's blessing on those who welcome visitors the whole time in which a table is prepared.[8]

---

are nearest to him. We should not consider this recommendation as an invitation to discriminate against those further away or unknown, but rather as an exhortation to translate every day concern into hospitality, beginning with those with whom one deals more frequently (cf. Al-Ghazali, *On the Manners Relating to Eating—Kitāb ādāb al-akl*, Book xi of the Revival of the Religious Sciences— *Ihya' 'ulūm al-dīn*, D Johnson-Davies (introduction and note), [Cambridge: Islamic Texts Society, 2000], XIII).

5. Al-Bukhari (810–870 AD) is a celebrated chronicler who has authored a monumental collection of traditions, the *Sahīh*, which was compiled over a period of sixteen years and contains 7397 *hadith* (which are reduced to 2762 when the countless repetitions are excluded).

6. The most eloquent *hadith* in this regard is presented in the collection *Riyad as-Salihim*, The Gardens of the Righteous, of the Imam Muhyi al-Dīn al-Nawawī (d.1277). "According to Abou Hourayra, someone said to the Prophet: 'I am exhausted by hunger'. [. . .] The Prophet then said: 'Who wishes, then, to give hospitality to this man?' An Ançarita says: 'I do, O Messenger of God!' He then went to his house accompanied by his guest and said to his wife, 'Do you have anything to eat?' She replied, 'Only what I have prepared for the children'. He said, 'Let them wait on some pretext and if they ask for dinner, put them to sleep. Then, when our guest comes to our house, turn off the light and let him believe that we eat with him'. So they set the table and the invited ate while they spent the night with an empty stomach" (Quoted by L Ibrahi-Ouali, 'L'hospitalité comme une oasis au milieu du désert', 169).

7. G-H Bousquet, 111. This *hadith* surprisingly draws on the biblical hospitality of Abraham, whose extraordinary opening to hospitality is an essential condition for his encounter with God's messengers.

8. This *hadith* is reported by Al-Tabarānī (873–971), a leading compiler of traditions who was born in Syria and lived most of his life in Isfahan, present day Iran, where he died.

We offer a few other excerpts from the *Kitāb ādāb al-akl* that bear resemblance to certain practices we have already widely analysed in the course of this paper:

> The host will make [an invitation] for pious purposes [. . .] He will invite the poor without the rich and not forget his neighbours. He must gradate his friends and acquaintances. He ought not invite for the purpose of competing in pride or beauty. Nor invite someone whom it would be painful to accept.[9].

As for the course of the meal, the head of the household must make known the list of dishes to be served so that the invitees can determine accordingly how much to accept. But once more, it is well to recall that hospitality is not judged by the abundance of food but by the generosity of the gesture. In this sense, some traditions maintain that serving sweets at the end of the meal is more important than serving a large number of dishes overall; or again, the comfortable seating of chairs is of greater value than increasing the amount of food offered. Both the reception of guests and their departure is strictly regulated and the Sunnah states that a householder must accompany his guests to the door as a sign of respect, a respect that is expressed in a pleasant attitude and the ability to animate interesting conversations. Nevertheless, for his part, the guest ought not take advantage of hospitality for more than three days so that the householder is not importuned and forced to ask him to leave. Concerning this latter, Al-Bukhārī provides us with one last interesting detail: 'Hospitality is for three days; any prolongation becomes a charity.'[10]

---

9. G-H Bousquet, 111. Shortly after, referring to the invited guest, however, he adds: 'It is shameful not to rejoice on receiving an invitation. It should be considered an obligation to accept. But it should not be accepted if it is known that the host is acting under constraint. An invitation should not be turned down because of the distance. Nor remain away because one is fasting; the fast must be broken to give joy to your brother' (111). It is important to note that, according to these rules, the guest is required to observe if the host behaves reprehensibly or if there is anything untoward in the place of welcome (meaning 'the possible existence of figurative representations' . . .). In grave cases, or when unable to change an unacceptable situation, the guest is obligated to leave the house that receives him without having to further justify his action (*cf* D Johnson-Davies, 37–38).

10. Al-Bukhārī, *Ādāb*, 6019, quoted by D. Johnson-Davies, 44.

Conclusion

The above statement just quoted reconfirms the basic distinction between hospitality and charity, which has already been mentioned several times, and to which we will return. Hospitality expresses a relationship among peers; charity instead marks a profound difference between the giver and the receiver, the latter completely dependent on the former for succor. That is why, as already mentioned, an act of charity is a direct expression of an ethical requirement of faith. Returning to the Islamic interpretation in this regard, a *hadith*, reported six times in Al-Bukhārī's canonical redaction and four times in the Muslim collection[11] (highlighting its importance), reads: 'Whoever believes in God and the day of the Resurrection does no harm to his neighbors. Whoever believes in God and the final Day of Judgement will treat his guest with respect. He who believes in God and the final Day of Judgement will speak only what is good or remain silent.'[12] If ethics in the Qur'an are expressed as an appeal to respect, it is the very fact of the other, his mere presence, that is at issue. Here we understand one of the essential foundations of the Islamic religion—that it is more of an orthopraxis than an orthodoxy. This explains why Islam will speak more of 'proximity' than of 'communion;' and why it is preferred to define the action of the believer toward his neighbor more in terms of charity than of hospitality. We point out once again that the prescriptions of the Qur'an concerning the attitude to be adopted towards a traveller or pilgrim has more to do with protection than with welcome[13] and alludes more to the duties of social ethics than to a real theological hospitality. Theologically understood, hospitality receives God in every guest who is welcomed and is not simply an expression of an ethical requirement towards the needy. In other words, a truly theological hospitality will grant a welcome to God who never tires of knocking on the doors of humanity in the guise of the stranger and the pilgrim.

---

11. The full title, *al-Musnad al-Sahīh bi-naklīl 'adlī*, is one of the six major *hadith* collections of the Sunni oral traditions containing the sayings and works of the prophet Muhammad. It is second in importance to *Sahīh* of Al-Bukhari. It was compiled by Muslim ibn al-Hajjaj, also known as Imam Muslim. The authentic translation of *Sahīh* is 'whole' or 'correct.'
12. The Italian translation is taken from Al-Bukhari, *Les traditions islamiques*, (translated Houdas O, IV, (Paris: Ernest Leroux, 1914), 151.
13. 'And give the relative his rights, and the poor, and the wayfarer, and do not squander wastefully. The extravagant are brethren of the devils, and the devil is ever ungrateful to his Lord' (Qr XVII, 26–27).

Hospitality in the Christian World

The Theology of the New Testament

The Incarnation: The Son of God pleads for a human welcome

It would be impossible to analyse all of the texts of the New Testament and patristic tradition which directly refer to the duty of hospitality or indirectly outline a meaningful portrait. We limit ourselves to taking up a number of texts that enable us to give an overview of the issue.

If the Old Testament manifests the sacredness of the rights of a visitor in a general way, to the extent that even a fugitive may be able to find an inviolable shelter beneath the tent of an enemy, the New Testament ratifies the importance of the practice of hospitality by clarifying and deepening the principles on which it rests, with no display of novelty or surprise in a ritual well established over the centuries and in all cultures.

Even so, as Giuseppe Danesi notes, after the concept of 'stranger' was eliminated from the vision of Christian life, the term hospitality underwent an essential semantic transformation: hospitality (*philoxenia* or love for the stranger) became a fundamental expression of love of neighbour (*cf* 1 Jn 4:19), the most solemn manifestation of charity; and the 'stranger' is equated to the 'guest', the 'one to be welcomed'.[1] Faith in the God who took on human nature in Christ necessarily changes not only the divine / human relationship but also inter-human relations as well. That is why, even more clearly than in

---

1. *Cf* G Danesi, 'Per una teologia delle migrazioni', in *People on the Move*. 9 (1979). The author of this article has co-authored a substantial scriptural study of migrations and welcome (G Danesi, S Garofalo, *Migrazioni ed accoglienza nella Sacra Scrittura* (Padova: Edizioni Messaggero, 1987), the second part of which is dedicated to the New Testament.

the Old Testament, it is evident that hospitality is not expressed in rhetorical, abstract formulas but is translated into concrete attitudes that are a revelation of a divine plan of salvation.

So, if on the one hand there is a continuity with the Greco-Roman tradition of hospitality and the conventions common to the entire Mediterranean basin, the New Testament reflections translate God's saving plan into a spiritual incentive as the foundation of a welcoming kindness. This can be inferred from the prologue of Luke's Gospel, who alone lingers on the Nativity and the infancy of Christ. In the first two chapters of Luke, every theological-symbolic reflection is rooted in a historical and sociological background. Mary and Joseph look for shelter in Bethlehem but no one welcomes them. It is therefore in a stable, outside the city walls, that Jesus will be born 'because there was no room for them at the inn' (Lk 2:7). The Christ, the Son of the living God, the God who is with us (Emmanuel), entered into human history despite being refused the hospitality of his fellows. This is but the beginning of a search for a welcome that Jesus, throughout his entire public life, will continue to lead in company with his disciples. An itinerant life that progressively provokes differing gestures of hospitality: in the home of friends such as that of Lazarus and his sisters (cf. Lk 10:38-42) or a simple reception like that of Zacchaeus (cf Lk 19:5-9) but also shuttered doors which become symbolic of the rejection of the Good News itself.[2]

The episode of the Nativity, as well as the entire life story of the Son of God who has nowhere to lay his head in this world (*cf* Matt 8:20), becomes the essential hermeneutical criterion of hospitality as the New Testament understands the meaning of the term. The reception of 'the other', wanderer and refugee, known or unknown, is no longer roused merely by any joy experienced in the gods' mysterious protection of the visitor, as in pagan antiquity; nor is it sufficient even to say, as in the Old Testament, that the welcomed guest is a messenger of Yahweh. The grand revelation on which hospitality is

---

2. An emblematic episode is narrated by the evangelist Luke in the context of the great journey of the Messiah to Jerusalem, the place of his passion and death. Jesus sends messengers ahead with instructions to find him shelter. '[T]hey went into a Samaritan village to make preparations for him but the people would not receive him because he was making for Jerusalem [. . .] and they went off to another village' (9:52b-53:56).

established is the radical oneness of God in Christ in his declared identification with the small and needy: 'I was a stranger and you made me welcome' (Matt 25:35). 'This solidarity is rooted in the fact that Christ, by his incarnation, is in his very person the basis, the place and the concrete realization of the relationship between God the Father and the Son of God in his humanity'.[3]

In the course of this study, we have often mentioned the crucial role of the theological motif of 'foreignness'—the 'foreignness' of the patriarch Abraham which becomes the 'foreignness' of the Chosen People in their own land and which becomes, finally, the condition of humanity in this world: pilgrims toward an unknown destiny. In some foundational texts of the New Testament, the experience of the Patriarch and the Chosen People is repeated, in part, in the theology of the incarnation. 'Where do you come from?' (Jn 19:9): This great question asked of Christ by Pilate reveals his 'foreignness', because the very definition of the stranger is one's place of origin. It is obviously a question that goes beyond a simple inquiry into the human origins of Christ and approaches the greater theme of his ontological identity: '[S]ome of the people of Jerusalem were saying [. . .] "Can it be true the authorities have made up their minds that he is the Christ? Yet we all know where he comes from, but when the Christ appears no one will know where he comes from"' (Jn 7: 25, 26b–27). Lucio Cilia correctly points out that for the Jews Christ is not a stranger because they are persuaded they well know his origin; that is precisely why they are unable to recognise in him the Messiah! Paradoxically, we could say that the Lord is rejected by the Jewish world because his origin is too well known! And the Lord himself will refute this claim to knowledge, on the one hand with irony: "Yes, you know me and you know where I came from. Yet I have not come of myself; no, there is one who sent me and I really came from him, and you do not know him" (Jn 7:28); on the other hand, he protests allowing no rebuttal: 'It is true that I am testifying on my own behalf, but my testimony is still valid, because I know where I came from and where I am going; but you do not know where I come from or where I am going' (Jn 8:14). To conclude, God is not a stranger geographically or

---

3. P Miquel, 'Hospitalité', in Viller M, editor, *Dictionnaire de Spiritualité*, VII, (Paris: Beauchesne, 1969), coll. 808–819 (814).

ethnically; instead, his 'foreignness' pertains to his very nature: He is the one who comes from heaven.[4] In the Christological hymn of the letter to the Philippians (2:5–8), Jesus is rightly presented as a model of 'self-emptying', in what is theologically termed *kenosis* or abasement.[5] It is legitimate to ask why would God become a stranger in the incarnation? The response is clear: God became a stranger to encounter humanity, to welcome those who are strangers to this world into the universe of divine citizenship: 'So you are no longer aliens or foreign visitors: you are citizens like all the saints, and part of God's household' (Ep 2:19).[6] God rejects 'ethnicization', that identification with a people (the circumcised) that represented for the Jews the very meaning of election. God rejects this exclusive choice and realizes an inclusive preferment in the blood of Christ, already anticipated in some ways in the original call of Abraham.[7] In the theology of the New Testament, this unlimited value of salvation brought by Christ is expressed in the universalism of the proclamation made even to the uncircumcised, to the Gentiles or pagans; to these especially is the preaching of St Paul directed, but it is already evident in the synoptic Gospels.[8] Going even further, the theology of the Gospels suggests that those who receive Christ receive the Father who sent him: 'Anyone who welcomes you welcomes me; and those who welcome me welcome the one who sent me' (Matt 10: 40).

---

4. *Cf* L Cilia, 'Gesù straniero tra i suoi nel Vangelo di Giovanni', in I Cardellini, editor, *Lo straniero nella Bibbia*, 233–250 (236–237). The author, biblical scholar and rector of the Patriarchal Seminary of Venice, makes us realize that the failure to welcome Christ is due to his 'foreignness' and not vice versa!

5. This term recurs on almost every page of the New Testament, as an essential expression of Christ's relinquishment of the glory due his divinity (but not his divinity itself).

6. A Rizzi, 'Lo straniero nella Bibbia. Meditazione teologica', in *Servitium*, 25 (1991): 51. We are able to say that 'foreignness' becomes a category of Revelation because, Jesus, as a stranger, can still be reecognised thanks to God's gift which manifests itself freely.

7. *Cf* M Grilli, 'L'universalismo nei sinottici', in I Cardellini, editor, *Lo straniero nella Bibbia*, 297–315.

8. It would, however, be simplistic and reductive to speak of a universalist Christianity as distinguished from a particularistic Judaism, if only because the diverse currents of biblical Judaism already contain differing positions with respect to the problem of the Gentiles and their salvation.

Hospitality in the Gospels: Welcoming the Father in the Son

The Christian law of hospitality finds its inspiration in the attitudes and conduct of Christ who, in turn, acts in accord with God's plan for the salvation of all peoples. At this level, the situation of the children of Israel differs from that of the Gentiles, and Jesus does not cease to recall this fact to the foreigners he meets. Particularly well-known and significant here are the Gospel accounts relating his relationship with the Syro-Phoenician woman ('The children should be fed first, because it is not fair to take the children's food and throw it to the house dogs'; Mk 7:27), and with the Canaanite woman ('I was sent only to the lost sheep of the house of Israel'; Matt 15:24).[9] But the cultural and ethnic differences, never dismissed by Christ, are superseded by a level of faith that manifests itself as *the* determinant of a person's identity.[10] The Gospels present Jesus as an itinerant prophet in the classical sense: without money or bag or sandals or a staff for the journey (*cf* Matt 10: 9-10); no set place or apostolic center wherein to receive people; the preference is rather to solicit hospitality. However, as already mentioned in the previous paragraph, the Lord seems to have the usual logistical references: the home of the Apostle Simon of Capernaum[11] or that of his friends

---

9. But the best-known example remains that of the encounter between Jesus and the Samaritan woman at the well of Sychar, in the fourth chapter of the Gospel of John: "The Samaritan woman said to him, 'What? You are a Jew and you ask me, a Samaritan for a drink?' Jews, in fact, do not associate with Samaritans" (Jn 4:9). To pursue this issue of the relationship between Jesus and foreigners in the Gospel accounts, we refer to the article of E Manicardi, 'Gesù e gli stranieri', in I Cardellini, editor, *Lo straniero nella Bibbia*, 197–231.

10. 'Woman, you have great faith! Let your wish be granted' (Matt 15:28); 'I tell you solemnly, nowhere in Israel have I found faith like this' (Matt 8, 10). Jesus is frequently represented as the eschatological horizon before the final entry of the foreigners who are not yet the immediate recipients of his public ministry: 'I tell you that many will come from east and west to take their places with Abraham and Isaac and Jacob at the feast in the kingdom of heaven' (Matt 8:11). If there will not be many foreigners brought to salvation by Christ prior to the Easter mystery, after his public life they seem to be the better disposed to accept the gift of God.

11. *Cf* Matt 8:14–15; Mk 1:29–39; Lk 4:38–39. 'When he returned to Capernaum some time later, word went round that he was back' (Mk 2:1). This notation of Mark the Evangelist is very surprising because there is nothing that would lead us to think that the Lord had his own home in the city. It is reasonable to think that the evangelist would make allusion to the house of Simon Peter, as a stopping place quite usual for Jesus and his disciples.

Martha, Mary and Lazarus of Bethany[12] (we do not address the complex question of the existence of family ties as not of primary value in this study). In the periscope of the healing of Peter's mother-in-law, mentioned by all the Synoptics, Christ, after having attended the Jewish synagogue on the Sabbath,[13] comes to the house of the first of his apostles, whose mother-in-law is lying sick in bed. This story of healing linked to an act of kind hospitality is a re-reading of the Old Testament accounts of the prophets Elijah and Elisha.[14] In Capernaum, despite having virtually requested his reception, the Lord seems to stay only one night before continuing on his way. There is one more interesting detail: the entire city of Capernaum gathers before the door of the house of hospitality, not to abuse the guest, as happened at Sodom (*cf* Gen 19:4–9) and Gibeah (*cf* Jg 19:22–25) but, on the contrary, to solicit the aid of Jesus and, more specifically, his healing powers. Jesus responds only partially to these demands and, well before dawn of the following day, leaves everyone and goes apart for a time of prayer in solitude. As already mentioned, Christ would also often visit at Bethany (a village three kilometers from Jerusalem) at the home of Martha and Mary and their brother Lazarus; the frequency of these visits explains the importance given to this place by all the evangelists (their accounts differ only in minor details).[15] At Bethany, Martha is revealed as the head of the household, the hostess attentive to the exigencies of the ritual of hospitality. However, Jesus does not conceal his greater appreciation for the attitude of her sister

---

12. *Cf* Matt 26:6–13; Mc 14:3–9; Jn 12:1–11.
13. Andrew Arterbury points out that this visit to the synagogue for a passing traveler could also respond to a practical need: it was the perfect place to go first, even before the public square in the center of the village, to find a welcoming host (*Cf* A Arterbury, *The Custom of Hospitality in Antiquity and its Importance for Interpreting Acts 9:43-11:18*, Doctoral Thesis, Baylor University, Waco Texas 2003, 236).
14. In both cases (*cf* 1 Kgs 17:17–24; 2 Kgs 4:18–33), we have an account of family members of a welcoming host being raised from the dead.
15. Luke does not mention the name of the village, as does John (*cf* 11:1), nor does he speak of Lazarus; he is more attentive to Martha's activity in welcoming Jesus. According to Andrew Arterbury, the most popular New Testament description of hospitality is the scene of the Visitation of Mary to her cousin Elizabeth, also given us by Luke (*cf* 1:39–56). However, this story, despite the length of the stay (three months), appears lacking in the details of the various phases of the ritual of welcome, as already noted, across the centuries and in different cultural contexts.

Mary who, alone, is not absorbed by the many practical concerns of hospitality and is able to recognise in him not only a simple passer-by but an 'itinerant missionary', the bearer of a message of salvation to be listened to and internalized.[16] Again in Luke's Gospel, the figure of Zacchaeus seems to sum up the attitude of both Martha and Mary (*cf* 19:1–10). His hurried joy in welcoming repeats not only that of Martha, but also that of the patriarch Abraham at Mamre (Gen 18:1–8), even though at Jericho it is Christ who as guest elicits the reception (as it befits of necessity a true pilgrim). Zacchaeus not only receives his guest, but also welcomes his message demonstrating concretely a change of heart: and therefore his generosity deserves a reward (*cf* Lk 19:9). This encounter at Jericho is among those termed that 'scandalous hospitality' that characterizes the life of the Messiah who accepts and sometimes personally offers invitation to meet at the highly reprehensible homes of publicans and public sinners.[17] This behaviour is the cause of the growing hostility against him ('This man', [the Pharisees and scribes] said, 'welcomes sinners and eats with them'; Lk 15:2); Christ is soon identified with the people with whom he associates ('The Son of Man came, eating and drinking, and they say, 'Look, a glutton and a drunkard, a friend of tax collectors and sinners''' Matt 11:19). Nevertheless, the Messiah, who has no possibility of offering material hospitality, teaches his disciples to offer it to all without exception. He who was made welcome, who shared the same table with those who were excluded from the ultra-orthodox, by this same gesture integrates them into the communion of Abraham, restoring their human and spiritual dignity: 'Today salvation has come to this house, because this man too is a son of Abraham; for the Son of Man has come to seek out and save what was lost' (Lk 19:9–10). And this completes the radical revision of the definition of the foreigner.

On what basis can we speak of a 'foreigner' as a person? The well-known parable of the Good Samaritan, again found only in Luke's

---

16. There is another reception that precedes all others: that of Christ the *Logos*, God's very Word. The fourth Gospel converges on this very point with the dramatic statement that: 'He came to his own domain and his own people did not receive him' (Jn 1:11); the Greek verb *paralambáno* does not mean 'to receive into one's home' or 'to make sit at table' but simply 'to believe'.
17. 'When the Pharisees saw this, they said to his disciples, "Why does your master eat with tax collectors and sinners?"' (Matt 9:11).

Gospel (*cf* Lk 10:29–37), is probably the best response to this question. This Gospel begins with a question: 'And who is my neighbor?' The answer is only implied. A stranger who shows mercy is no longer a foreigner but becomes a 'neighbour' or, rather, becomes an example for understanding what it means to be a neighbour to another . . . Ethnic and cultural differences, from now on, cannot be the criteria for separation or exclusion. To have compassion (cf. Lk 10:37) means participating in the divine action itself, and this nearness to the 'God of compassion' becomes the foundation stone of the relationship of one person to another, especially those in situations of need and hardship. Here also is found the hermeneutical key to understanding the parable of the Last Judgment (*cf* Matt 25:31–46), where the Judge of the universe is formally identified with the wretched of this world and calls them 'his younger brothers [and sisters] ('I tell you solemnly, in so far as you did this to one of the least of these brothers of mine, you did it to me'; v 40). The interpretation of this text is very complex. Surely Jesus is represented in a special way by the poor and lowly and these become, as such, brothers and sisters of the Lord, *The* Humble One among the humble of the earth. In other words, the poor and lowly have privileged access to the mystery of the Son of Man by their very insignificance and because of the appeal to a neighbour's love that their smallness must inspire.

From this premise, we can return to the question asked in the parable of the Good Samaritan, 'And who is my neighbour?' (Lk 10:29) to understand why its answer is completely different from that given by Judaism.

> In fact, according to the will of Jesus, a new fraternal community—of the spiritual order—has simply replaced the old nationalistic community of Israel, so that instead of finding a neighbour in compatriotism, one finds him now in a shared faith. But Jesus really expects more: one's neighbour is any unfortunate person encountered who, simply because of his or her need as such, makes the Master present; the least among us is his brother and sister and therefore mine as well.[18]

---

18. J Ratzinger, 'Fraternité', in *Dictionnaire de Spiritualité* (Paris: Beauchesne, 1964), V, coll. 1141–1167 (1146).

The Theology of the New Testament 117

This then is the foundation of a hospitality which seems universal, all the more so since very often, again, as the parable of the Last Judgment emphasizes, the just do not realize that they were serving the Son of Man in the person of the stranger they welcomed (*cf* Matt 25:38).[19] This Christological foundation of welcoming the other converts a simple 'human solidarity' into a true 'Christian brotherhood', the difference of which is well summarized by Joseph Ratzinger: 'Christians, by the very fact of believing in the Father of Jesus Christ, have recognised their brotherhood and show hospitality while others, on the contrary, are unaware of it'.[20] Hospitality in the Christian sense of the term is a participation in the fortune of Christ who laid down his life for humanity, thus bestowing a sacramental character (sign) and a re-reading of the profound meaning of the banquet, symbol of joy and pinnacle of hospitality, which now becomes the privileged place of encounter with Christ himself ('When the hour came, he took his place at table, and the apostles with him. And he said to them, "I have

---

19. This observation partially contradicts the claim that the poor concretize the presence of the Lord, independently of any ethical claim, simply by their littleness and poverty. In fact, as just mentioned, Jesus, in the parable of the Good Samaritan, completely overturns the notion of 'neighbour'. If the man of the law asked: 'Who is my neighbour?' (in the passive sense), Jesus responds by asking him (in the active sense): 'Which of these three, do you think, proved himself a neighbour to the man who fell into the brigands' hands?' (Lk 10:36). Stated otherwise, it is not the representative character of poverty which is essential (the fact that someone is poor or not does not make Christ present), but the neighbourliness of the one who receives them. We must be as neighbour to each other; and it is enough to realize that we are neighbours when we approach one another in love.

20. J Ratzinger, 'Fraternité', col. 1158. *Frater* (brother) was the most common name among the early Christians. As Ivan Illich emphasised: 'This fraternity was seen as a completely new reality, unprecedented. If Christians were brothers, it was not because they had a common city as matrix as in Plato, or the earth or the universe for mother, as among the Stoics. Christians called each other 'brothers' because the recognition of God as Father was their common vocation: a God who adopts them. And this brotherhood takes form with individual acts of mercy. [...] *Adelphos* and *frater* are fully signified in only two ways: the liturgical binding together of fraternity with the *osculum pacis*, the kiss of peace 'from mouth to mouth' (literally breathing together), and in the breaking and sharing of bread, thus becoming one body. The use of the term 'brother' clearly cuts short every allusion to a biological relationship, any vague stoic sympathy and, obviously, to the current sense of Greek male chauvinism. *Adelphos* was in fact free from any connotation of status, gender or origin' (I Illich, *La perdita dei sensi*, [Firenze: Libreria Editrice Fiorentina, 2009] 24–25).

longed to eat this Passover with you before I suffer'", Lk 22:14–15). That is why a refusal to participate in the messianic banquet becomes at the same time a sign of the lack of openness to hospitality.

Festive Gospel meals

In the Gospels the recurrence of festive scenes is striking: As a practice, Jesus frequently 'shared a meal'. How many miracles and teachings of Jesus are set in the convivial intimacy of a home, are inspired by a gesture of hospitality and very often take place around a dinner table! From the first miracle at Cana during a wedding party (the beginning of the public ministry of Christ according to the Johannine tradition; *cf* Jn 2:1–11), through the meal in the home of Simon the leper (exclusively told in Luke's Gospel, 7:36-48) that inaugurates a series of 'embarrassing invitations' from the Pharisees (we find a second in Lk 11:37–54 and a third in Lk 14:1–34), or among the publicans (Levi's feast in Lk 5:29–32; Matt 10:12; Mk 2:15–17), to the Last Supper that Jesus shares with his disciples (Mk 14:12 to 26; Matt 26:17 to 19; Lk 22:7 to 13).[21] In an essay titled The Meals of Jesus: Table Fellowship in the Gospel,[22] Mark Moore examined four basic functions of the meal in the context of community, functions that Jesus often interprets and sometimes upsets:

---

21. But the list could be much longer, not to mention some texts which, although with no direct reference to a meal, are suggestive of an experience of festivity by the context and vocabulary (for example, in the case of the healing of Peter's mother-in-law, already mentioned, the meal is not described but simply stated; *cf* Mk 1:29–31). Even the accounts of the appearances of the Risen One present a meal as an integral part of the experience of His presence (*cf* EJ Hammes, 'Pietre trasformate in pane: perché no?', in *Concilium*, 2 (2005): 31–43). Finally, we remember that the only miracle worked by the Lord that is unanimously reported by all four evangelists is that of the so-called first multiplication of the loaves (*cf* Mk 6:30–44; Matt 14:13–21; Lk 9:11–17; and Jn 6:5–13). It is once again the sharing of a meal, an extraordinary sharing because it involves an immense crowd of people invited by Christ himself who have the experience of a super-abundance of grace, an overflowing sign of God's mercy (in a deserted place, beginning with only five loaves and two fish, yet everyone has enough with some left over; in other words, God's abundance satisfies every human being, there, wherever a meal of hospitality is celebrated).

22. Professor Moore teaches at Ozark Christian College in Maine, USA. The source is the Internet: markmoore.org/resources/essays/meals.shtml (consulted on 21/02/2012).

1. Meals consolidate one's family and friends; they establish boundaries, discriminate between the 'in' group and those who are 'out.' During his festive meals, however, Jesus, however, reconfigured the relationships of kinship and belonging, creating an extended family based on listening to and obeying the Word of salvation (*cf* Mk 3:31–35 and parallels).
2. Generally, meals also reinforce hierarchies and privileges that distinguish people by assigned seating arrangements at table. Jesus upsets these exclusive hierarchies and challenges every social and religious prejudice (for example the bias that discriminates against women).
3. Meals impose very rigid rituals of legalities, prayers and symbols. Jesus questions the absolutism of a number of these requirements concerning ablutions, fasting and the laws of the Sabbath, especially when these precepts take priority over the people.
4. Meals in a Jewish context are reminiscent of the symposia of ancient Greece, where the guests, especially the more notable, exhibit an eloquence and benevolence in order to curry the favour of those present. Jesus often offends both the host and the guests, unmasking their true purposes and intentions.

Still according to Mark Moore, the Lord makes use of festive meals almost subversively for teachings which often become critical of social and religious practices, but at the same time is establishing a new relationship to God and among one's fellows. Chapter 14 of Luke's Gospel is an eloquent example of what we are saying. We are in the course of a banquet on the Sabbath day when the Jews usually prolong their encounter in the synagogue with a meal prepared the evening before in preparation for the weekly day of rest. At this meal there are often invited guests and Jesus personally benefits from this hospitality, taking advantage of the occasion to offer instruction. It is a prolongation of his itinerant preaching in an often hostile environment and it becomes the decisive confrontation with his opponents and, in particular, with members of the observant Jewish world, the Pharisees.[23] In only thirty verses (most likely the work of an editor), the Lord takes up a controversy on the legality or not of healing on the Sabbath (in this case of a man with dropsy), and

---

23. *Cf* S Garofalo, 'L'ospitalità nella vita e nell'inseGenamento di Gesù', in G Danesi and S Garofalo, *Migrazioni ed Accoglienza nella Sacra Scrittura*, 197–239.

then links together a series of short parables of a didactic nature. To emphasise the importance of humility, Jesus tells the parable of a wedding feast where all the guests rush to take the first place; then he proposes the possibility of a gratuitous invitation to guests who will be unable to return the favor; and finally, one last parable is presented in an eschatological perspective, a kind of prophecy of the triumph of justice and love of God who opens the doors of the Kingdom to the excluded of this world after those invited first refuse to come to the wedding feast—the wedding feast itself being an image of the eschatological banquet. In fact, the joyful encounters and the festive meals, assume a theological meaning and in them anticipate the messianic future.

> The image of the eschatological banquet (*cf* Isa 25:6) forms part of the Jewish tradition, in the same way as giving food to the hungry supplements hope in the Lord (*cf* Ps 132/131:15; 146/145:7) who takes care of her and provides food throughout the year (Ps 104/103:27ff).[24]

Christ, by integrating the celebration of a festive meal into his preaching and practice, and especially as table communion with the poor and those otherwise excluded, anticipates of joy of ultimate kinship or mutual hospitality between humanity and God in his mystery. The message is clear: 'To live for others, with a view to their lives, and to consider the lives of others as a part of one's own, is an expression of faith in him who came to serve at table and not to be served.'[25] That is why the account of the Last Supper is the apogee of the festal practices of Jesus; He is the true *diakonos*, that is, the one who serves, who prepares food accessible to all peoples and who founded the community of those who share a single table, both human and spiritual (*koinonia*). Yet beyond this fundamental theological meaning, in which Jewish history and culture cohabit the scene of the Last Supper, elements of the ritual of hospitality are to be found, the legacy of a practice that spans many centuries and cultures, now reinterpreted in the ambit of a new era inaugurated by Christ. Moreover, the New Testament inherits many Old Testament elements of hospitality. For example, the offering of water to a guest for ablutions

---

24. EJ Hammes, 'Pietre trasformate in pane: perché no?', 35.
25. EJ Hammes, 'Pietre trasformate in pane: perché no?', 42.

(a gesture that will be taken over by Christ in John 13, when he will wash the feet of the Twelve disciples); and his own head is anointed with perfumed oil. Both gestures are implicitly evoked in the account of the sinful woman in the house of Simon the leper (*cf* Lk 7:44–46, 49); thanks to which we also learn that guests were greeted with the kiss of peace, and that, during the meal, guests did not usually sit at a table but rather reclined on a mat or carpet. There is another Gospel story, also in Luke, a kind of parable, totally centered on the theme of hospitality and with a symbolic title: 'The importunate friend' (*cf* Lk 11:5–8). More than a description of the ritual of hospitality, it reconstructs the preliminaries to a typical gesture of welcome. The traveler who needs to be received arrives at night when, during the summer, the easterner prefers to travel to avoid the heat of the day. Despite the unorthodox hours, the traveller knocks on the door of his potential host because the sacredness of hospitality cannot be limited in time or space. In fact, not only is the time inopportune, but the very structure of the house of those who ought to receive him makes the gesture of solidarity extremely awkward. The entire family shares one room and all the members are lying on mats: It is impossible to get up without rousing everyone! The traveller will, however, obtain at least three loaves (one person's allowance) due to his insistence, symbolic of the persevering trust we must always have in the Father, as well as consequently the indispensable duty to respond to the needs of others when we are asked for help.

We return now to the account of the Last Supper as given to us by St Paul (*cf* 1 Co 11:23–26) and the Synoptics. We refer here to the account as given by Mark the Evangelist.

> On the first day of Unleavened Bread, when the Passover lamb was sacrificed, his disciples said to him, 'Where do you want us to go and make the preparations for you to eat the Passover?' So he sent two of his disciples, saying to them, 'Go into the city and you will meet a man carrying a pitcher of water. Follow him, and say to the owner of the house which he enters, 'The Master says: "Where is my dining room in which I can eat the Passover with my disciples?" He will show you a large upper room furnished with couches, all prepared. Make the preparations for us there.' The disciples set out and went to the city and found everything as he had told them, and prepared the Passover (14:12–16).

We cannot learn much about the homeowner through this description, except that, even if he had not been a disciple, he probably knew Christ (because he needed only to hear 'the Master' to identify the person who sent the messengers). Noteworthy persons at this time ordinarily sent messengers ahead to verify the possibility of a worthy reception before continuing on themselves. On his part, the person holding the reception would more easily grant hospitality to visitors with whom he was already on good terms. Most likely, in the account we are analysing, Jesus' disciples met a servant of the owner of the upper room, since only a servant would go to the city to draw water, surely not the owner himself![26] 'The Master says: "Where is my dining room in which I can eat the Passover with my disciples?"' (v 14). It had to be a very large group to eat a year-old male lamb without blemish;[27] there are in these details, apparently marginal, the fundamental elements of the Jewish Passover celebration and Jesus seems preoccupied with providing good arrangements according to the needs of the ritual.[28] If there are undeniable references to the Jewish Passover, at the same time there are lacking many elements typical of this celebration, replaced in part by others that are absolutely new. One cannot but see that Christ does not simply follow the Jewish Passover ritual, but celebrates his own Passover, giving at the same time a new meaning to the Old Testament Passover.[29] Returning

---

26. How many encounters, especially in the Old Testament, are held in proximity to a source of water and, in particular, to a well! This was already mentioned in an earlier chapter. What is quite rare is the fact of speaking about a man carrying a water pitcher, as normally it is the women who carry out this task; the men, at most, carry the wine. This irregularity was probably a distinctive enough trait to enable the disciples to recognise him as a guide amidst a crowd of people.

27. *Cf* Ex 12:5. Also in Exus, 'If the household is too small to eat the animal, a man must join with his neighbor, the nearest to his house, as the number of persons requires. You must take into account what each can eat in deciding the number for the animal' (12:4).

28. We do not enter here into the merits of the thorny historical-theological debate about the true nature of the farewell meal that Jesus celebrated in the company of his disciples: the problem is knowing whether or not it was a Passover meal, even if a few days in advance of the Jewish calendar.

29. This latter, moreover, no longer corresponded to the ancient usage of a brief meal eaten standing and rushed in the memory of the Exus from Egypt during the night. In first century CE Palestine, the Passover meal had become a veritable sumptuous banquet to which even the very poor were invited.

to the descriptive elements of the Last Supper, certain details of the place setting and décor reproduce a very typical portrait in the Semitic context. For example, in the story of the hospitality given by the Shunemite woman to Elisha in the Second Book of Kings, there is mention of a reception room for him when he passes by, located on the second floor. 'She [the Shunemite woman] said to her husband, "Look, I am sure the man who is constantly passing our way must be a holy man of God. Let us build him a small room on the roof and put a bed in it for him, and a table and chair and lamp; whenever he comes he can rest there"' (2 Kgs 4:9–10).

We began with the text of Mark's Gospel but we cannot omit the symbolic action of great theological as well as sociological significance at the very heart of the ritual of hospitality: the washing of the feet of the disciples as described in John's Gospel, and probably placed exactly during the Last Supper. We know that the Fourth Gospel does not give an account of the institution of the Eucharist as do the Synoptics; but instead devotes an entire chapter to a long discourse on the Bread of Life (*cf* Jn 6) and a second chapter as a farewell discourse which may be described as Christ's spiritual testament (*cf* Jn 17), accompanied by the unusual and shocking washing of the feet. If the content of the catechesis on the Bread of Life already gave a new and unexpected understanding of the Messiahship of Christ, his washing of the disciples' feet is a gesture even more puzzling and ambiguous, because it is a service normally accomplished by slaves and not only an expression of extreme hospitality and total dedication.[30] Love to the end becomes service to the end. By accomplishing this act of service and exhorting the disciples to do the same (cf. Jn 13:15), the washing of one another's feet becomes symbolic of the acceptance of a love received as such, completely free and not in the logic of a gift to reciprocate.

---

30. The great Rudolf Schnakenburg partially dissents from this analysis stating that the washing of feet, despite its being a humble gesture, is not only the duty of slaves but also that of wives for their husbands and those of the children for their parents (*cf* R Schnakenburg, *Il Vangelo di Giovanni: Commento ai capitoli 13–21*, (Bresica: Paideia, 1981).

The apostolic communities: the welcome given the messengers of the Gospel

> Then he summoned the Twelve and began to send them out in pairs, giving them authority over unclean spirits. And he instructed them to take nothing for the journey except a staff—no bread, no haversack, no copper for their purses. They were to wear sandals but, he added, 'Do not take a spare tunic.' And he said to them, 'If you enter a house anywhere, stay there until you leave the district. And if the place does not welcome you and people refuse to listen to you, as you walk away shake off the dust from under your feet as a sign to them' (Mk 6:7–11).

Box 2 Ancient Roads and Caravanserais

Towards the end of the first century CE,, there were no less than 372 land arteries for a total of 78,000 kilometers (some 50,000 miles) in the Mediterranean. These road networks offered excellent connections between Palestine, Phoenicia, Syria, Asia Minor, Macedonia, Greece and Italy (a necessity when boats were used only for the transport of goods and only rarely for passengers.) In general, one could not travel more than 50 kilometers a day and, for this reason, caravans advancing by stages took advantage of hostels or shelters, if they were fortunate enough, and sometimes even the most renown caravanserais. These latter consisted of an open space and were surrounded by a rather high wall. Within, around the courtyard, ran a portico that offered shelter and was, at times, enclosed by walls, thus creating small room compartments, reserved for those who could afford to pay for more privacy (this is probably the context in which Mary of Nazareth gave birth to the Messiah; cf. Lk 2:6-7). This was no small advantage in often overcrowded conditions, which were characterized by promiscuity in the public places of the time. The Ottoman caravanserai, called han, became extremely important and increasingly elaborate, especially since the fifteenth century, offering hospitality to passing merchants and their animals and serving as a warehouse for their goods. It was comprised of rectangular buildings that included a large courtyard and, originally of two levels, came to include a third since the eighteenth century. The stables, shops and craft rooms were located mainly on the first (ground) floor. The shelters were located on the second floor, rooms surmounted by cross beams that all faced a pergola and beyond that was the inner courtyard. The rooms were completely bare of furniture, each sleeping on his own carpet amidst his bags and luggage. Often, in the middle of the courtyard, there was a small mescit (prayer room) with a fountain for the ritual washings. All the structures were equipped with their own tea room, an essential drink for the correct ritual of hospitality for all social contacts and trade in the East. Everyone, including animals and goods, was safe in these shelters: at night the doors were shut and the sentries kept watch, maintaining order and peace both within and without. The safety of the caravanserai was legendary, to the point that by the seventeenth century the buildings erected were intended explicitly for the storage of valuables and money, thereby eliminating the need for banks. It is easy to see their social purpose and not only their commercial value (they were often created in connection with a large mosque), which corresponded to a fixed monthly sustenance for the religious community, including educational activities and preparation of food for the poor.

The directives given by Jesus to his disciples at the moment of assigning them their mission shift now from the obligation of hospitality towards Christ himself to that which will benefit those who are commissioned to spread the Gospel message throughout the world. In other words, as Jesus benefited from the law of hospitality in the carrying out of his public mission, in the same way, so may his disciples after him. After a first mission experience within the borders of Palestine and more specifically in Galilee ('These twelve Jesus sent out, instructing them as follows: "Do not turn your steps to pagan territory, and do not enter any Samaritan town; go rather to the lost sheep of the House of Israel"', Matt 10:5–6), the Twelve, heeding their Master, travelled the streets of the world to bring the message of salvation 'to the ends of the earth' (Acts 1:8). But they are not alone, because after them and following their example are inspired a great multitude of 'ministers of the Word' (Lk 1:2) and collaborators animated with apostolic zeal. Certainly, the Church of the first century reflects the mobility of Roman society and is able to spread thanks to the practice of hospitality which is of benefit to them as they pass through. The rapid expansion of Christianity, particularly in the Mediterranean region, however, remains surprising. Rainer Kampling tells us that it was particularly favored by the presence of pre-existing Jewish communities in all the great cities of the Roman

126   *Strangers With God*

Empire and by excellent connections between the various groups.[31] Another factor favouring the spread of the Gospel, was a very compact communications network across land, seas and rivers, essential for the commercial traffic of the time but also favourable for the mobility of peoples.

Returning to the opening text of this section, we note first of all that the disciples were sent out two by two (*cf* Mk 6:7), no doubt to help each other, but also to be able to testify according to the law of Moses: 'A single witness cannot suffice to convict a man of a crime or offense of any kind; whatever the misdemeanour, the evidence of two witnesses or three is required to sustain the charge' (Deut 19:15). Sent to announce the Good News, the disciples are also to be witnesses of the quality of hospitality offered: a testimony of salvation or condemnation, depending on whether they were welcomed or not (*cf* Mk 6:11). As for the more material provisions, those who choose to follow Christ in proclaiming his Gospel are fundamentally exhorted to a radical detachment, trusting totally in Divine Providence. The terms of this detachment diverge slightly between the three synoptic versions, Mark's being a bit more accommodating: differences that are easily realized by reference to the various audiences to whom they are writing. For Mark's readers of non-Jewish culture, traveling without staff or sandals was a sign of wandering. The staff especially was considered a necessary defense, to the extent that the evangelist would not have been able to be asked for its surrender. However, the paucity of the itinerant preacher's equipage, evident in all the Gospels, demands an adequate and urgent hospitality in exchange for the spiritual profit their hearers receive 'for the laborer deserves his wages' (Lk 10:7). This principle, established as a vital necessity even for so great a traveller as St Paul,[32] seems, however, to be questioned as

---

31. *Cf* J Schreiner and R Kampling, *Il prossimo, lo straniero, il nemico*, 127. Salvatore Garofalo recalls that by now there were only a small number of Jews living in Palestine and that there were scattered communities of the Jewish diaspora along the coastal regions of the Mediterranean and Aegean Seas, travelled by St Paul. In these communities, the Apostle always received a warm welcome, as long as his preaching, quite open to the Gentiles, did not provoke violent reactions by those Jews of pharisaical obedience (*cf* S Garofalo, 'L'ospitalità nella vita e nell'inseGenamento degli Apostoli', in G Danesi and S Garofalo, *Migrazioni ed Accoglienza nella Sacra Scrittura*, 247–250).

32. 'People under instruction should always contribute something to the support of the man instructing them', (Gal 6:6); *cf* also 1 Tm 5:18.

The Theology of the New Testament

to its binding force by the Apostle to the Gentiles. To understand this reticence of Paul we must perhaps refer to his concrete experience at Philippi, in Macedonia, during his second missionary journey. It is here that he comes to know Lydia, a wealthy trader in purple goods from Thyatira (well-known for its production of purple cloth). Of pagan birth, Lydia was already associated with the Jewish community before receiving baptism with all her family and servants. To extend her knowledge of the Good News, she offered hospitality to Paul and Silas by referring to her faithfulness in the Lord: "'If you really think me a true believer in the Lord", she said, "come and stay with us.'" This passage from the book of Acts concludes with: 'And she would take no refusal' (Acts 16:14–15). According to Salvatore Garofalo, the use of the word 'force' or 'constraint' refers to Paul's intent not to live at the expense of third parties (even though Christian) but to meet his needs and those of his companions by the work of his own hands.[33]

'I have never asked anyone—said the Apostle to the Gentiles—for money or clothes; you know for yourselves that the work I did earned enough to meet my needs and those of my companions' (Acts 20:33–34). On the one hand, Paul is proposing himself with these statements as a model for Christians who, misled by false announcements of an imminent Parousia, were living in idleness as if the time of the Spirit had already come. To them, the Apostle says bluntly: 'You know how you are supposed to imitate us: now we were not idle when we were among you, nor did we ever have our meals at anyone's table without paying for them [. . .] We gave you a rule when we were with you: not to let anyone have any food if he refused to work' (2 Thes 3:7–10). In both posture and by word, Paul has also the personal concern about not becoming a burden to anyone;[34] rather, he would prefer to bring the gifts of the Christian community to those who are really in need of it: as in the case of the collection solicited in the churches

---

33. However, the Greek word used here (παρεβιάδαντο) is exactly the same as that used by Luke to describe the invitation of the two disciples on the road to Emmaus to the mysterious pilgrim they met along the way. The word suggests an urgent proposal rather than a compulsion (cf Lk 24:29): In the same way Lydia allowed Paul and Silas to accept her hospitality by insisting they would not be a burden to her (cf S Garofalo, 'L'ospitalità nella vita e nell'insegenamento degli Apostoli', 254–255).

34. Paul, for example, stayed more than three weeks in Thessalonica while he was preaching in the synagogue but worked for his own maintenance at the same time.

of Galatia for the community of Jerusalem (*cf* 1 Co 16:1-4); or for the more personal needs of disciples of the Gospel such as Mark (cf Col 4:10) and Epaphroditus (*cf* Phil 2:29); or the women associated with the mission such as Phoebe, the deaconess of Cenchreae (*cf* Rm 16:1-2). Finally, in all of Paul's hesitance to accept anyone's invitation there is undoubtedly also a concern to safeguard the gratuity of the Word, freeing it from any sort of ulterior motive or material interest, as could be in the case of false prophets who, on the contrary, profit as parasites from a generous hospitality.[35] This attitude of the Apostle to the Gentiles, in comparison, does not contradict his gratitude to those who were mindful of his hours of extreme poverty, as was the community of Philippi during his multiple imprisonments (*cf* Ph 4:10-19). Paul even likens his circumstances to an accounting system—which is quite improper both in the classical vision of Christian charity and in the ritual of hospitality. In other words, if the Philippians make an offer of material goods, he makes the point to reciprocate with spiritual goods (*cf* 1 Cor 9:11).

In the Gospel passage about the commission of the Twelve, there is further data to be emphasized: that hospitality ought not to be accepted indiscriminately upon arrival. In Matthew's version of this passage, he writes: 'Whatever town or village you go into, ask for someone trustworthy and stay with him until you leave' (10:11). If one thinks of the sometimes very precarious condition of hostels along the major roads of the time, this exhortation may be understood as a warning against overnight stays in disreputable places, which would preclude any credibility of announcing the Good News in the future... But the adjective 'worthy', used differently by the evangelist Matthew a few verses later (*cf* v 13), can also be understood in the sense of 'hospitable' or, more exactly, a 'believer in the gospel'. About this latter, one must remember that the natural repugnance of the disciples toward the pagan world (given greater emphasis in Matthew's Gospel, which is addressed primarily to the Judeo-Christian world) decreased only very slowly, to the measure that these witnesses began to really encounter the non-Jewish world. It was then discovered that if the person who accepted them was not yet in the truth, it was the practice

---

35. Paul's monologue in First Corinthians is very significant here. Paul presents himself as a model preacher legitimized by a personal apparition of the Risen Christ and rich only the Word itself which he announces free of charge (*cf* 1 Col 9:1-18).

of hospitality that opened the door to faith.[36] Moreover, for Paul this opening to the pagan world will begin as a real need and only later become his choice, because the Jews will become increasingly hostile at hearing the content of his preaching. The experience of the Apostle at Ephesus indicates this hostility:

> He began by entering the synagogue, where he spoke out boldly and argued persuasively about the kingdom of God. He did this for three months, till the attitude of some of the congregation hardened into unbelief. As soon as they began attacking the Way in front of the others, he broke with them and took his disciples apart to hold daily discussions in the lecture room of Tyrannus (Acts 19:8–9).

Tyrannus was probably the owner, if not himself a professor of rhetoric, who lent the premises of the city's school of philosophy to Paul during the times free from official courses! Of course, this instance does not eliminate the fact that the relationship between the preachers of the Gospel and the pagan world will know serious moments of crisis and that there will always be a certain fragility of presence and communal cohesion outside the traditional geographical boundaries of Judaism. That is why there will never be lacking continuous warnings against heresy, sensuality and idolatry, alongside the repeated calls to a New Testament reception of missionaries of the Gospel.[37] In a Christian

---

36. *Cf* G Danesi, 'Per una teologia delle migrazioni', 36. Concerning this the author recalls the illustrious examples of Simon the tanner with whom Paul himself spent the night (*cf* Acts 9:43); of Cornelius, a centurion of the Italica cohort stationed in Caesarea, who welcomed Peter (*cf* Acts 10); or the already mentioned Lydia of Thyatira (*cf* Acts 16).

37. Among the many biblical references possible are included the Second Letter of John: 'If anybody does not keep within the teaching of Christ but goes beyond it, he cannot have God with him: only those who keep to what he taught can have the Father and the Son with them. If anyone comes to you bringing a different doctrine, you must not receive him into your house or even give him a greeting. To greet him would make you a partner in his evil work' (vv 9–11); and the Letter to Titus: 'If a man disputes what you teach [literally, 'is a heretic'], then after a first and second warning, have no more to do with him' (3:10); or, again, the First Letter to the Corinthians: 'What I wrote was that you should not associate with a brother Christian who is leading an immoral life, or is a usurer, or idolatrous, or a slanderer, or a drunkard, or is dishonest; you should not even eat a meal with people like that' (5:11).

community still in its infancy, attempting to structure itself in light of the Good News still being preached by the last direct witnesses of Christ, there is growing concern to stem any false interpretations and to isolate those in error. This requirement would appear difficult to reconcile with the message of Christ himself but is simply evidence of a context now different from that of the ministry of the Son of God. It would take centuries to rediscover in the Church, and return to, a reflection on the importance of an unconditional welcome in the bosom in the community: a welcome set free from religious discrimination and called forth by religious motivations.

Box 3 Paul's Understanding of Hospitality: A 'Selective' Practice?

If Paul considers hospitality a duty and not an option for the true Christian, going so far as to speak of it as one's 'special care' (cf. Rm 13:13)—implying that such solicitude does not flounder in the face of difficulty, nor even before the risks posed by a total availability to welcome—nevertheless, it is questionable whether this availability is totally unlimited. Paul is speaking of an attention ordinarily reserved for the needs of the 'saints,' those who are members of the Christian community called by God in baptism to be part of a holy people, and thus consecrated unto perfection (cf. 1 Th 5:23). In other words, this hospitality seems to be a duty of one Christian toward another. Where Paul emphasizes that Christians are called to bless their persecutors, there is no mention of a duty to also welcome them ("Bless those who persecute you: never curse them, bless them [. . .] Never repay evil with evil;" Rm 12:14.17). Paul even seems to refer to a precise hierarchy of travelers who need to be given a priority of welcome: he speaks of apostles, prophets and teachers (Cf. 1 Co 12:27-28). For teachers he means those responsible for catechesis in general; rather, the apostles are missionaries and preachers of the Good News. All must be received as the Lord, Paul says, as long as their teaching is 'orthodox' (i.e., according to tradition), a teaching that promotes justice and knowledge of the Lord himself. It is necessary, therefore, to discern between true and false apostles and prophets. These cited exceptions to the duty of hospitality, which seem to indulge Paul himself, must be located in the context of the first century CE when the routes of the Roman Empire were crowded with propagandists of religious and philosophical doctrines. Obviously, not all enjoyed a good reputation; among them those who could prey on the good

The Theology of the New Testament

131

faith of the people were not lacking, those who were quick to appeal to flattery and deception, and take possession of their money in a cheap market of glory. Therefore, as an itinerant missionary, Paul had much company and could easily be mistaken for one of the many imposters who called themselves bearers of the message of truth and salvation. This framework will contribute not a little to form the combative character and determination of the Apostle of the Gentiles. His missionary activity needed a careful strategy and solid organization. We limit ourself to recalling that this mission was exclusively urban, mainly because only the cities could be reached by land, along the main Roman roads, or by sea. Similarly, a preacher could make himself understood in Greek only in city centers. Then, there was a matter of opportunity because by choosing a large city as a missionary center, one could hope that the Christian message would radiate out to the surrounding rural areas (This is what Paul tried to do in Corinth and especially in Ephesus). It was not, then, only a question of choosing the most suitable locations for the proclamation of the message, but also of finding suitable housing, as well as helpers, points of reference and the means to effectively preach. Moreover, urban cosmopolitanism would contribute greatly to the creation of the universalist dimension of the Pauline vision.

Interior dispositions and gestures of welcome

The account of the mission of the Twelve, already highlighted, does not offer many details about the ritual of hospitality. Nor do the apostolic writings allow us to know much more about a practice which, however, would not have deviated very much from the customs of their Semitic world. Probably the ablutions followed the opening greetings ('wash the saints' feet', as Paul mentions in 1 Tim 5:10) and all the kindly attentions typical of a warm welcome such as preparing the food to eat, providing for the night and the whole ensemble of special needs, rarely described in detail.[38] Once one has been received into a home it is not permitted to change accommodation until the end of the sojourn in a given city or geographically limited location (*cf* Mk 6:10), except when constrained because of some indignity (that which ought not to be acceptable for a preacher of the Gospel). Any velleity to settle elsewhere for trivial reasons would be considered deeply disrespectful towards the host.

---

38. Paul, referring to the arrival of the deaconess Phoebe, says generically, 'help her with anything she needs' (Rom 16:2).

'As you enter his house salute it, and if the house deserves it, let your peace descend upon it; if it does not, let your peace come back to you' (Matt 10:12–13). The wishing of peace at the moment of the initial greetings (*shalom* in Hebrew, *she-lam* in Aramaic and *salām* in Arabic) is much more than a simple formality. It includes every kind of blessing both spiritual and temporal and, above all, is convinced that this peace, a true gift of God, cannot remain without effect.[39] Again, from the Biblical perspective, hospitality assumes a significance that goes far beyond a mere sociological practice. That is why all the evangelists associate hospitality with listening to the Word brought by its messengers: ('If anyone does not welcome you or listen to what you have to say . . .' Matt 10:14; and 'If any place does not welcome you and people refuse to listen to you . . .' Mk 6:11). To deny hospitality, therefore, automatically also means a rejection of the Good News and the One from whom it came ('Anyone who welcomes you welcomes me, and those who welcome me welcome him who sent me', Matt 10:40; or 'Jesus declared publicly: "Whoever believes in me believes not in me but in the one who sent me"', Jn 12:44), which accentuates the severity of the resulting judgment. The symbolic gesture of shaking the dust from their feet, noted by all the Synoptics (*cf* Matt 10:14; Mk 6:11; Lk 9:5), was very familiar with the Jews; and they will experience it at their expense when Paul and Barnabas, persecuted and driven from Antioch in Pisidia, 'shook the dust from their feet in defiance and went off to Iconium' (Acts 13:51). In fact, those who refuse to welcome the Word and its messengers are like the pagans and even the dust itself of a pagan land can contaminate the soil of the Holy Land; one must disencumber oneself before leaving hostile ground. In short, shaking the dust from one's sandals is a gesture that takes on the meaning of a judgment which Matthew makes particularly severe by comparing it to that pronounced upon Sodom and Gomorrah (*cf* Matt 10:15), cities inhospitable towards the messengers of God, and above all for the Jews the prototype of a merciless punishment of impenitent sinners.[40]

Among the few details concerning the ritual of hospitality provided us by the New Testament texts, particular importance is assigned to describing the preliminaries for a traveller preparing his journey: from the necessary information about the route, the supply of food and water, and money, to letters of recommendation or 'credentials'. Paul,

---

39. *Cf* S Garofalo, 'L'ospitalità nella vita e nell'inseGenamento di Gesù', 234.
40. S Garofalo, 'L'ospitalità nella vita e nell'inseGenamento di Gesù', 235.

The Theology of the New Testament 133

in particular, was always particularly attentive in ensuring the good treatment of his collaborators in evangelization. In his final directives to Titus he stipulates: 'See to all the travelling arrangements for Zenas the lawyer and Apollos, and make sure they have everything they need. All our people are to learn to occupy themselves in doing good works for their practical needs as well' (Tit 3:13–14). These cryptic admonitions are not limited to the deportment of the Gospel messengers from the moment of arrival and simple greetings to their departure but contribute in a very concrete way to the success of their mission.[41]

The New Testament redactors linger still more on the interior dispositions required by the practice of hospitality, upholding its importance and necessity. Paul offers a real catechesis on the Christian duty of hospitality which is taken up also in the Catholic epistles. We offer here some salient points.[42] In Chapter 12 of the Letter to the Romans, the Apostle describes several qualities and expressions of sincere love (or charity without pretense) including that of hospitality ('If any of the saints are in need you must share with them; and you should make hospitality your special care', v 13).[43] The love of strangers φιλοξενία (*philoxenia*) therefore is an expression of φιλαδελφία (*philadelphia*) or love of brother and sister.[44] In the well-known Sermon on the Mount, Christ had already proposed the primacy of this brotherly love as part of the same love for God (*cf* Matt 5). Of course, if fraternal charity is realized as Christians encounter one

---

41. Multiple references are possible in this regard: 1 Cor 16:6.11; 2 Cor 1:16; Rom 15:24.

42. For a more exhaustive analysis refer to Salvatore Garofalo, 'Esortazioni apostoliche sull'ospitalità', in G Danesi and S Garofalo, *Migrazioni ed accoglienza nella Sacra Scrittura*, 274–290.

43. The Greek term used here is κοινωνούντες (koinōnoúntes) which is derived from the same root κοινωνία (koinonia, society, communion). It also means to communicate, to show solidarity, verbs that Paul often uses in reference to more material goods (Gal 6:6; Phil 4:15), without neglecting those of a spiritual and moral nature.

44. This association of terms is also proposed in the letter to the Hebrews: 'Continue always to love each other like brothers (φιλαδελφία, philadelphia) and remember always to welcome strangers (φιλοξενία, philoxenia) . . .' (Heb 13:1–2). Garofalo tells us that the use of the Greek term φιλαδελφία, in the metaphorical sense of a purely spiritual brotherhood, is a feature of the New Testament in contrast with an exclusively secular Jewish usage. The sophist Lucian (c 125–190 CE) had already stressed with amazement that the first Christian legislators tried to convince all their disciples to be brothers (*cf De morte Peregrini*, 13). Tertullian, on his part, noted that the pagans reacted negatively to this manifestation of a Christian brotherhood, because it was synonymous with an unheard of affection and they associated brotherhood with kinship (*cf Apologia del cristianesimo*, XXXIX, 8).

another as members of a single body and as travellers together on the way to the heavenly homeland to which Christ introduces them, it is hospitality, from this perspective, that creates and develops the Body of Christ. That is why Paul speaks of 'in union with the Lord' (*cf* Rom 16:2a) and why hospitality introduces us to the concept of αγάπη (*agápē*) in the Greek sense of shared love.[45] Now, it is interesting to note that the latter term in the plural, αγάπαι (*agápai*), has assumed the sense of 'common banquet' or 'fraternal meal' since apostolic times. We read in the Book of Acts that: 'They went as a body to the Temple every day but met in their homes for the breaking of bread; they shared their food gladly and generously' (Acts 2:46). Thus, the prepared table is representative of that fraternal charity which must unite Christians. Verse 46 just mentioned is the natural result of verse 42 of the same chapter, Acts 2: 'These remained faithful to the teachings of the apostles, to the brotherhood, to the breaking of bread and to the prayers.' The author draws a parallel between the Jewish religious meetings (which took place in the Temple) and those of the Christians (at home). Throughout the first century CE, Christianity, not yet considered a licit religion, had no public places of worship which is why the celebrations were held in private homes[46] and it was because of this practice that the early Church was defined as a 'domestic church'. These Christians distributed the food provided by the community and from that originated the sharing of goods (*cf* Acts 2:45). The faithful probably celebrated the breaking of bread during a normal meal (*cf* 1 Cor 11:26–34), which was proposed as an alternative to the official cult of the Temple.[47]

---

45. The Bible borrows the term αγαπη (*agape*, later translated into Latin *caritas*) from the Greek αγαπάω (*agapao*, love) that characterises Matt 5:43–46.

46. In the house of Phoebe (Rm 16:1), in that of Prisca and Aquila (Acts 18:2–3), of Aristobulus (Rm 16:10) and even of Philemon (Phil 1–2). Paul himself, during his captivity in Rome, welcomed all who came to visit him in his own rented lodging (Ac 28:30): on these occasions most likely even the Eucharist was celebrated.

47. It is not necessary to always imagine a Eucharistic celebration at these daily meals in Judeo-Christian homes. They were ordinary Semitic meals, centered on the recollection of the risen Master and in anticipation of his coming, during which, at times, the Eucharist itself was a part, when it renewed the words and actions of the Lord that transformed a normal banquet into 'the Lord's Supper' (1 Cor 11:20–34). Freed definitively from the celebration of the Jewish Passover, this Eucharist took place certainly more than once a year, probably weekly (Acts 20:7.11). Abuse and degeneration, reported by Paul himself (1 Cor 11:20–22), led later to a final separation between the daily profane feast and the celebration of 'the Lord's Supper'.

The Church's thinking on hospitality:
An historical overview

The second century: The Fathers of the Church

The early Church takes up the biblical teaching on hospitality without adding any really new elements to the reflection. Towards the end of the first century of our era, an anonymous author in Syria drew up a small treatise in Greek entitled *The Doctrine of the Twelve Apostles*, better known as the *Didaché*.[1] Very soon it became the object of great veneration, to the point that, for a certain period of time, it was read alongside the Epistles of the New Testament during the liturgies of the primitive Church.[2] The *Didaché* is the first extra-canonical document of early Christianity, appearing at the same time as the books which make up the New Testament. The sociological and cultural setting is the same as that of the Pastoral Letters: hospitality is described as a precise duty and not as an option for a Christian. Notwithstanding, it must be practiced with both generosity and great caution.

> Let every apostle who comes to you be received as the Lord. But he must not remain more than one day, or two, if there's a need. If he stays three days, he is a false prophet. And when

---

1. The Greek term precisely means 'teaching' or 'doctrine.' It was probably the work of a scribe since, despite the title which refers to the twelve Apostles, the apostles are never mentioned in the text in question!
2. The Church Fathers (Irenaeus, Clement of Alexandria, Athanasius, Origen . . .) frequently referred to it as did Eusebius, the author of *Ecclesiastical History*. Because of its renown, the *Didaché* was soon translated into Latin and Arabic. However, the document disappeared from circulation for centuries and was found again only around 1873 in Constantinople, by Philotheos Bryennios, Patriarch of Nicomedia and dean of the School of Phanar.

136 *Strangers With God*

the apostle goes away, let him take nothing but bread to last him until his next night of lodging. If he asks for money, he is a false prophet.[3]

These details are particularly interesting because they implicitly testify to possible abuses of hospitality, which are underscored by the *Didaché* as well:

Welcome anyone coming in the name of the Lord. Receive everyone who comes in the name of the Lord, but then, test them and use your discretion[4]. If he who comes is a transient, assist him as far as you are able; but he should not remain with you more than two or three days, if need be. If he wants to stay with you, and is a craftsman, let him work for his living. But if he has no trade, use your judgment in providing for him; for a Christian should not live idle in your midst. If he is dissatisfied with this sort of an arrangement, he is a Christ peddler. Watch that you keep away from such people.[5].

There is in these lines an echo of certain recommendations made by St Paul to the first Christian communities, testifying to a commonality of issues between the *Didaché* and the New Testament writings. Beside the denunciations of abuse, there is constant preoccupation about protecting the true faith from the risk of heretical contamination. Already Tertullian, towards the end of the second century CE, maintained that the profession of the one Credo was the best guarantee in the case of receiving strangers. But it must be noted that there are two levels of the meaning of hospitality as used by Tertullian and the Church Fathers in general: one that refers to the doctrine of salvation, very restrictive with regard to those who are 'outsiders'; and, within the Church, the proper rules of communion. It is at this second level that the theology of *contesseratio hospitalitatis* lies. In other words, towards the end of the second century and into the third, Christian literature is largely polemical and is engaged in a double

---

3. The Doctrine of the Twelve Apostles (*Didaché*), XI, 4–6. The translation is by Tony Jones and is under the protection of 'Creative Commons license'. Found on-line.
4. There is here an allusion to the gift of discernment but also, and more specifically, to the ability to distinguish good from evil (*cf* Matt 25:33).
5. *Didaché*, XII, 1–5.

battle: *ad extra* against idolaters, philosophers, Jews and heretics; and, *ad intra*, against disciplinary deviations within the Christian communities. The main purpose of this double combat is to draw the lines that separate the Christian from his adversaries and to define, implicitly, the Christian identity. A very complex reality is reduced to a simplistic dichotomy: those who are in the truth and those who are in error. Now, Tertullian and the Fathers regarded the Church—the community, those who, in fact, are in the truth—as a 'family', with all that this term implies. Christians are God's household (as St Paul says: 'You are citizens like all the saints, and part of God's household' Ep 2:19); pagans, heretics and Jews, on the contrary, were 'outsiders'. This idea and these terms are, moreover, of biblical origin and much used by the Fathers of the Church. It is in this intra-ecclesial context and the practice of the letters of communion (*litterae communicatoriae* in Latin, *koinônikà grammata* in Greek), as well known in the West as in the East, that Tertullian evokes the *contesseratio hospitalitatis*, a Latin expression that could be translated as a 'mutual exchange of the duty of hospitality'. Now, these *litterae communitoriae* both expressed and guaranteed communion between the bishops and local churches. Tertullian mentions this latter stating that 'to all these is the Title of Primitive, and Apostolick Churches due also, while they live in the Unity of the same Faith and Discipline; and while they religiously observe, and strictly keep up true brotherly Love, and constant Communion one with another. And Nothing could make them do so, and preserve these sacred Rites entire, but the Tradition and Observation of one and the same Doctrine and Discipline'.[6] In addition to these *litterae communicatoriae*, each community had lists of names and addresses to be consulted, to know to which church and to which bishop to turn while traveling through a given region; this was to ensure remaining within the *koinônia-communio* of Christ's Church. These different signs of communion allowed mutual understanding among communities around the world and protected

---

6. Tertullian, *De Praescriptione haereticorum*, XX, 8–9, translated by Joseph Betty, 1722 and found online www.tertullian.org/works/de_praescriptione_ haereticorum.htm. The Latin text is more significant than the English translation: '*Sic primae omnes, et omnes apostolicae, dum a omnes. Probant Unitatem communicatio et Pacis appellatio fraternitatis, et contesseratio hospitalitatis. Quae jura not alia ratio regit quam eiusdem sacraments a traditio*' (De praescriptione haereticorum XX, 8: PL 2, 32).

against a false communion with those who did not share the ecclesial unity. As regards the aforementioned *contesseratio hospitalitatis,* the word was fashioned by Tertullian adding *con* to the noun *tesserae,* forming an original *contesseratio.* The image is very concrete and refers to a practice of Greco-Roman hospitality. Essentially it consisted of a tablet, a cube and a small bone, half of each held by each party, to be passed on to one's descendants. Bringing the two halves together would demonstrate the existence of links, even those of a much earlier time. Whoever had a complementary part could then, even after many years, claim a right to hospitality. In short, the *tesserae* were signs of recognition and communion between the members of the faith community.

Another term borrowed from the ancient Greek culture and brought into Christian usage is that of the *symbolon.* The term was used originally in a commercial context, bringing with it the idea of a contract or the seal that guarantees the contract. Since the early centuries of Christianity, the baptismal profession of faith was called the *symbolon,* and later, using a formula now more developed, 'the Apostles' Creed'. Now, Tertullian considers that the sign of recognitionion among Christians is this profession of faith: the new intangible *tessera hospitalitatis* that Christians must display among themselves is to live as brothers and sisters and practice mutual hospitality; it remains, therefore, fundamentally intra-Community.

The third century: The development of the practice of hospitality

If the first two centuries of Christianity were very cautious insofar as expanding the concept of hospitality, the third century in particular developed a rich literature favoring its practice. Although there are no specific writings on this topic, there are several exhortations of general encouragement. *The Shepherd of Hermas*[7] lists hospitality among the good works and, in particular, correlates it with the good conscience of those among the 'saints' or 'brothers'—the elders (bishops or

---

7. Written in the second century, the work enjoyed a great success, despite never having been integrated into the list of canonical books. The original text is in Greek, written in Rome, and translated into Latin very quickly (perhaps by the same Hermas). Only this last edition has come down to us complete. The text consists of five visions, twelve precepts (or commandments) and ten similitudes (or parables).

deacons)—who have special duties in the community.[8] According to Hermas: 'And from the tenth mountain,[9] where were trees which overshadowed certain sheep, they who believed were the following: bishops given to hospitality (*philoxenoi*), who always gladly received into their houses the servants of God, without dissimulation.[10]

Clement of Rome (35–97 AD), for his part, inspired by the Third Epistle of St John (3 Jn 5–8), congratulated the Christian community of Corinth for their well-known hospitality: 'For who-ever dwelt even for a short time among you, and did not find your faith to be as fruitful of virtue as it was firmly established? Who did not admire the sobriety and moderation of your godliness in Christ? Who did not proclaim the magnificence of your habitual hospitality? And who did not rejoice over your perfect and well-grounded knowledge?'[11] In his *Epistle to the Corinthians*, Clement calls upon the divine rewards ever

---

8. This was already exhorted in the Pastoral Letters (*cf* 1 Tm 3:2 and 1:8; Ti, written primarily to bishops). The best known Fathers confirm that hospitality must be a characteristic trait of the shepherds: for example, Jerome in his Epistles and Chrysostom in his Second Homily on Genesis advise bishops to leave their homes open to strangers and to those suffering for the cause of truth and their table available to the poor because, by so doing, they are sure to spend time with the Lord hidden under the guise of a pilgrim (*cf* G Bonet-Maury, 'Hospitality. Christian', in J Hastings, editor, *Encyclopaedia of Religion and Ethics*, XIII [Edinburgh-New York: T&T Clark-Charles Scribner's Sons, 1908–1927], VI, 804–808). Elsewhere the Pastoral Letters also speak of widows (a woman "at least sixty years old who has had only one husband. She must be [. . .] known for her good works and for the way she has brought up her children, shown hospitality to strangers and washed the saints' feet, helped people who are in trouble and been active in all kinds of good work (*cf* 1 Tm 5:10).

9. In this passage of the ninth similitude, Hermas is speaking of twelve mountains which correspond to the twelve tribes, the twelve nations, all the nations of the world and, above all, to the twelve categories of Christians (but it is clearly a reference to the twelve tribes of Israel), even before the final purification of the Church from every type of sinner (Hermas begins by noting that not all Christians will come to salvation).

10. The Shepherd of Hermas, Similitude IX, 27 (1–2), found on-line at Early Christian Writers, http://www.earlychristianwritings.com/churchfathers.html. The author situates hospitality among the Christian virtues, among which are principally assistance given to widows, visiting orphans and the poor, rescuing God's People from slavery and, simply, hospitality because in being hospitable there is often opportunity to do more.

11. Clement of Rome, Epistle to the Corinthians, I, 2. Found on-line, http://www.earlychristianwritings.com/text/1clement-roberts.html

enjoyed by the patriarch Abraham, model of hospitality. He continues by referring to the stories of Lot and Rahab as further examples.[12] Also in the second century, Justin Martyr, in his *Apology*, provides an overview of the different types of transient guests, listing all who need help and support from others who have not only the means, but even the simple good will, according to their resources; the community will be responsible to allocate resources offered to widows, orphans and the needy, the sick, prisoners, passers-by.[13] Nor was there any difference made between treatment given to Christians of Jewish origin and those of Gentile origin. Tertullian too, in his treatise *Ad Uxorem*, states that his wife, assuming that he will precede her in death, should waive her right to remarry a pagan because a brother pilgrim could not be received into an unbelieving household.[14] Nor do we forget Origen among the authors of the second and third centuries, who touches on the theme of hospitality especially in his *Homilies on Genesis*, and more exactly in Homilies IV and V dedicated to the characters of Abraham and Lot, with which we will deal directly in the next chapter.

Hospitality as an act of justice

Among the Fathers of the Church of the fourth and fifth centuries, certainly it is St John Chrysostom (ca 344–407), the first Patriarch of Constantinople, who offers the most significant contributions to hospitality. Chrysostom contrasts the 'philanthropy' of Christ to the inhumanity of those who do not welcome the stranger and the pilgrim. We refer specifically to his *Homilies on the Acts of the Apostles* where he appeals directly to the term 'humanity' in the sense of 'hospitality;' Pierre Miquel wonders if there is not some trace of a stoic influence in this detail.[15] We offer here some extracts from the writings of this great preacher, a native of Antioch, which give an ideal synthesis of Patristic thought on the subject.

---

12. Clement of Rome, Epistle to the Corinthians, I, 2. X, 6–7; XI, XII and 1, 1.3.
13. *Cf* Justin Martyr, *Apology*, I, 67. Found on-line *http://www.earlychristianwritings. com/text/justinmartyr-firstapology.html*
14. *Cf* Tertullian, *To His Wife*, Book II, IV. Found on-line http://www. earlychristianwritings.com/text/tertullian29.html
15. *Cf* P Miquel, 'Hospitalité' in M Viller, editor, *Dictionnaire de Spiritualité*, 815. If an inhospitable person is described as unhuman, it goes without saying that someone who is hospitable is then 'rich in humanness,' substituting humanity for hospitality.

The Church's thinking on hospitality: An historical overview

> Aye, if it were given me to entertain Paul as a guest, I readily and with much eagerness would do this. Lo! It is in your power to entertain Paul's Master for your guest, and you will not: for he that receives one of these least, he says, receives Me (Matt 18:5; Lk 9:48). How much the brother may be least, so much the more does Christ come to you through him. For he that receives the great, often does it from vainglory also; but he that receives the small, does it purely for Christ's sake.[16]

The author continues by offering scriptural quotes in support of his proposal, alluding to the eschatological reward given to those who accept Christ in their needy brothers and sisters, before moving on to more concrete suggestions in the practice of hospitality.

> Make for yourself a guest-chamber in your own house: set up a bed there, set up a table there and a candlestick (*Cf* 2 Kgs 4:10). For is it not absurd, that whereas, if soldiers should come, you have rooms set apart for them, and show much care for them, and furnish them with everything, because they keep off from you the visible war of this world, yet strangers have no place where they might abide? Gain a victory over the Church. Would you put us to shame? This do: surpass us in liberality: have a room, to which Christ may come; say, This is Christ's cell; this building is set apart for Him. Be it but an underground chamber, and mean, He disdains it not [. . .] For you ought indeed to receive them in the upper part of your house;[17] but if you will not do this, then though it be below, though but where your mules are housed, and your servants, there receive Christ.[18]

John Chrysostom had himself been exiled and undergone hardship and insecurity; he himself had suffered the loss of family and friends, been suspected and accused unjustly. He is, therefore, a connoisseur of the psychology of the refugee, the passing stranger, with his hopes and fears. That is why he insists so strongly on the need for a host to be welcoming and conscious of assuming a 'Christological attitude', which necessarily requires both joy and gratitude. The Desert

---

16. St John Chrysostom, *Homily 45 on Acts*. Found on-line at http://www.newadvent.org/fathers/210145.htm

17. This is probably an allusion to the room reserved for the prophet Elijah in the house of the widow of Zarephath in 1 Kgs 17:19.

18. St John Chrysostom, *Homily 45 on Acts*.

Fathers also understood this exigency; after an initial period of strict eremitism, they progressively moved to a cenobitic way of life, chosen also in compliance with the obligation of hospitality. Certainly, giving oneself to visiting the sick and offering hospitality to those in need and to travelers does disturb the quiet of contemplation and occasions certain exceptions to the usual austerities of their way of life; still, in welcoming the poor and needy it is Christ who is welcomed, the same Christ whom one is seeking in those very austerities!

Thanks to the testimony of St Ambrose (340–397), we are able to apprehend the need for a hospitable sensitivity which not only characterizes a Christian environment in general, but also feeds a lively debate in the secular world and political institutions.[19] Ambrose maintains that hospitality is essentially a feature that should characterize everyone (*publica species humanitatis*) and not Christians only; this must be done then, first of all, for love of Justice.[20]

> Hospitality also serves to recommend many. For it is a kind of open display of kindly feelings: so that the stranger may not want hospitality, but be courteously received, and that the door may be open to him when he comes. It is most seemly in the eyes of the whole world that the stranger should be received with honour; that the charm of hospitality should not fail at our table; that we should greet a guest with ready and free service, and look out for his arrival [. . .]

19. We refer in particular to the most important moral writing of the bishop of Milan, *De Officiis Ministrorum* (written after 386), which describes the duties of the clergy and at the same time puts forth the whole of Christian morality; his object was to correct and expand the homonymous pagan ethics of Cicero. The latter, speaking of Justice, denounced among other things the immorality of expulsing foreigners.

20. *Cf* St Ambrose, Abraham, 1, 5, 32. Similar ideas, in a discourse that has become ever more theological, are also found in a number of texts of St Augustine and other Fathers, especially those of the Western tradition. We cannot account for all of them in the space of this research, because the multiplication of citations will not add much to what is already given here. The bishop of Hippo in his Rule (which probably dates back to 397 and is, for this reason, the oldest Rule known in the West) is concerned not so much with the classical forms of hospitality towards a stranger as with the life of the community more widely and its needs. As regards interactions of everyday life, however, the Rule lays the foundation for new relationships that inspire a hospitality that could be qualified as 'social emergencies.' Common life, says St. Augustine, is a permanent solicitude to an acceptance of 'the other' with whom one shares daily life and who is different.

> A man ought therefore to be hospitable, kind, upright, not desirous of what belongs to another, willing to give up his own rights if assailed, rather than take away another's [. . .] When a good man gives up any of his rights, it is not only a sign of liberality, but is also accompanied by great advantages. To start with, it is no small gain to be free from the cost of a lawsuit. Then it also brings in good results, by an increase of friendship, from which many advantages arise [. . .]
>
> In all the duties of hospitality kindly feeling must be shown to all, but greater respect must be given to the upright. For 'Whosoever receiveth a righteous man, shall receive a righteous man's reward', as the Lord has said. Such is the favour in which hospitality stands with God, that not even a draught of cold water shall fail of getting a reward.[21]

The text just quoted sounds surprisingly modern as it replaces exclusively theological considerations with a socio-political analysis. It also anticipates some fundamental rules of the coexistence and rights of peoples. We have here a clear sign of the progressive 'exportation' of hospitality beyond the Christian circle. While some Church Fathers of the fourth century note a weakening of the ardor of Christian charity, the pagan world, by contrast, seems to have become much more responsive to the practice of hospitality, which was regarded as the secret principle behind Christian advancement. In fact, a little poem, *The Death of a Pilgrim*, by Lucian, a sophist, rhetorician and satirist of the second century, tells the story of an adventurer who is introduced to the Christian community, is converted and is welcomed and surrounded with the greatest veneration. In summary, these Christians are described in unforgiving terms as naive and gullible, more ridiculous than dangerous; also, however, confirmed as formidably welcoming and fraternal, allowing the pilgrim to take advantage of their generosity. Another pagan testimony at a much later date, is that of Julian the Apostate who urges his governors to practice the hospitality that is characteristic of Christianity since that seems to have been a means of propagating their faith while, on the contrary, Hellenism was struggling to expand. Here is his recommendation to Arsacius, the High-priest of Galatia:

---

21. St Ambrose, *De Officiis Ministrorum*, Book II, 103–107. Taken from *The Sacred Writings of St. Ambrose*, edited by Philip Schaff, Kindle edition 2012.

144   *Strangers With God*

> Why do we not observe that it is their benevolence[22] to strangers, their care for the graves of the dead and the pretended holiness of their lives that have done most to increase atheism [that is Christianity, editor]? [. . ..] For it is disgraceful that, when no Jew ever has to beg, and the impious Galileans support not only their own poor but ours as well, all men see that our people lack aid from us.[23]

The emperor alludes to the situation that arose at the time of the Peace of Constantine (the Edict of Milan, 313) which allowed the Church to legally inherit and own property. Within only a half century of its propagation, *xenodocheia* had been established throughout the Empire: hospices set up along the main thoroughfares of communication which, under the authority of the Bishop, offered hospitality to the entire community. The foundation of the first *xenodocheia* was originally attributed to St Benedict of Nursia (ca 480–547), but it goes back, in fact, already to the origins of Eastern monasticism, which also introduces the tradition of the washing of feet.[24] This custom was perhaps introduced by St Pachomius (292–346) who established the first Christian coenobium that we know of in approximately 328. The great ascetic instituted an office of brothers entrusted with hospitality on behalf of the community and determined the first rule of the monastic ritual of welcome which meant, exactly, the washing of feet at the doorstep and the possibility of allowing a guest to join in the common prayers after having duly examined his morality and orthodoxy. If priests and religious enjoyed, initially, a special treatment allowing them easy incorporation into the life of

---

22. We find the term *humanitas* replacing that of *hospitalitas*; it is quite interesting to note that copyists have sometimes confused the two (as mentioned in note 15).

23. Julian the Apostate, Letter 22. To Arsacius, High-priest of Galatia [362, on his way to Antioch in June?] Found on line http://www.tertullian.org/fathers/julian_apostate_letters_1_trans.htm.

24. Evelyne Patlegean, a specialist in Byzantine history, maintains that the establishment of *xenodocheia* not only quickly became the means of social transformation, but also fostered a situation of opposition between the rich and the poor; no longer merely linked to economic and material circumstances, those without means now acquired a legal and social classification (*cf* E Patlagean, *Structure sociale, famille, chrétienté à Byzance, ive-xie siècle* [London: Variurum Reprints, 1981], 71).

the monastery, later the requirements became more stringent. In short, Julian the Apostate dreamt of reproducing in a pagan context a Christian institution that represented the transition from simple personal hospitality to a hospitality that was publicly organized. This is an evolution that deserves to be briefly analysed and that allows us to delineate the basic characteristics of medieval, then modern, Christian hospitality.

Hospitality as an institution

Evolution or degeneration?

> I will describe the first institutionalization of hospitality towards the middle of the fourth century CE. About that time, the first few shelters for the homeless were constructed under a Christian influence, and financed by the community. What I want to emphasize is the effect on the practice of hospitality, from this point on, occasioned by this well-meaning institutionalization of Christian charity, in the form of public care centers. We must clearly see that these public care centers are the dramatic reversal of hospitality as we understand it in the Christian sense, of that hospitality towards one's 'neighbor' which exists at the very heart of what we call the Gospel. And for this reason, public care progressively effects a metamorphosis of the Samaritan neighbour into a client of humanitarian services.[1]

These words of Ivan Illich, with which we choose to introduce this chapter, are quite provocative in that they propose the concept that the evolution of hospitality is at the same time the source of its degeneration and, ultimately, of its disappearance. Now, if a greater public establishment of hospitality does involve, quite logically, a decrease in an individual, personal involvement with this responsibility, it seems to us that Illich is somewhat too categorical in his conclusions. We will attempt to demonstrate in the remainder of this paper that the ancient virtue of hospitality toward the needy

---

1. I Illich, *La perdita dei sensi*, 15.

can be neither replaced nor permanently abolished by any form of its institutionalization. Certainly, admission to a hospital is the social expression of a new way of thinking and perceiving the human body (and secondarily the person who inhabits this body) as an object of services rather than as the sign of a transcendent presence. It is very difficult to say whether we can speak of the existence of shelters set aside for care of the needy prior to the Peace of Constantine. However, a number of documents, especially since the fourth century, certify that the legal recognitionion of the Church by the Empire represents a turning point in the evolution of the practice of hospitality.

Since Greco-Roman antiquity, the first step toward institutionalizing hospitality corresponded to a formal mandate delegating it: a role played, first in Greece and then in Rome, by the *proxenos*, literally the 'protector'[2]. Individual persons entrusted the task of welcome progressively more and more to the civil institutions, among which, from the beginning of the Christian era, was the Church. According to the historian Sozomen, the first public hostel for pilgrims was built in Edessa (then Syria, today Turkey) in 370 CE, although the most renowned is the one erected by Basil of Caesarea in 375, a construction so innovative as to give his name to all those that followed: *basiléiadas*.[3] In 325 the Council of Nicaea officially required of every city the building of separate hostels for strangers and travellers, for the sick and the poor. This same Council entrusted the institutionalized ministry of hospitality to monastics, requiring that there be in every monastery a monk specifically assigned to this office. From this time on, public Christian hospitality spread on a large scale, although it was more popular in the East, where there was a particularly strong memory of this practice since the beginnings of

---

2. The main duty of the *proxenos* was to assist travellers coming from foreign lands, becoming their advocate with the establishment of the receiving country. Concretely, he could be called upon to materially accommodate the stranger, assisting his entry among the people or to the hostel, loaning him money or even administering the assets of a visitor who died in a foreign land. Sometimes the *proxenos* was paid for his services, but more often he was a volunteer. Very soon, however, his role was officially recognised and his name carved on the stone inscriptions in the central square of the city.

3. This was not a simple edifice, but a complex structure that Gregory Nazianzen described as a veritable city of hospitality. Without reaching to so grand a structure, other bishops too and many superiors of religious communities followed in Basil's footsteps.

Christianity. In 530, Justinian accorded to the Eastern *xenodocheia* (hostels for travelers) their own legal personality distinct from ordinary ecclesiastical institutions, with the right to possess annuities and lands and to receive inheritances; they remained, however, under the protection of the Church. In Constantinople alone, under the influence of John Chrysostom, between 400 and 403 seven different facilities for the various categories of need could be counted: a nursery for abandoned children (*orphanotrophium*), a hospital (*nosocomium*), a home for the elderly (*gerontocomium*), an asylum for the disabled (*colobotrophium*), a refuge for strangers (*xenodochium*), a shelter for the poor (*ptochotrophium*) and generically a place for all *(pandochium)*. But as Ivan Illich notes, to apply the notion of hospice or hospital to what existed in Greek or Roman antiquity is anachronistic.

> At Pompeii—he writes—excavations have shown that the houses of doctors often had a special room that could accommodate two patients. The temples permitted travelers to sleep or, more precisely, 'to stretch out' or to 'lie down' for diverse days within their precincts. [. . .] The Greek city-state formalized a welcome given to foreign ambassadors. Nowhere, however, was there talk of a refuge for the indigent. Nor has there been any inscription alluding to a similar institution.[4]

The idea is still widespread that hospitality is to be allocated to one's peers and that, once this equality is established, only then may the visitor be invited to cross the threshold.

Hospitality in the Western monastic tradition

It is within the monastic setting that the practice of hospitality resumes importance in the West; the delay in comparison to the East is due, among other things, to the barbarian invasions. If coenobitism was certainly not created to meet the needs of hospitality, it is nevertheless true that it was soon characterized by this practice. The fellowship of welcome was the evangelical response first of all to internal needs of the various monasteries because there were hundreds of itinerant monks who made visits to their brothers or spiritual masters among

---

4. I Illich, *La perdita dei sensi*, 27.

the pilgrims and travellers of the time; or again, on their way to the main sites of pilgrimage.[5] It was only later that monastic hospitality became officially open to accommodate the common pilgrim, ascetic and wanderer.

Following Pachomius and Basil who inspired the first rules of monastic hospitality in the East, we have the Rule of the Master holding first place in the West. It was probably written about ten years in advance of that of St. Benedict who makes reference to it.[6] The text is very wary of transient visitors, describing at length and sometimes with biting irony the questionable behavior of wandering monks who abuse the hospitality accorded to them: a daily pilgrimage more to satisfy the appetite than for the soul; and keeping watch to prevent anyone from coming or going at will or leaving the monastery clandestinely. The Rule of St Benedict—a unique code of Western monasticism in the high Middle Ages—undoubtedly represents a thorough rethinking of this vision and sketches the outlines of a ritual that play a key role, according to its own expression, in 'the instruments of good works'. Benedict of Nursia does not claim to reinvent monastic life, but simply adapts the original Eastern practice to the Western mind. The Rule in its 73 chapters, arranged in no logical order, provides the essential elements for the organization of a community. Two chapters in particular are devoted to hospitality: Chapter 53 describes the reception of guests while chapter 61 refers specifically to comportment toward unknown visiting monks. We find, of course, many of the issues already addressed in our study. There is, first of all, the Christological motive that encourages the obligation of hospitality: 'Let all guests who arrive be received as Christ, because He will say: "I was a stranger and you took Me in"' (53 . . . 1). 'In the greeting let all humility be shown to the guests, whether coming or

---

5. Pilgrimages, generally undertaken voluntarily or imposed to obtain pardon of grave sins, very soon became customary among European Christians. If the travels were often hazardous, it is also true that along the footpaths as well as at the ports of embarkation, there was no lack of hostels. These were ensembles of shelters for pilgrims which were attached to the well-known range of Cluniac monasteries scattered along the French *camino* to Santiago de Compostela.

6. This legislation, exceptionally ample, seems to have been born not far from Rome in the first quarter of the sixth century. Its author is anonymous and owes its name to the fact that almost all the chapters are framed by two parallel columns: 'The Disciples' Question' and 'The Lord replies through the Master', making the text look like an oracle pronounced by this unknown Master.

going; with the head bowed down or the whole body prostrate on the ground, let Christ be adored in them as He is also received' (53:6–7). The Rule also states: 'Let the greatest care be taken, especially in the reception of the poor and travellers, because Christ is received more specially in them; whereas regard for the wealthy itself procures them respect' (53:15). The ritual of welcome therefore conveys an especial kindness: it is the monks who receive the announced guest and it is the entire community that participates, not merely a single brother (the *receptor hospitum*) deputed to the task: 'When, therefore, a guest is announced, let him be met by the Superior and the brethren with every mark of charity' (53.3). 'And let them first pray together,[7] and then let them associate with one another in peace. This kiss of peace should not be given before a prayer hath first been said, on account of satanic deception' (*cf* 53. 5). The initial greetings end with the washing of the guest's hands and feet. The guest, then, eats at the table of the abbot who breaks the fast in his honor (unless it is a day of solemn fast that cannot be broken (*cf* 53:10).[8] There is, in short, a carefulness to ensure that the obligations of hospitality not disrupt the monastic rhythm and customs; at the same time affirming a basic compatibility between the tasks and duties of hospitality and those of monastic life.

Over the course of centuries, monasteries in general have managed to preserve and even to reconcile Christian brotherhood and the pagan tradition of hospitality inherited from the past. This seems to us an important consideration because the *xenodocheia*, on the contrary, became more and more shelters for travelers and traditional social structures to meet the needs of the poor and, first of all, the sick. This trend is associated with a change in sensitivity where 'in the name of mercy alms supplanted hospitality'.[9] It is important to remember that the biblical Greek term *eleêmosunê* (literally alms) is close but not identical to the Latin *misericordia* (mercy). In ecclesiastical language, the term 'charity' or 'almsgiving' has a double significance: in a broad

---

7. This beginning in prayer is very unusual as compared to the classic ritual of hospitality.
8. The Rule states that the kitchen of the Abbot and the guests is apart (*cf* 53:16) and that only the abbot can break the fast; as for the other monks, they keep the customary fast (*cf* 53:11). Moreover, apart from the initial moment of the welcome and greetings, 'On no account let anyone who is not ordered to do so, associate or speak with guests' (53:23).
9. I Illich, *La perdita dei sensi*, 32.

152   *Strangers With God*

sense, it refers to any work of compassion and mercy intended to assist others in need of soul or body;[10] in a narrower sense, it addresses only corporal goods, excluding the spiritual realm.

Hospitality and charity: An evolution in terms

It is interesting to further investigate the issue of the evolution of the practice of charity as it relates to hospitality. 'In the Judeo-Christian tradition, hospitality constantly intersects with charity which has not remained a particular aspect or concrete application of it and with which it has become confused, as the words of Luke strongly suggest. However, the story is far from being so straightforward'[11] Sociologist Anne Gotman here leads us to rethink the relationship between the two terms that, until now, had been considered as practically synonymous. Above all, up to a certain era, hospitality was offered to all possible categories of beneficiaries, to one's equals as well as to the poor, as has already been addressed in these pages. In the sixteenth century work, however, there is a gradual evolution of terminology, establishing a clear distinction between hospitality given to one's peers and that extended to the needy.[12] Anne Gotman continues to inspire us in this analysis:

> When hospitality extended to the needy is secularized—if not irreparably severed from charity—it loses its component of friendship (today we would say its relational aspect), for the sake of a purely material benefit. [. . .] Hospitality and charity will each progressively operate in a specific social space.

---

10. St Thomas Aquinas in his *Summa Theologica* defines charity as 'any act of giving to the needy out of compassion and for love of God'.
11. A Gotman, *Le sens de l'hospitalité* (Paris: PUF, 2001), 1–21.
12. The dating proposed here is definitely questionable because, although Anne Gotman specifies that in the sixteenth century there is a remarkable diversity of motivations inspiring hospitality: within the family (necessary); towards strangers (courtesy); and with the needy (charity), the division between a welcome reserved for one's fellows and that extended to others was already in place. In fact, monastic hospitality has presented different ambiences since Carolingian times (eighth century): there were lodgings for the poor (*hospitale pauperum*) and for guests properly understood (*hospitale* or *hospitum nobilium*). It is from this time forward that these two kinds of comers are greeted outside the walls of the monastery, a prelude to a progressive secularization of the practice of hospitality.

> Hospitality, limited to convent or shelter, ends at the gates
> where the poor are fed with leftovers from the tables of the
> great; charity and almsgiving, meanwhile, are conceived as
> outside of these borders and consist mainly of gifts of money.[13]

In short, hospitality seems increasingly limited to people who are known (family, friends) while charity is extended to the poor, beggars, the sick and, in general, the marginalized. Over the centuries, continues Gotman, hospitality is increasingly driven from the religious sentiment which is its source, risking its identification with charity, mercy and compassion; instead, hospitality itself becomes opposed to religiosity. Each of these terms, moreover, merits closer examination, because each expresses a particular aspect of the same problem. For example, charity (benevolence), born of mercy (sympathy), is transformed into compassion (the offering of aid). And it is the inclination to share the physical suffering of the Crucified Lord, manifested in the person of the sick, which led the Western Church to create the first hospitals in the strict sense.[14]

Beyond these general considerations, we cannot linger with further details of the Church's practice of hospitality through the ages because it would take us too far from the heart of our research. We recall only some essential dates corresponding to the many milestones in the history of its organization. The Fifth Council of Orléans (549) annexed the assets of hospices to church property, declaring them inalienable. During the second Council of Mâcon (585) the importance of the practice of hospitality for the atonement of sins and to avoid the punishment of an angry God was affirmed. In support of this declaration, even lack of means could not be seen as an excuse to not offer hospitality, however simply. About this same time, the towering figure of Pope Gregory the Great (c. 540–604) urged the virtue of hospitality in a homily on the Gospel episode of the disciples of Emmaus, making explicit references

---

13. A Gotman, *Le sens de l'hospitalité*, 21.
14. In the vocabulary of Christian spirituality, the word 'compassion' refers specifically to the participation of Mary in the Passion and the redeeming sacrifice of Christ. But it also applies to the acts of love of all those who, by intention or in fact, follow the example of the Sorrowful Virgin. In a more general sense, compassion includes reparation that Christians offer to God in union with the Passion of God's Son. It is also exercised as charity and mercy in the face of the sorrows and pain of their fellows (*cf* R Brouillard, 'Compassion', in *Catholicisme. Hier, aujourd'hui, demain*, XV (Paris: Letouzey et Ané, 1948–2000), II, coll. 1417.

to the letter to the Hebrews (13:1), the First Letter Peter (4:9) and Matthew (25:36). Coming back to France, the first of the great reform councils held in Aachen (816) during the reign of Louis the Pious, ordered the creation of hospitals at the expense of the Church, under the direct administration of bishops, the secular clergy or the abbeys. The eleventh century is characterized by the first wave of religious congregations founded as hospitallers, including the Hospitallers of St Antony (sometimes also called Antoniti). A second wave will coincide with the post-Tridentine Catholic revival of the sixteenth century. In the twelfth century, the Crusades of the East led to the birth of several other Orders devoted in particular to the care of hospitalized patients (among the first of these is the Order of St. John of Jerusalem). The Knights Hospitallers, as we are reminded again by Ivan Illich, created the first foundation in Jerusalem in 1195, after observing the Greek hospitals in Byzantium. Being among Muslim physicians it is very likely that the founders of this hospital were already aware of the Islamic *maristan*.[15] Near the shelters for pilgrims which, thanks to Charlemagne, had obtained the protection of the Muslims chiefs, the Hospitallers of the Order of St. John of Jerusalem were to give refuge to wounded crusaders too sick or old to return home.[16] But the Church is no longer the only one to create these structures, despite having opened the way: hospitality, more or less institutional, had become a widespread phenomenon at the center of medieval society. The vocational brotherhoods devote a part of their financial resources to the creation of hospitals, often in existing structures, which are at the same time places of care for their own families. Not even the civil powers remain indifferent and, especially in France, donations and proceeds are multiplied to create these foundations.

Two decrees of the Fourth Lateran Council (1215) contribute to the common religious orientation of the various hospital statutes of the thirteenth century. The first, more general, requires that any founding of a new religious house must accept the rule of orders already established and approved. The second decree concerns us more directly in that it is a reminder to keep watch over the soul of the sick before taking care

---

15. Also called *bimāristān,* these are real hospitals. The first was created in Baghdad, by order of the Caliph Hārūn al-Rashīd (786–809), a Christian doctor of Jundichapour in Iran, where there was already a similar foundation due to the Sasanid dynasty of Persia (224–651).

16. *Cf* I Illich, *La perdita dei sensi,* 29–30.

of the body (a clarification rather superfluous for institutions already entrusted to religious orders but of obvious importance for new secular foundations). From this decree we infer that the staff of hospitals designated as Maison-Dieu or Hôtel-Dieu, were obliged to be 'of a religious mind,' that is, required not only to observe the commandments of God as does every good Christian but were also advised to strive for evangelical perfection. We see here one more argument that the importance of individual hospitality was gradually being lost.

The Council of Trent, in its fifteenth session of December 3–4, 1563, appealed in a general manner for 'prompt and kind' hospitality to be exercised by all who had been endowed with an ecclesiastical benefice. But despite these measures taken at the highest level of the Catholic Church, the movement toward secularisation in the sixteenth century, accompanied by a progression of centralizing ideas and the actual crisis of many religious orders, led to a general laicization of hospital services. As often happens, a compromise was worked out: the temporal management of hospitals was entrusted to the laity working in the name of the State; but the spiritual direction was to remain with the Church; and members of religious orders, men and women, were to retain the care of the sick. In effect, it was primarily the management of the assets of the houses of charity that were progressively removed from ecclesiastical authority.

However, alongside this secularization of administrative management, another new factor appeared on the horizon: the search for new forms of assistance in response to the reality of mounting poverty. In the sixteenth century there was a formidable increase in begging as a consequence of both the economic crises as well as the disasters of the religious wars. In this new situation, hospitals were no longer central in assisting the needy; instead, the religious orders (especially the new congregations to be established in the following three centuries) assumed a leading role in helping the poor in a specialized way. St Charles Borromeo, Archbishop of Milan and passionate champion of the Council of Trent (1538–1584), considered hospitality at his own home one of his essential duties as bishop. In Rome in 1575, he was receiving three hundred guests a month; in Milan, he was receiving upwards of thirty to forty every day.[17] This example was followed in Italy chiefly by lay groups such as the Society

---

17. *Cf* GP Giussano, *Vita di S. Carlo Borromeo*, VIII, chapter 26 'Dell'ospitalità', Roma 1610; the book is kept at the Biblioteca Ambrosiana di Milano (f.185 inf.).

of Divine Love, founded in Genoa in 1497 and inspired by Ettore Vernazza. This association offered its members a group meeting every week, opportunities for fasting, monthly confession and Eucharistic communion four times a year, in addition to Christmas and Easter. They were also committed to works of charity towards the most underprivileged, especially the terminally and chronically ill of Genoa, where the company had taken over their management. The Society of Divine Love also operated in Rome (St Cajetan of Thiene [1480–1547] was among its members), in Vicenza, Venice and Naples. The seventeenth century saw a lively rebirth of Christian charity, especially in France. The Society of the Blessed Sacrament,[18] with its organization and its charitable initiatives, prepared the way for the admirable work of St. Vincent de Paul who was the founder, along with Louise de Marillac, of the Daughters of Charity. The latter, originally devoted to care of the sick and poor in their homes and popular teaching in the countryside, later took care of orphans, the management of hospitals, homes for the elderly and asylums for the mentally ill.[19]

After the upheavals of the Revolution, there was a return to the option of religious charities. At the same time, public assistance was further organized. 'The real ideological foundation—writes Marsot— was not the duty of charity nor the philanthropy of the late eighteenth century, nor the idealistic brotherhood of 1848, but solidarity, interdependence of the members of the same social body.'[20]

---

18. An important society of lay persons and secular priests, founded in 1627 by the young duke, Henri de Levis de Ventadour, who devoted himself to the practice of humble and hidden works of charity in imitation of Christ hidden in the Blessed Sacrament.

19. 'The oldest term which refers to the function of both "hospital" and "hospice" is always "hospitality". Further, in affirmation of their therapeutic vocation, general hospitals fully accomplish this double task of welcome and aid, intending both to encompass and comfort the soul as they care for the body. But in addition to these general hospitals, certain institutes fulfill a further role of retirement homes or a direct link to social rehabilitation, as is the case of the Hotel Royal des Invalides founded in 1670' [J-P Bois, B Puijalon and J Trincaz, 'Modèles institutionnels de protection sociale', in A Montandon, editor, *Le livre de l'hospitalité*, 736–761 (739). The comparison between 'hospital' and 'hospice' highlights the growing separation between the medical and the social functions that are imposed as a part of hospitality. Hospitals will increasingly become the place where medical care is dispensed, while a hospice identifies as a place of welcome for the elderly, the sick, abandoned children, and all who are in need of social, but not necessarily medical, assistance.

20. G Marsot, 'Hospitaliers. Etablissements', in *Catholicisme, Hier, aujourd'hui, demain*, V, coll. 966–971.

Conclusion

The reception of the poor has always been one of the noblest forms of social hospitality. In a Western context, primarily inspired by Christian culture, we should perhaps speak of a certain decline of the sacred sense of hospitality, especially by comparison with the Arab world or, more broadly, the Middle East (characterised as it is by a predominantly Islamic religious and cultural imprint). At the same time, we must consider the need to redefine hospitality, noting that there was a certain semantic change from the more classical term which understood hospitality as a freely exercised and gratuitous accommodation of strangers. One could also add to this already generous gesture the imperative of a warm and unconditional openness. This semantic search, however, cannot ignore the factors that have led to a weakening of the sense of hospitality in the West as early as the sixteenth century: we refer to the progressive substitution of public hospitality in place of personalized hospitality[21] and the advent of so-called 'modern civilization' with its quest for a marked social distance over integration. For the French Encyclopaedists, it was the very movement of history and civilization itself to condemn the ancient bond of hospitality which had more or less characterized all peoples and cultures. Essentially, shelters of welcome for the poor whatever their human misery as well as for the passing traveller suddenly became obsolete. Their functions would gradually have been taken over by a multitude of specialized institutes, private and public. Although the personnel of these institutions remained predominantly religious, particularly in countries with an ancient Catholic tradition, the control once exercised almost exclusively by the Church was greatly reduced. It also became difficult to retain an evangelical motivation behind hospitality: a service executed in the spirit of Christ, respecting every person as created in the image of God and caring for him or her. Associated, if not identified, with charity, hospitality in the Christian tradition became, along with faith and hope, one of the three theological virtues and, as such, was the center

---

21. By this term we mean to refer to the 'social question' which, towards the end of the nineteenth century, expressed, among other things, the need to deal with structural discomfort (and not only accidental or temporary), with political and rational planning and not only with the spontaneous generosity of private individuals.

of the concerns and activities of the early Church. But the believer had begun to live in an increasingly dichotomous relationship between the social and spiritual dimensions of hospitality: a dichotomy unthinkable when monastic hospitality was being developed. We do not forget that, in medieval times, the Church itself, with its dependencies and properties, was a place of asylum, mitigating the inadequacies and injustices of human structures. At this time, charity, including its form of hospitality, always prevailed in the right. It is surprising, then, that the separation of church and state in several Western European countries, a separation that could have allowed the Church to fully assume the role of counter-power, instead assisted paradoxically in the progressive disappearance of the notion of the right to asylum in the Catholic Code of Canon Law.[22] The obvious risk of over spiritualizing an appeal for solidarity in the Christian world was the advance of a significant decline in appreciating the social role of the Church. Furthermore, since the beginning of the nineteenth century, the extraordinary development of private and secular philanthropy, born of the sentimental humanitarianism of the Enlightenment with the new bourgeoisie's social role, should be noted. These phenomena, in conjunction with the aforementioned developments in the Christian world, led to a kind of 'manipulation' of individual charity. The latter is elicited, in fact, more and more from a humanistic rather than from an evangelical perspective.[23] In a word, the unconditional gift is increasingly supplanted by law and is no longer inspired to exceed the latter.

Of course, government assistance does not pretend to nullify Christian charity, because it not infrequently solicits its cooperation; for example directly, by volunteers helping at public functions. The real problem is to overcome a certain one-sidedness of institutionalized

---

22. *Cf* P Godi, 'La maison de miséricorde', in A Montandon, editor, *Le livre de l'hospitalité*, 831–850 (843). Most likely concerned not to derogate from the common law as well as to avoid abuse, the Church does not even mention religious asylum since the 1893 Code of Canon Law.

23. The idea of charity and/or a humanistic hospitality appears to be founded on a theory that makes humanity, as a human species, the origin and purpose of rights. Here the 'philanthropic societies' claim to replace the Church, no longer in the name of God, but in the name of human rights, often considered, in fact quite rightly, as antagonistic. In the first Declaration of Human Rights (1793), 'public emergency' is defined as a 'sacred duty' of the nation (*cf* P Godi, 'La maison de miséricorde', 843

hospitality in order to rediscover the reciprocity of the gift exchanged (which goes far beyond the material plane) in an unconditional welcome. Further, the poor, the stranger, the weak, once understood almost as sacred, are transformed over time into a potential threat to the social order, to health and security. There is need, therefore, to reduce their impact, to control and channel their possible ill effects. Already in the Renaissance, we remember, poverty was seen as the worst of evils; as is reminiscent of Leon Battista Alberti's dialogue *Paupertas*, Italy's courts were the most luxurious. It is also in this period that the interdict against begging was imposed and vagrancy repressed in a general context of growing social inequality, especially in the cities. The Reformation also contributed to this vision: Luther criticized the practice of pilgrimages and the existence of mendicant clerics. Where assistance was given to the poor, the tendency was to emphasize their fundamental difference rather than to welcome them as guests.

> The rituals of admission to a place of shelter—writes Jacques Carré—already highlight the dissimilarity of the poor: at the Hospice of the Ponte Sisto, these unfortunates were immediately shaved and clothed in gray. The offer of food itself and accommodation was officially made in exchange for work. Even if it was, very often, only a threat, this economic exchange introduced the logic of the market-place, completely foreign to the medieval practice of hospitality, to reception of the poor[24].

Finally, can we speak of an irreversible decline of hospitality following the loss of the original purity of the sacred rite of welcome? This conclusion would be too hasty and superficial. Society as a whole has not ceased to be sensitive to the necessity of accommodating the poor, even from a moral and religious perspective, characteristic of Christian charity. However, it is very difficult to surpass a utilitarian gesture of hospitality when, on the contrary, daily practice seems to show a greater spiritual advantage given to those who receive hospitality than to those who offer it. If the payment following a service, replace the salt alliance and the two pieces of card to be matched, the true mutuality in a spiritual sense belongs to a completely different order.

---

24. J Carré, 'Entre charité et enfermement', in A Montandon, editor, *Le livre de l'hospitalité*, 789–800 (792).

At the same time, how can we ignore the wealth of unconditional charitable initiatives that continue to multiply in the world of care? Must we speak of a kind of charitable and gratuitous hospitality, formed in an ancient ambience and now, later, denatured by paid service? Certainly, over the centuries money has created a sort of watershed and hospitality in its own right became limited to the gates and sites of charity.

It is probably possible to continue to speak of new forms of hospitality where effective institutionalised assistance lends 'additional' care of the soul in terms of humane relations and general recognition of the dignity of the needy. Here is the exercise of charity which can never go on vacation and which is always required not only to go beyond the law but also to precede it.

Part Two

History of the Acceptance and Interpretation of Genesis 18

Abraham, The Uncertain Origins of an Ancestor

After analysing the importance of Hospitality in the Traditions of the Three Abrahamic Religions that look to Abraham, we now move to a comparative reading of the well-known sacred narrative essential to the heart of our research: the hospitality of Abraham at the oak of Mamre, handed down in the biblical tradition of Genesis 18, and present in both the Jewish and Islamic traditions.

The Keeper of a Common Memory

The contested historicity of the biblical cycle of the Patriarchs

It is well known that Jews, Christians and Muslims all revere and honor Abraham as the founder of the monotheistic religions. Although for different reasons, these three great religions each essentially consider themselves as the legitimate posterity of the Patriarch, heirs of the divine covenant and promises proclaimed by God to his descendants, and the blessing granted to all nations in him. At the same time, none of these three traditions can claim an exclusive monopoly on the figure of the Patriarch. 'Abraham was neither a Jew nor a Christian: he was a *hanīf* [the first among believers], dedicated entirely to God and was not an idol worshiper' (Qur'an III, 67).[1] We will return to this Qur'anic passage regarding the definition of Abraham as the father of all believers; for now, we limit ourselves to noting the undeniable influence of the biblical tradition, especially the earlier Jewish tradition, on Muslim theology regarding the Patriarch and his 'native foreignness'.[2]

---

1. This text introduces the Quranic concept of *hanīf* that will be treated in verse 95 of the same chapter. *Hanīf* (plural *hunafā*) is a term which in Islamic literature indicates a follower of the original true religion, that is, one who, even before Islam itself, perceived the Oneness of God and who practiced a 'natural monotheism.' In the Qur'an the term is used most often to describe Abraham as a model of pure worship of God. In the more controversial quotes, the *hanīf* opposes idol worshipers. In fact, Muslims must defend themselves against criticism of Islam, stating that their religion is the pure worship of God, revealed already to prophets prior to Muhammad, but partially corrupted over the centuries by Judaism and Christianity (cf. M. Watt, "Hanīf" *Encyclopédie de l'Islam, op. cit.*, III, 1990, pp. 169–170).
2. We refer to our reflection in the chapter concerning Jewish hospitality.

We cannot linger here on a comparative research of the theological significance of the character of Abraham at the heart of the three monotheistic religions. The task is exciting but has already been the object of several studies of some importance.[3] Nevertheless, we do ask some questions about the main protagonist of the meeting at Mamre.

Exegetes explain that the 'cycle of Abraham' (Gen 12–25) is based on various oral and written sources and has undergone different levels of editing. This literary corpus gravitates around the unifying theme of the divine promises to the Patriarch: a progeny, a country and a blessing. It is a rich and varied content issuing from different periods and situations. Research on the Pentateuch has not yet reached a conclusive theory on the formation of Genesis from Chapters 12 to 25. This task, moreover, goes not only beyond our expertise but also the scope of this study. The literary question in its complexity, however, is no stranger to the problem of the historical value of the narrative, and as far as we are concerned more directly, of the historicity of the person of Abraham, as well as of all the biblical Patriarchs. The archaeological findings do not permit us to reconstruct precisely

---

3. Even in Italian, the general bibliography for Abraham is substantial. Here are some titles. For the biblical character of the Patriarch in the most general sense: B Costacurta, *Abramo* (Milano: Jaca Book, 2001); A. Sicari, *Abramo, Mosé, Elia. Ritratti biblici* (Milano: Jaca Book, 1995); G Lafon, *Abramo o l'invezione della Fede* (Milano: Gribaudi 1998); M Tibaldi, *Il codice Abramo. Personaggi in cerca di attore: Abramo e Sara*, (BoloGena: Pardes Edizion, 2009). For a more exegetical and literary approach to the Genesis stories of the Patriarch: G Von Rad, *Il sacrificio di Abramo*, Morcelliana (Brescia: Queriniana, 2009); A Wénin, *Da Adamo ad Abramo o l'errare dell'uomo. Lettura narrativa e antropologica della Genesi. I. Gen 1, 1-12, 4* EDB, BoloGena: Pardes Edizion, 2008); A Wénin, *Isacco o la prova di Abramo. Approccio narrativo a Genesi 22*, Cittadella, Assisi 2005; F. Gentiloni, *Abramo contro Ulisse. Un itinerario alla ricerca di Dio* (Torrino: Claudiana, 2003). Finally, regarding a comparative study of the Patriarch in the three montheistic religions: J-L Ska, *Abramo e i suoi ospiti. Il patriarca e i credenti nel Dio unico*, (BoloGena: EDB, 2003); H-Pons, J Jiménez Hernandez, *Abramo il credente. Secondo la Scrittura e il Midrash*, (Napoli: Chirico, 2007); M Giuliani, *Le tende di Abramo. Un'eredità comune*, (trentpo: Il Margine, 2007); G Dal Ferro, *Nel seGeno di Abramo. Ebraismo e Islam a confronto con il cristianesimo* (Padova: Edizioni Messaggero, 2002); L Massignon, *L'ospitalità di Abramo. All'origine di ebraismo, cristianesimo e islam*, (Napoli: Medusa, 2002); L Ginzberg, *Le leggende degli ebrei*, Vol 2: *Da Abramo e Giacobbe*, (Milano: Adelphi, 1997); K-J Kuschel, *La controversia su Abramo. Ciò che divide e ciò che unisce ebrei, cristiani e musulmani* (Bresica: Queriniana, 1996); J Riemer, G Dreifuss, *Abramo: l'uomo e il simbolo*, La (Firenze: Giuntina, 1994).

the concrete history of a man (Abraham) who would have lived in the second millennium before Christ. It may, however, determine, at this time, the existence of a historical-sociological context absolutely compatible with what would be at the origins of the traditions on Abraham. The theory of the literary genres can help us since the stories of the Patriarchs correspond to family sagas: thus, we can also speak of 'a legend of Abraham'. A legend normally arises around a character or an important historical event; it is narrated and handed down from generation to generation. A legend of a religious nature, like that of Abraham, is enriched by the values and beliefs of those who pass it on. The cycle of Abraham therefore contains credible events which are traceable by an historian, such as the journey to Egypt because of the famine that struck the land of Canaan (*cf* Gen 12:10). Conversely, there are also highly unlikely wondrous episodes, such as the transformation of Lot's wife into a pillar of salt (*cf* Gen 19:26). Walter Vogels, moreover, highlights the fact that in the cycle of the Patriarchs there are passages that are neither historical nor unbelievable. They are situated merely in another order of ideas: that of the experience of faith.[4] In essence, the stature of the character of Abraham goes beyond the religious context to become the cultural archetype of the father: a character that, for more than a millennium, raises many questions and stimulates many diverse enquiries. For our part, we merely note, as all three monotheistic religions have realised, that the importance of the Patriarch goes far beyond the question of his historicity. The stories concerning him have transmitted and continue to transmit to generations of believers a model with which to identify oneself as well as messages of hope for the future, in spite of contemporary difficulties.[5]

The example of Abraham in comparative religions

The legitimisation of Abraham as the common father of the believers of the three monotheistic religions is at least theologically questionable, although the formula 'Abraham, father of believers,' appears to be unanimously used in all three traditions. Actually, according to Jacques Jomier, the title 'father of believers' is attributed to the

---

4. *Cf* W Vogels, 'Le personnage d'Abraham est-il historique?', in 'Abraham, père des croyants', *Biblia*, 16 (2003): 6–7 (7).

5. *Cf* T Römer, 'Figures d'un ancêtre', in *Le monde de la Bible,* 140 (2002): 15–19.

Patriarch especially by Christians and is not absolutely characteristic of the vocabulary of the Qur'an.[6] In short, we can say that any reference to Abraham in Islam, Judaism and Christianity is in general approached more in a strategic sense that is not truly objective and, especially in the Muslim-Christian dialogue, it is better to use it with great caution. Jean-Louis Ska says that Abraham is not in any way the 'founder' of the three monotheistic religions. The 'founder,' that is, the personality that gave Judaism its physiognomy is Moses, just as Jesus Christ and Muhammad are, respectively, the persons of reference for Christianity and Islam. But Abraham, Father Ska notes, 'is like the only source of these three rivers that later took different directions, under the impulse of their "founder" or "initiator". If Moses, Muhammad and Jesus are at the origin of the fundamental traits of each of the three monotheistic religions, Abraham is the guardian of their common memory.'[7] In the introduction to his famous work *La controversia su Abramo (The Controversy on Abraham)*, Karl-Josef Kuschel speaks of 'Abrahamic ecumenism': an expression that for him does not eliminate or ignore the differences among religions. Noting that, to the contrary, they have very often been violently opposed, Kuschel identifies a reason for everything especially in the disputes that revolve around Abraham's birthright and loyalty to his legacy.

---

6. *Cf* J Jomier, *Dieu et l'homme dans le Coran. L'aspect religieux de la nature humaine joint à l'au obéissance Prophete de l'islam* (Paris: Cerf, 1996), 68. In a footnote, Father Jomier states that, in the land of Islam, Abraham is often referred to as 'the Father of the Prophets'. Another title used by Islam to designate the Patriarch, also found in the Bible, is 'Friend (*khalīl*) of God', as in the Qur'anic passage, 'God chose Abraham as Friend' (Quran IV, 125). In a French translation Jacques Berque interprets *khalīl* as 'intimate friend'—which seems to stretch a term already very strong—in the context of a vision that accentuates theological transcendence and therefore the natural separation between God and humankind (*cf* Jomier, *Dieu et l'homme dans le Coran*, 79). Finally, to the extent that in the Islamic tradition the ancient prophets announce and prefigure Muhammad, embodiments of the perfect ideal and becoming examples themselves, Abraham is presented as 'the model' for having broken with the idolatry of the people. The term 'model' (*Uswa*) appears only three times in the Qur'an, twice in sura LX, 4, and again in reference to the Prophet of Islam (Quran XXXIII, 21). In general, the major characters are evoked as role models for a particular feature and not globally, as in the case of Abraham (Joseph for his chastity, when resisting the blandishments of Potiphar's wife; Mary for her purity in the virginal conception ...) (*cf* J Jomier, *Dieu et l'homme dans le Coran*, 80).

7. J-L Ska, *Abramo e i suoi ospiti*, 21.

Therefore, it is as if the Patriarch plays a dual, apparently contradictory role: he is simultaneously both a factor of unity and a factor of division. Hans Küng resumes these considerations and speaks of a real conflict around the Abrahamic heritage: Abraham as a common heritage but also as an element of differentiation and, therefore, the starting point of a 'trialogue' that could be constructed.[8] For these reasons, the 'case of Abraham' is a veritable stumbling block for interreligious comparison, revealing all its complexities. It is precisely this formula, 'Abraham, father of believers,' that we must have the courage to put to a comparative test. Only then, after having appreciated the actual differences, we may also highlight the complementarities or even the common points. The following are some fundamental features of this diversified presence of the Patriarch in the heart of the three monotheistic religions.

---

8. *Cf* H Küng, *Ebraismo* (Milano: BUR, 1999).

Abraham in the theological interpretation of the three monotheistic religions

Abraham in the Christian tradition

> And I tell you that many will come from east and west to take their places with Abraham and Isaac and Jacob at the feast in the kingdom of heaven; but the subjects of the kingdom will be turned out into the dark where there will be weeping and grinding of teeth (Matt 8:11–12).

In the evangelical redaction of St Matthew, we are dealing with the oldest Christian reference to Abraham, the announcement of a salvation now extended to the pagan peoples after the defection of the Chosen People. We cannot linger here to analyse the theological scope of these affirmations of Christ that sound so severe to the people of Israel. It is not so much a dispute of Israel as Abraham's firstborn but of a radical reinterpretation of the meaning of the 'paternity' of the Patriarch. In Israel's theology the election is, in practical terms, reserved only to the descendants of Abraham, therefore to the children of Abraham 'according to the flesh' (*cf* Rom 4:1). On the contrary, in the Gospel passage just quoted, Christ makes us understand that salvation regards those who believe in the Messiah beyond a simple 'Abrahamic filiation;' in other words, the Gentiles will be saved while the children of Abraham themselves may be excluded from the kingdom of heaven.[1] The emphasis is therefore placed on faith; St Paul founded his entire argument relative to 'salvation by faith alone' precisely on this basis in the letters to the Galatians and Romans. The Apostle of the Gentiles must, then, show

---

1. *Cf* J-L Ska, *Abramo e i suoi ospiti*, 49–52.

172 *Strangers With God*

the chronological anteriority of Abraham's faith to that of the Mosaic law in its linkage to the divine promise (*cf* Gen 15:6). Beginning from the same chronological criterion, Paul then states the primacy of faith over circumcision (Abraham was circumcised only after believing the promises of God; cf. Gen 17:1–26) because, according to Jean-Louis Ska, if faith is anterior to the Law of Sinai, as well as to circumcision, it is then superior in importance and, according to faith, Abraham can therefore be considered the father of the circumcised and uncircumcised (*cf* Rm 4:9–12).[2] This universal fatherhood of Abraham anticipates the universal brotherhood secured in Christ, in whom there is 'no more distinctions between Jew and Greek, slave and free, male and female' (Gal 3:28).

Beyond the simple 'Abrahamic filiation in the flesh', as highlighted in the theology of Paul, is its theological completion in the Letter to the Hebrews and the Gospel of John, as demonstrated once again synthetically by Father Ska.[3] In a historical period particularly difficult, marked by the destruction of the temple in Jerusalem and the transition to the practice of an exclusively Jewish synagogue where observance of the Law has become the hallmark of Jewish identity, Abraham becomes the first rabbi of Israel, faithful not only to the written Torah but also the oral tradition that precedes it.[4] In chapter 8 of his Gospel St John presents a dispute of Jesus in opposition to this Jewish tradition: a controversy that reaches unprecedented levels of violence. In the first place, those who threaten the life of Christ, saying they are faithful to the tradition of the Fathers (*cf* 8:39–44) are called 'children of the devil' and not 'children of Abraham'. In the second place, it is not Christ who must look to Abraham to benefit from the privileges granted to the descendants of the Patriarch, but Abraham himself who must receive salvation retrospectively from the true Son promised by God (*cf* 8:56). For the Jewish world, it is a theologically unacceptable position, not to say blasphemous, because it implies the affirmation of the pre-existence of Christ over the Father of the Chosen People: 'I tell you solemnly, before Abraham ever was, I am' (8:58). Again, temporal anteriority implies ontological superiority: 'If Jesus preexists Abraham, and from all eternity, he is therefore

---

2. J-L Ska, *Abramo e i suoi ospiti*, 58.
3. J-L Ska, *Abramo e i suoi ospiti*, 53–57.
4. *Cf* K-J Kusche, *La controversia su Abramo,* 112–115.

infinitely superior. Similarly, there is no possible comparison between the race of Abraham and faith in Jesus Christ, especially if one admits that Abraham himself waited for the coming of Jesus.[5] It is easy to imagine that, contrary to what St Paul says, faith in Jesus becomes, in this context, a major source of division between Christians and Jews instead of breaking down religious and cultural barriers (a paradox that we have already evidenced in our reflection on the figure of Abraham).

A study of the role of Abraham in the Christian tradition ought not be limited to the New Testament in which his theological relationship with Christ is established. Instead, as Jean Danielou points out, there are very important further developments in the literal, moral and mystical senses of his figure even though, as compared to that of Jewish reflection, the 'theology of Abraham' appears to be characteristically traditional.[6]

Abraham in the rabbinic tradition

The Rabbinic tradition is definitely heir to the biblical tradition, while emphasizing particular aspects.[7] The Jewish interpretation presents Abraham as a seeker of the true God since his childhood and, later, as the scourge of the vanity of the worship of stars and idols. The story

---

5. J-L Ska, *Abramo e i suoi ospiti*, 56.
6. *Cf* J Daniélou, 'Abraham dans la tradition chrétienne', in *Cahiers Sioniens,* 2 (1951): 68–87 (68). Jean Daniélou contests in part the claims of David Lerch *(Isaaks Opferung christlich gedeutet,* Tubingen, 1949), who states that from the second to the twentieth century, the whole tradition concerning Abraham presented virtually no really significant theological development.
7. 'The Jewish tradition seeks above all to exalt the figure of Abraham in ways that make him a precursor and a model for the pious Jew of all times' (J-L Ska, *Abramo e i suoi ospiti,* 23). This aspect is deepened in the midrashic comments on Gen 18:1–15. We recall that the oldest post-biblical Jewish traditions of Abraham are contained mainly in some rabbinical midrash that gloss the order of the verses of the Pentateuch and following, as is the case of the Midrash Rabbah on Genesis. Some texts called apocryphal are preserved in languages other than Hebrew and Aramaic, as is the case also of the Book of Jubilees. There are still some writings written in Greek but whose authors are deeply influenced by Jewish culture: for example, the historian Josephus and Philo, especially the Apocalypse and the Testament of Abraham.

174   *Strangers With God*

of *Beresit Rabba* (38) is very suggestive.[8] Seeing the sun rise, Abraham believed himself to be in front at the Teacher of the World and began to worship him; but the sun went down and Abraham began to worship the moon. The moon then disappeared and Abraham understood that the luminaries were only servants of the true Master. In essence, post-biblical Judaism sees Abraham as the initiator of the adventure of faith in a simultaneous act of uprooting its traditions to indulge to the unpredictable projects of God.[9] The Patriarch remains, evidently, the emblematic father, the living attestation, before God and before humankind, of the faith of the Jewish people, to the point that one can no longer conceive the existence of Judaism without a reference to Abraham.[10] This fact is particularly true after the Babylonian exile, as recorded in the book of Nehemiah, the primitive text of the post exile.

> Yahweh, you are the God who chose Abram, brought him out from Ur in Chaldea, and gave him the name Abraham. Finding him faithful of heart before you, you made a covenant with him, to give him the land of the Canaanite, of the Hittite and the Amorite, of the Perezzite, Jebusiste, Girgashite, to him and his posterity. And you kept your promise because you are just (Ne 9:7–8).

According to this text, the God who was worshiped in Israel was already identified as the God who acted on Abraham's behalf. The latter becomes an instrument in God's plan (the name change certifies this 'divine possession') that chooses him and draws him out of an ancient land to lead him to a new land. Since Abraham becomes

---

8.   T Federici, editor, *Commento alla Genesi, Beresit Rabba* (Torino: UTET, 1978), XLVIII, 371–382.
9.   It is important to highlight an evolution in the interpretation of the role of the Jewish patriarch because, at the time of Christ and St. Paul, Abraham was still seen as an observer of the Law. As we have already pointed out, it is the Jewish Paul who redirects, in the context of the biblical sources, the description of Abraham as the 'first of the believers' ('Abraham put his faith in Yahweh, who counted this as making him justified', Gen 15:6. This justice is the deep righteousness that conforms us to God's will).
10. This is here a theological consideration and not historic because, as already stated, historians have little to say in relation to the character of Abraham and the cycle of the Patriarchs in general; we are at the level of what Jean Botta Tero defines as the 'prehistory' of the religion of Israel (*cf* J Bottéro, *Naissance de Dieu: la Bible et l'historien* (Paris: Gallimard, 1986).

a 'partner' in a covenant with God, he is also the pledge of God's faithfulness toward his people, despite the betrayals of the latter. The itinerancy of Abraham is 'a parable of faith:' if on the one hand it is characterized by stages, encounters obstacles and moments of crisis, on the other hand it is reecognised above all for overcoming these obstacles. Abraham rises to the role of universal intercessor ('Father of all believers') and, more than any other biblical figure, to that of archetype. As we already mentioned at the beginning of this section, and as confirmed by Father Jean De Menasce,

> We will refrain from systematically delineating the rabbinic traits of Abraham's story, for this would suggests deviations with respect to the biblical narrative, and it is from the Bible itself that are taken the epithets that in the *midrash* accompany the name of the Patriarch: the beloved of God, the only one, the perfect one, the most powerful among the giants, the light of the orient, the chosen one, the fruit of splendors. Also Biblical is the title 'God of Abraham', which essentially means the living and true God.[11]

Abraham in the Islamic tradition

This last observation offers us a perfect transition into the scope of the Islamic tradition, so as to really capture its Abrahamic universality. From the point of view of the history of religions, the Islamic roots in the faith of Abraham depend to a large extent on the Jewish tradition. Despite the fact that Muslims theologically refute a dependence of their revelation on the Bible, the scholars of Islam do not hesitate to define the Islamic rereading of the Bible as a kind of return to the past. There is evidence of a Hebraic influence in their theological interpretation but the same is not true of a Christian biblical and theological influence of the first centuries.[12] In the perception of

---

11. PJ De Menasce, 'Traditions juives sur Abraham', in *Cahiers Sioniens,* 2 (1951): 96–103 (103).

12. Concerning Abraham in the Islamic traditions and the Qur'an, we refer to J-L Ska, 'Abramo nella tradizione ebraica', in *La Civiltà Cattolica,* IV (2000): 341–349; Y Moubarac, *Abraham dans le Coran. L'histoire d'Abrabam dans le Coran et la naissance de l'islam* (Paris: Vrin, 1958, resumed in a concise article 'Abraham en Islam', in *Cahiers Sioniens,* 2 (1951): 104–120; R Martin-Achard, *Actualité d'Abraham*, Delachaux et Niestlé, (Paris: Neuchâtel, 1969), 161–175; K-J Kuschel,

Islam, Abraham was and remains the *imam* (the one who gives direction, the guide) of all the true believers and in particular 'the obedient one', that is the true *muslim*, the one who lives Islam (*cf* Qr III: 67).[13] The richest Qur'anic description of the Patriarch is found in surah IV: "And who could choose a better religion than to give oneself entirely to God and to do good to one's fellow men and follow the community of Abraham, in pious faith? Because God chose Abraham as a friend" (v 125).[14] This Medinan verse[15] summarises the essential qualities attributed to Abraham in the Islamic tradition. We find the Muslim terms (the authentic *muslim*, the submissive or abandoned one) and *hanīf* (the pure monotheist, one who is not an

---

La controversia su Abramo, 231–293; D Masson, *Monothéisme coranique et monothéisme biblique. Doctrines comparées*, (Paris: Desclée de Brouwer, 1976)— in particular, on Abraham *cf* 350–371. We cannot undertake the question of the Qur'anic understanding of the relationship between Abraham and the characters that surround the biblical metaphors: we are concerned solely with the figure of Sarah and the story of hospitality at Mamre. Jean-Louis Ska also deals with the relationship between Sarah and Hagar, mother of Ishmael, and the relationship between him and Isaac, who in the biblical tradition receives the totality of the inheritance of Abraham. Ishmael, in the Qur'anic tradition of Medina, becomes the undisputed star next to his father, and with the latter shares the role of co-founder of the sanctuary of the Ka'ba, the black stone temple in Mecca. In his book *Abraham dans le Coran*, Youakim Moubarac questions the total silence of the Meccan suras on the foundation of the sanctuary of the Ka'ba by Abraham and Ishmael. Is this tradition a patent invention of the late prophet, justified by political reasons and not strictly theological? Moubarac expresses doubts about it. 'It is difficult to assume a priori that the Qur'anic preaching may have imposed on its listeners a matter so new, so alien to their tradition. On the contrary, it seems to be presented as known and accepted by all' (73). Emilio Platti reinforces this view, evoking the existence of a number of sources that show how certain tribes of the Northern Arabian Peninsula recognise Ishmael as the founding ancestor. It is likewise easy to assume that the followers of Muhammad should also know certain traditions concerning the origin of the Abrahamic sanctuary of the Ka'ba (*cf* E Platti, *Islam . . . étrange?* (Paris: Cerf, 2000), 157–158.

13. A Muslim believer will generally choose 'abandonment' over 'submission' in the interpretation of the Act of Islam, a concept borrowed from Christian mysticism.

14. Emilio Platti proposes a more literal translation in French which reads: 'Who is better in religion than one who submits his being (*aslama*) to Allah, conforming to the revealed law and following the religion of the righteous man (*muhsin*) Abraham? And Allah had chosen Abraham as a privileged friend (*khalīl*)' E Platti, *Islam . . . étrange?*, 151).

15. *Cf* the chart on the following pages .

'idol worshiper'[16]), already present in the sura III, but there are also added words *muhsin* (one who does good) and *khalīl*, 'the friend of God'. Abraham is the only character to whom the Qur'an attributes this title which, among others, can also be found in the Bible (*Cf* Isa 41:8; 2 Chr 20:7; Dn 3:35; and even once in the New Testament in Jam 2:23). Joachim Moubarac states, however, that the Arabic root of the word *khalīl* has no trace in biblical usage, while the opposite is true. Surely, the qur'anic use of the term denotes a clear choice, the fruit of theological study. Mu'tazilite Muslim theology (a nationalist ideology of primitive Islam, founded in the eighth century and considered the origin of Islamic jurisprudence) 'found unworthy of divine transcendence that a man can be called a friend of God, and proposed for the Qur'anic *khalīl the* sense of "poor", according to a possible interpretation of the Arabic root of the word'.[17] The very name of the patriarch Abraham occurs sixty-nine times in the Qur'an and he is among the biblical characters more often cited, but not as often as Moses. Abraham is less present in the suras of Mecca than in those of Medina; in the first he appears primarily as the prophet of an imminent Judgment even though he is still defined as 'the righteous one' (*siddīk*). In contrast, the Medina suras develop more fully the institutional, legal and liturgical initiatives of the Patriarch as founder or reformer of the monotheistic cult of the Ka'ba. This is however not a double qur'anic portrait of Abraham but rather an evolution in the description of the same character, whose essential features are already present from the Meccan period of the revelation. Essentially, it is not whether Muhammad was already attracted by Abraham at Mecca or only later in Medina that is important, but the fact that he was looking to the Patriarch as a source of pure faith that could represent a brotherly bond between all monotheistic believers. Thus, the evolution between the Meccan revelation and that of Medina becomes very important: in Medina, Abraham is no longer just the restorer of an original monotheistic worship, but the model of the Muslim believer. This is not to be intended, according to the Qur'an, as a restriction but as the expression of a universal vocation:

---

16. This expression refers implicitly to those who damage the unity and oneness of radical Islamic monotheism. Evidently, even the Christian dogma of the Trinity is regarded as the heresy of idolatry in the Islamic view.
17. IGenace Goldziher, citing Y Moubarac, *Abraham dans le Coran,* 111, note 30.

Box 4 The Compiling of the Qur'an: The Meccan and Medinan Suras

The history of the redactions of the 114 suras of the Qur'an is extremely complex. According to a classification adopted by the most popular edition of Cairo, 'of King Fu'âd' (1924), 86 suras belong to the Meccan period and 28 to that of Medina. A sura is referred to as Meccan if its first verses were revealed to Muhammad in Mecca between 610 and 622 of the Hijrah, even if its continuation held verses revealed in Medina. These suras are very concise compositions that speak of justice, responsibility and remuneration. They can be divided into three distinct periods. The Medinan suras, on the contrary, are so called if their first verses were revealed in Medina, between 622 and the death of Muhammad around 631. These latter are longer, and pertain especially to legal and social norms. The very hypothesis of different stages in the preparation of the Qur'an indicates an evolution not only of revelation but also of Muhammad's own interpretation. Today we must admit that it is probably impossible to ascertain the real chronological order of the writing of the Qur'an. There is currently only one Qur'anic translation, that of Abu-Sahlief Aldeeb in French (Editions de l'Aire, 2008), that attempts to present the suras in the order in which they would have been revealed to Muhammad. The Qur'anic text, 'of Uthman,' classifies the suras in order of length (with some rare exceptions) and certain Muslim authors are convinced that this order had been approved by Muhammadhimself on the advice of the Angel Gabriel (the dominant opinion, however, is that Muhammad would have only approved the order of verses in each sura).

> O you who believe! Bow down, prostrate and worship your Lord and do good, so that you may prosper. And strive in the way of God[18] as becomes you. God has chosen you, and has not imposed on you a heavy burden in religion *(dīn)*, the religion *(milla)* of your father Abraham. He has already called you *Muslim* from antiquity, and in this revelation still . . . (Qr XXII: 77–78).

According to the Qur'an, since the creation there have been persons who have reecognised their true relationship with God; in other

---

18. Some translators, as Jacques Berque, more faithful to the sense of interior jihad (spiritual effort or warfare), translate: 'Strive for God'.

words, 'Islam' exists from the beginning but this faith has faded over the course of history. The advent of the Prophet Muhammad restores it in its purity and rediscovers in Abraham his role as archetypal model of the believer:

> [Remember] when the Lord tested Abraham with certain commands and he obeyed[19] and God said to him, 'Truly, I will make you the prince of the people', and he asked, 'And what will become of my posterity?' 'My covenant', God replied, 'shall not apply to the wicked' (Qr II: 124).

This citation from the Qur'an is particularly important because Abraham's request, that Allah extend his promise (that of a large posterity) to all his descendants according to the flesh, is answered in the order of overcoming the 'genealogical significance of salvation'. Since Abraham is the model of all believers, the salvation and the promise cannot become the hereditary privilege of a single family. There is, in this observation, Muhammad's radical opposition to the exclusion of Jews and Christians in relationship to Abraham.

> [They who hold to the Scriptures] will say again: 'Become Jews or Christians and you will be rightly guided.' But you say, 'No, we are of the Nation (*milla*) of Abraham, who was a *hanif*, and not an idol worshiper [a polytheist]' (Qr II:135).

It would seem in such statements that Islam is attempting to annex Abraham as a representative of pure faith that cannot be connected to any particular membership. Karl-Josef Kuschel tries to answer this objection by referencing the self-consciousness of Islam as the seal of revelation. Stated differently, Islam considers itself not merely the only true religion, but as the most authentic, the 'final religion' that corrects the errors and misrepresentations of revelations that came before it. Now, for the Muslim Abraham is proof of the existence of an 'Islam before Islam:' Islam, understood as surrender before God, would in fact be the original form of human adoration of God; and, through the founding of the Ka'ba by Abraham and Ishmael, has

---

19. This refers to the tests that Abraham had to face, including the request to sacrifice his son (Isaac or Ishmael, depending on whether one is Judeo-Christian or Islamic).

become an historical reality even while remaining metahistorical.[20] Of course, this view is not without an attempt at annexation, an attempt that is not lacking also in the Jewish and Christian traditions,[21] an aspect that once again puts into question 'Abrahamic ecumenism'. According to Pim Valkenberg, 'relations between the religions are marked by [these] conflicting interpretations and use their common ancestry to mark their own identity thereby rejecting the claims of the other [identity], in the same way as children fight among themselves for their parents' inheritance'.[22] These considerations make us realize that any reference to Abraham as a central figure in attempting interreligious dialogue needs to be always contextualized and is not easily acceptable by all three monotheistic religions simultaneously. For example, Jews, claiming a lineage of Abraham according to the flesh, feel excluded when one refers to the Patriarch as a model believer, emphasising especially a spiritual kinship with him. That is why the concept of 'the religions of Abraham' can have a future only if it involves a shared willinGeness among Jews, Christians and Muslims, to work together on the stories relating to the Patriarch, accepting as well the differing interpretations that may help to expose the negative preconceived notions that one has of the others. It remains true that, despite their diversity, the Talmudic, Apostolic and Qur'anic commentaries coincide on certain points relative to the character of Abraham, including the tale of hospitality at Mamre with which we will deal in the next pages.

---

20. *Cf* K-J Kuschel, *La controversia su Abramo,* 277–282. It should be noted that, from the outset, Muhammad considered Abraham as the model of true faith that every believer can imitate, regardless of belonging to a people or a precise history of salvation.

21. Kuschel coins the terms the 'halakahization' and 'ecclesialization' of Abraham to talk about the attempted annexation of the Jewish and Christian Patriarch.

22. P Valkenberg, 'Il concetto di 'religioni abramitiche' ha un futuro?', in *Concilium,* 5 (2005): 124–135 (127).

Genesis 18:1–15: Abraham ad His Mysterious Guests

The Structure of the Biblical Account

The story of chapter 18 of the book of Genesis also has partial echoes in the Qur'an. It is therefore common, at least in its essence, to the sacred writings of all three of Abraham's monotheistic religions. It offers the ideal setting for the direction of our research. We have already stressed that all three interpretations—Jewish, Christian and Muslim—traditionally assign the title 'Friend of God' to the Patriarch.[1] The story of Genesis 18, in fact, seems to be the origin of the attribution of this title to Patriarch.[2] We refer to verse 19 in particular, where Yahweh declares to have known Abraham. In actual fact, the biblical translations differ and in general we prefer the expression 'I have chosen him'. The Hebrew verb *yāda'* literally means 'to know' but it can also be understood in the sense of 'to love' in the sense of personal knowledge (*cf* Am 3:2). Occasionally, it designates the conjugal act, as in Genesis 4:1, or it may even refer to 'enlightenment', as interpreted by the Hellenizing Philo. Yet, there is a further possibility of interpretation in the sense of 'election'. The

---

1. 'The theme of divine friendship has a long history and we find traces of it in Mesopotamia as well as in ancient Egypt. It is of particular importance in the Greek world. The terminology varies from one time and place to another, as well as its meaning. Here the notion 'friend of God' may have erotic nuances; there it may evoke a mystical character of deep intimacy; elsewhere, it denotes the benevolence of the gods to a human creature; and in still other circumstances, the same concept is, finally, the piety of the faithful towards God' (R Martin-Achard, *Actualité d'Abraham*, 176).

2. It should be remembered that, although the Targum of Jerusalem and Philo of Alexandria (De Sobrietate, § 56) seem to use this expression (with especial reference to Gen 18:17), it is not found in the Masoretic version nor in the Greek Septuagint.

verb *yāda'* is then translated as 'to distinguish', 'to recognise', then in fact, 'to elect', 'to choose'. What is important to emphasize in all these variant interpretations is the insistence on the primacy of the divine initiative. If the Old Testament, as a whole, highlights the initiative taken by Yahweh with regard to humanity, in this specific case God's friendship with Abraham corresponds to a free gift which comes from above. Therefore, in Genesis 18 we find not only a paradigm of hospitality and a gem of Old Testament literature; but also and above all, a symbolic illustration of the love of God that precedes and gives rise to the 'Theophany'.

The delimitation of the text and its context

The story of Abraham's hospitality is part of a much larger literary whole: one grand combined narrative named 'the history of the Patriarchs' (*cf* Gen 12–50); this in turn is made up of smaller narrative accounts called 'the cycles of the great Patriarchs'.[3] These units had existed separately before being assembled to compose the Book of Genesis. The account of Abraham's hospitality is included in a longer, complex story and is developed over two chapters centered

---

3. Specifically, we need to distinguish the cycles of Abraham (Gen 12–25), of which we have already thoroughly spoken; some of the tradition of Isaac (Gen 26); the cycle of Jacob (Gen 25–35); and the story of Joseph (37–50). The cycles of Abraham and Jacob are quite different from one another, as shown by the plots, the atmosphere, the geographical settings and many other details. Generally speaking, the accounts of the Patriarchs of Israel are characterized by precise literary genres: the anthology (Abraham), the epic (Jacob), the novella (Joseph). In addition, the narratives of Genesis 12–50 contain other literary genres, specifically: 'lists' (that manifest the genealogical preoccupations of the authors of Genesis); 'the tribal judgments' (attempts to characterize a clan or tribe, very often by drawing a comparison from the animal world); 'the travel records' (the various stages of a journey, to indicate the presence of the Patriarchs at places and shrines important to the future kingdoms of Israel and Judah); and, above all, 'the stories', which make up the dominant literary genre. Among these we can distinguish: 'stories of conflict'—between two women: Sarah and Hagar (Gen 16) and Leah and Rachel (Gen 29–30); or between brothers: Jacob and Esau, Joseph and his brothers; there are also 'etiological narratives.' These latter are especially numerous in the history of the Patriarchs. Their function is to explain both the name of a place or a person, and the origin of a practice or costume. This polyphony of literary genres and themes demonstrates implicitly the multiplicity of authors telling the stories of the ancestors of Israel (*cf* P Quesnel and M Gruson, editors, *La Bible et sa culture. Ancien Testament*, 82–83).

on two main characters: specifically, Yahweh and Abraham. We have already noted that the difference between the historical data and the biblical texts on the Patriarchs is considerable. Caution, therefore, is an imperative when we speak of the 'historicity' of the biblical texts; it is necessary to read them with a pair of eyes different from that of a historian. In short, the purpose of these stories is not to impart information about history or what really happened, rather, they are intended to form the religious consciousness of a people. This objective, of course, does not exclude the fact that there may also be historical elements. Yet the manner of telling it is different; what matters most to the authors is not so much the objectivity of the data, but the significance of the events for the addressees. These stories of the Patriarchs in Genesis chapters 12–50 represent, for the Jewish people, a way to give an account of their origins by tracing their genealogy. To be more specific, the cycle of Abraham is a composite, made up of an assemblage of shorter narratives,[4] driven forward by the question of descent (which also forms the setting in which our analysis is placed). Already found in the genealogy of Genesis (11:27–30) is this remark—quite usual in a genealogical framework—'Sarai was barren, having no child' (Gen 11:30). The situation is again mentioned in Genesis 16:1. The very history of the Chosen People and the divine promise is threatened. The statement is repeated in several other passages of Genesis, at least until the birth of Isaac, and then again when God demanded of Abraham the fearsome sacrifice of his only son (Gen 22). Leaving this aside, we can define a smaller narrative unit running from Gen 11:33 to 21:7 (with particular attention to Gen 13), in order to contextualize the brief cycle of Abraham and Lot in Genesis chapters 18–19, keeping in mind the story of the birth of the child announced to Abraham and Sarah (Gen 21:2, 6–7), which is the logical culmination of the entire story.

Here is the text of Abraham's hospitality at Mamre in the Jerusalem Bible version:

---

4. Among the earliest we can include are: the cycle of Abraham and Lot (Gen 13:8–19); Abraham's sojourn in Egypt (Gen 12:10–20) and the two versions of the expulsion of Hagar (Gen 16:1–14; 21:8–20); and finally, Abraham's stay in Gerar (Gen 20:1–18; 21:22–34). The other episodes are typically newer, as are the different texts that connect the story of Abraham to the rest of the patriarchal traditions.

> [1]Yahweh appeared to him at the Oak of Mamre while he was sitting at the entrance of the tent during the hottest part of the day.[2] He looked up, and there he saw three men standing near him. As soon as he saw them he ran from the entrance of the tent, and bowed to the ground.[3] 'My lord,' he said, 'I beg you, if I find favor with you, kindly do not pass your servant by.[4] A little water shall be brought; you shall wash your feet and lie down under the tree.[5] Let me fetch a little bread and you shall refresh yourselves before going further. That is why you have come in your servant's direction.' They replied, 'Do as you say.'[6] Abraham hastened to the tent to find Sarah. "Hurry," he said, 'knead three bushels of flour and make loaves.'[7] Then running to the cattle Abraham took a fine and tender calf and gave it to the servant, who hurried to prepare it.[8] Then taking cream, milk and the calf he had prepared, he laid all before them, and they ate while he remained standing near them under the tree (Gen 18:1–8).

It is at this point in the story that the mysterious visitor, after asking about Sarah, announces to Abraham the birth of a child within the year;[5] Sarah, who was hidden from sight, was listening and laughed to herself, thinking of her advanced age and that of her husband. God, exposing her, censured the disrespect implicit in her snicker; nevertheless, the promise is confirmed. This is the third time that Yahweh promises an offspring of the patriarch (*cf* Gen 15:5; 17:4).

---

5. The second part of the story seems, at first sight, to have no particular ties to the foregoing. John Van Seters (*Abraham in History and Tradition* (New Haven-London: Yale University Press, 1975), 204–208, speaks of an earlier text made up of four parts: Gen 13:8 (the construction of an altar at Mamre); Gen 18 (the divine apparition near this shrine); Gen 18:10–14 (the announcement of a birth); Gen 21:2, 6–7 (the story of the birth). So, Gen 18:1b–9, the recounting of a hospitality that interests us, is not part of the original text. In fact, explains Van Seters, we must consider two narrative motifs: a 'theophany' near an altar or a sanctuary; and an 'incoGenito visit' of a deity (a literary theme very widespread in classical literature, well beyond and before the Semitic tradition, for example in classical Greece). Now, according to Van Seters, the announcement of a birth is linked much more logically to a theophany; only later will the scene of hospitality itself be transformed into a part of the theophany. The thesis of Van Seters does not have unanimous approval and is strongly opposed by a second school of interpretation related to German exegesis (Blum, Skinner, Gunkel and Von Rad). We will return to this issue because it is evidence of the relationship between hospitality given and the announcement of a birth as a reward for this generosity.

The Structure of the Biblical Account   187

Then, two of the mysterious visitors take leave of Abraham and depart for Sodom's punishment, while the third remains with him. Is this one the Lord, or at least a character that stands out from the other two? The biblical account seems to confirm this hypothesis: 'The men left there and went to Sodom while Abraham remained standing before Yahweh' (Gen 18:22). The mysterious personage forewarns Abraham about the punishment that is about to befall Sodom (vv 20–21). There follows Abraham's well-known intercession to dissuade God from the purpose of destroying the city where his nephew Lot and family live. The question is to determine how many righteous persons abide in the city so that God may renounce this terrible act of justice. Then God departs and Abraham returns to his tent.[6] The following chapter (Gen 19) tells of the destruction of Sodom, after God has promised to save the lives of Lot and his family.

The narrative structure

Returning to the ensemble of that which we have defined as the literary cycle of Abraham and Lot, the relationship between Mamre (Gen 18) and Sodom (Gen 19) has, at the same time, a great continuity and strong contrasts. According to Robert Ignatius Létellier,[7] the continuity is of a thematic and stylistic order. From the narrative point of view, the two chapters of Genesis have as common thread the 'journey of the messengers' (three in the first part of the story and only two thereafter), charged with carrying two separate tidings in stark contrast to each other: that of a birth (Gen 18:9–15) and that of destruction (Gen 18:20–21; 19:12–13).[8] From a stylistic point of

---

6. Chapters 18–19 seem to revolve around the character of Abraham (actually, around Abraham and Lot within the cycle of Abraham) but all the action is initiated by Yahweh. From beginning to end, Yahweh is the true, predominant agent; all the activity of Abraham, as also of the other characters, is in response to the initiative of Yahweh: Yahweh and Abraham (18:1–8), Yahweh and Sarah (18:9–15), Yahweh in monologue (18:17–21); and again Yahweh and Abraham (18:22–33). Beyond doubt, Yahweh is the protagonist: from the scene of hospitality in which a promise is given, through the formal soliloquy, to meeting Abraham's objections concerning the punishment of Sodom.

7. The author of a more comprehensive study on chapters 18 and 19 of Genesis, entitled *Day in Mamre, Night in Sodom: Abraham and Lot in Genesis 18 and 19* (Leiden-New York-Köln: Brill, 1995), an essential reference for our own study.

8. *Cf* RI Létellier, *Day in Mamre, Night in Sodom*, 37–41.

view, there are two introductory scenes of hospitality which present a surprising parallel and are very beneficial for a comprehensive understanding. We will try to analyze them briefly, assisted by a chart inspired by Létellier but by paralleling only the first eight verses of each chapter.

Gen 18:1-5, 8	Gen 19:1-3, 8
v 1. While he was sitting	v 1. Lot was sitting
v 2. He saw three men standing near him . . .. he ran to meet them	v 1. As soon as Lot saw them he rose to meet them
v 2. And bowed to the ground	v 1. And bowed to the ground
v 3. 'My lord', he said	v 2. 'I beg you, my lords', he said
v 3. 'kindly do not pass your servant by . . .'	v 2. "Please come down to your servant's house to stay the night . . ."
v 4. 'You shall wash your feet . . .'	v 2. 'and wash your feet.'
v 5. 'You shall refresh yourselves before going further.'	v 2. 'Then in the morning you can continue on your journey.'
v 8. Then taking cream, milk and the calf he had prepared	v 3. He prepared a meal for them, baking unleavened bread . . ..
v 8. And they ate.	v 3. And they ate.
v 5. That is why you have come in your servant's direction . . .'	v 8. 'They have come under the shadow of my roof . . .

After highlighting these parallels it is good to immediately clarify that there are also strongly contrasting elements in chapters 18 and 19 of Genesis: day and night, the tent and the city (i.e., a small community and a large urban area), the idyllic and the problematic, the announcement of the birth of a child and that of imminent destruction (allowing salvation accorded to only one family), and a fraternal welcome and violent hostility.[9] Two archetypes full of prophetic power are set against one another: an opposition that in technical parlance is called antithetical or structural parallelism (in other words, an arrangement of mirror opposites). This alternation

---

9. The repudiated and violent hospitality will make the natural Paradise of the Jordan Valley, chosen by Lot (Looking round, Lot saw all the Jordan plain, irrigated everywhere—this was before Yahweh destroyed Sodom and Gomorra—like the garden of Yahweh or the land of Egypt, as far as Zoar; Gen 13:10), a place of desolation and the reign of death (Gen 19:23-28).

The Structure of the Biblical Account
189

of analogy and opposition is accentuated throughout the narrative, in both time and space, as the story evolves into one grand succession. The visitors come to Abraham at high noon ('the hottest part of the day'; Gen 18:1b) and arrive at Sodom in the evening (Gen 19:1). At dawn ('When dawn broke'; Gen 19:15a), Lot and his family were urged to flee; they arrived at Zoar even before the sun appeared over the horizon (Gen 19:23). Finally, early in the morning, Abraham returned to the place where he pondered the destruction of the plains of Sodom and Gomorrah with Yahweh (Gen 19:27). How are we to interpret this structure elaborated with such care? We have first, in a general sense, a prophetic judgment on human history ('With the Lord, "a day" can mean a thousand years, and a thousand years is like a day', 2 P 3:8). In a single day, an archetypal day, the significance of which encompasses the entire story, a theological message is conveyed that makes hospitality the creator of history and much more than just an ethical imperative. The same judgment is rendered—in reverse— against those who despise hospitality. There is a second meaning, more immediate, in chapters 18 and 19 of Genesis: in the seemingly insignificant encounters of everyday human existence there may be a decisive moment in which life itself is altered.

Closely related to the measurement of time there is also the measurement of space. The location of the actions is described with so much precision because the symbolism of the place also bears important theological significance. We highlight two specific places and one fundamental focal axis. Genesis 18:1–15 is the first of these sites: Mamre (or Hebron), is a world unambiguously rustic, a place of peace and moral order, a place of quiet expectation where hospitality is freely given; we can easily imagine Mamre as a height above the surrounding plains that could be taken in at a glance (*cf* Gen 19:27-28).[10] The second site is Sodom (Gen 19), the city of the plain, a low place, a place of darkness (the facts described in the story of Genesis 19 are mostly held at night), a place of discord and moral disorder, and of inhospitable violence.[11] Between these two distinct sites, arranged in a kind of geographical collocation of theological significance, we can perceive a focal axis which we identify as the moment of intercession,

---

10. The exact geographical location of the sanctuary of Mamre still poses a problem for archaeologists and therefore also for exegetes (*cf* the chart on the next page).

11. We clearly recognise that this description is a bit forced, resembling a fictional film. Similarly, we recall that this literary style, at the heart of an antithetical parallelism, points to a symbolic power and not necessarily to the veracity of the story.

a face-to-face encounter between Abraham and the mysterious lone visitor who does not go to Sodom (Gen 18:16.22-33). In this case too, the physical space assumes a theological significance because the story of Abraham's intercession is, in effect, a veritable caesura, a point of transition between two worlds extremely different from each other. Verse 33 of Chapter 18 is a crossroads of space and time, a horizontal line formed by the decisive moment of the departure of Yahweh and the return of Abraham ('When he had finished talking to Abraham Yahweh went away, and Abraham returned home').

Around this pivotal narrative develops the dynamic of a great journey upwards, comprising the events of Genesis 18:1-15 and inaugurated by the arrival of Yahweh (18:1); this same journey continues, this time down and into the heart of night,[12] with Genesis 19:27-28 and 18:33. This kind of 'descent into hell,' a passing through the terrors of the night (19:1-14) and the befalling of the catastrophe (19:24-26), knows, however, two opposite movements: Lot's escape from the threatened city and finding refuge in another (19:17-23), and the return of Abraham to the place where he had spoken with Yahweh (19:27-28 and 18:33). Neverthelss, the night draws to a close and with the break of day (19:15) the judgment of God is finalized, as if the light itself is representative of God in some way. In Genesis 19:23 the arrival of full light completes the disaster.

An exegetical analysis

Relying on a Christian exegetical interpretation,[13] we turn now more directly to the scene of Abraham's hospitality in Genesis 18, in an attempt to highlight the main features of a story that effects a wealth of seemingly marginal details, but which are actually essential to an understanding of the entire ensemble.

---

12. The characteristics of day and night are used as a reflection of the themes of the plot. The entire episode at Sodom unfolds as the sun is setting and throughout the night: clearly, night is portrayed as a time of danger. The punishment of blindness inflicted by the messengers on the men who threaten sodomy (19:11) becomes, in this context, a darkness within the darkness, symbolic of guilt. The night, in short, becomes a correlative to the flagrant sin of Sodom (*cf* RI Létellier, *Day in Mamre, Night in Sodom*, 59).

13. We leave the comparative approach for the moment because it is only within the Christian tradition that we can speak of a critical edition of Genesis 18:1-18 and a real history of interpretation.

The Structure of the Biblical Account 191

Box 5 Mamre: Site of the Encounter

A site of strong religious sentiment, Mamre poses several problems for historians and exegetes, beginning from the very choice of its transcription into contemporary Western languages. Among the various translations, we prefer 'the Oak of Mamre', which is that of The Jerusalem Bible (originating from l'École biblique de Jérusalem which follows the Greek Septuagint text as well as, in this instance, the TOB). Yet there is a second problem: was Mamre a single oak, or several? The question might appear idle, but in reality it is significant because behind this detail is the vexing concern for the cult of the sacred tree (in the singular) of pagan origin, proscribed by Jewish law and denounced by the prophets. (As Father de Vaux states, "The account of Genesis 18: 4.8 speaks of a single tree. The plural used in the Jewish Masoretic text seems to be a tendentious correction to eliminate any reference to a sacred tree as the object of superstitious veneration;" cf. R. de Vaux, "Mambré", in Dictionnaire de la Bible-Supplément, V, Letouzey et Ané, Paris 1957, pp. 753–758 [753]). So does the prophet Hosea rail against idolatry as the prostitution of the people "under oak and poplar and terebinth, so pleasant is their shade" (cf. Ho 4: 13). Another question is whether the tree (or trees) is an oak or a terebinth. The two plants are very similar and have often been confused. Both versions are possible. Similarly, we prefer the Jerusalem Bible translation, which settles for the oak tree—in the singular. However, among the ensemble of different translations it is curious to note that the Palestinian Targum of the Penteteuch [R. Le Déaut, vol. 1, *Genèse, coll.* SC n°245, Paris 2006/19781].—known in two versions, the Neophytes Vatican Code and the version kept in London—speaks in both cases of an apparition made to Abraham "in the plain of Mamre" (Also called the "vision of the plains" in the Neophytes code); it no longer speaks, then, of either oak or terebinth. Furthermore, this same geographical location of Mamre poses problems for archaeologists. Genesis states: "After this, Abraham buried his wife Sarah in the cave of the field of Machpelah opposite Mamre, [a gloss adds 'namely Hebron'], in the country of Canaan" (23:19). 'Opposite' may refer to proximity or simply belonging to the same region. Similarly, perhaps it is on account of the forbidden worship of the sacred tree that Mamre, as a place, was gradually forgotten or assimilated into the city of Hebron.

192   *Strangers With God*

The scene consists of two basic parts:

vv 1–5: Abraham sees the arrival of visitors, solemnly greets them and invites them to accept his hospitality (or more precisely to rest a bit from their journey and to share a simple meal); there follows a positive response to the invitation;

vv 6–8: shows the stage of the material preparation of the meal, maGenifying the hospitality in its descriptive detail. Two new characters enter the scene: Sarah, the wife of Abraham, and a servant. The meal under the oak tree follows and this concludes the first part of the story of Mamre.

In the first five verses, the complexity of the plot and the narrative tension are very limited. The latter is considerably reduced because of the introductory verse, the importance of which is decisive for an understanding of the story: 'Yahweh appeared to him at the Oak of Mamre.' This central verse, which seems to be unconnected and even a bit extraneous as compared to what follows, is a figure of speech called a 'prolepsis'. The narrator provides the reader with a number of details that put him in a privileged position in comparison to the characters in the story itself. In this case, the reader knows from the beginning, well in advance, that it is Yahweh who appears to Abraham, long before the latter becomes aware of the divine presence.[14] As evidence of this fact, we find a very static description of the Patriarch, quietly sitting at the entrance of his tent, as would be expected of one who is trying to

---

14. 'Prolepses' correspond to the modern use of titles and subtitles that were unknown at the time (as well as punctuation, for that matter). We find the use of prolepses even in the literary writings of the ancient Middle East. The biblical authors use them on several occasions, particularly in the book of Genesis. We find an example already in Chapter 22:1, where the reader is informed that Abraham will be put to the test by God, which the protagonist himself will know only later. Continuing on, we find other examples of a prolepsis in the cycle of Jacob (*cf* Gen 27:23); and in the story of Joseph (Gen 37:18, 21a, 22b; Gen 42:7; Gen 45:1). Beyond the Book of Genesis, the best-known example of this figure of speech is at the beginning of the story of the call of Moses: 'There the angel of Yahweh appeared to him in the shape of a flame of fire, coming from the middle of a bush' (Ex 3:2); but Moses himself will understand only when God challenges him (Ex 2:4-6). For further details regarding this preliminary note, refer to the article by J-L Ska, 'Sommaires proleptiques en Gen 27 et dans l'histoire de Joseph', in *Biblica*, 73 (1992): 518–527; or 'Quelques exemples de sommaires proleptiques dans les récits bibliques', in JA Emerton, editor, *Congress Volume Paris 1992* (VTS 61), (Leiden: Brill, 1995), 315–326.

The Structure of the Biblical Account   193

get some rest, not awaiting a visit at the hottest time of the day (which would, moreover, be unlikely)[15]. With this introductory detail, the narrator establishes a gap between the point of view of the reader and that of Abraham, and in the next verse introduces the first twist in the story—the intrusion of three unexpected visitors: 'He looked up, and there he saw three men standing near him' (v 2a). In this verse there is a sudden change in point of view because the narrator describes what Abraham sees: three men standing in front of him.[16] The action of lifting his eyes signals the conclusion of Abraham's stillness. By the simple fact of standing in front of the Patriarch at the entrance of his tent, the visitors implicitly evoke a gesture of hospitality, because those who do not want to stop pass at a safe distance from the tent. All interest in the drama is now concentrated on Abraham's reaction: how will he behave towards his guests whose identity he does not yet know? The reader, in his turn is cannot but wonder how the Lord will reveal the protagonist and if the human actors will come or not to recognise the supernatural presence.[17]

Conscious or not of being before important guests, Abraham is set in motion: he then leaves his seated position at the entrance of the tent and runs to meet the unexpected visitors, approaching as near as possible. 'He is distant from them in terms of knowledge, but very close to them because of his hospitality'.[18] The appearance of the pilgrims on the scene brings with it a radical shift in the tempo of the action: Abraham abruptly bestirs himself in a succession of almost

---

15. The importance given to the time of the arrival of travelers in this unusual story is intended to extol the maGenanimous generosity of the hospitality and, at the same time, the absolute urgency of giving shelter to a wayfarer considering the extreme rigor of the heat of day in the desert.

16. In indirect speech there is a difference between the perspective of the narrator and the perception of the actor: the text does not say 'three men stood in front of me,' but 'three men stood in front of him.' The narrator is speaking in the third person, but the mention of three men makes us realize that we are seeing with the eyes of Abraham and not with our reader's perspective with prior knowledge of the identity of the visitors (*cf* RI Létellier, *Day in Mamre, Night in Sodom*, 81).

17. From these considerations, we can guess that the reader is forced to leave his 'all-knowing' position afforded by the initial prolepsis, in order not to lose the progressively dramatic story from the perspective of Abraham. It is only by adopting the Patriarch's point of view that the reader can grasp the radical nature of the act of hospitality in the nomadic and Semitic context.

18. J-L Ska, *Abramo e i suoi ospiti*, 121

194   *Strangers With God*

frantic actions (underscored stylistically by a succession of short sentence coordinates) in his desire to better receive his visitors. He greets them with ceremonial deference: 'My lord . . .' The Masoretic Hebrew version translates *ădōnāj* with 'lord,' actually adopting the reader's point of view while it may not yet be that of Abraham. Von Rad, in his exegetical commentary on Genesis, introduces the *'ădōnî*, which means 'my lord' (a generic singular that we assume is directed to one of the three visitors who takes on a prominent role among his fellows; we will come back to this question when we take up the rabbinical commentaries); this agrees with the result. There follows: 'I beg you, if I find favor with you,'[19] is a form of pure courtesy, always used in the singular and does not necessarily indicate an address to a person of higher rank.[20] Moreover, Abraham does not renounce his position of the bountiful landlord, as we see in v 4, making mention of the ritual ablutions. He does not personally take on the role of a servant or an 'inferior' (*cf* 1 Sir 25:41), to wash the feet of the travelers; he says instead: 'A little water shall be brought; you shall wash your feet . . .'[21]

---

19. The notion of grace, or favor, expressed by the Hebrew word *hēn* has two fundamental meanings: morally it signifies 'esteem', 'pleasure' and 'benevolence'; or, in a more aesthetic sense, 'grace', or that 'charm' which is at the origin of 'the beautiful' and 'gratuitousness'. In the biblical text the two meanings converge to express that special moment when someone suddenly becomes unique and important in the eyes of another (this does not mean that the 'bestower of *hēn* is necessarily of a superior dignity or social standing', *cf* L Di Pinto, 'Abramo e lo straniero. Gen 18, 1-16. I. Un'introduzione all'ospitalità', in *RasseGena di Teologia*, 38 (1997): 597–620). It should also be pointed out that the welcome and deferential attitude towards an unknown passer-by cannot depend on a previous investigation into his identity. On the contrary, any prior inquiry into his person would indicate a lack of true hospitality and is considered rude and inappropriate.

20. We leave, for the moment, the greatest theological and literary problem raised by the story at Mamre, which can be summarized in the following question: if it is Yahweh who appears to Abraham, why are there three mysterious pilgrims? What is the relationship between them? It is around this question that the entire history of the exegetical interpretation of the cycle of Abraham and Lot revolves; and it is this question that determines the most important differences in the reception of these two chapters of Genesis from the perspective of the three monotheistic religions.

21. This interpretation, shared by most commentators, does not prevent certain artists from representing Abraham as washing the feet of his guests: Rembrandt, for example, as well as Tiepolo, a century later. Moreover, from the literary point

After stressing the radical change of pace upon the arrival of the guests at the door of Abraham's tent, we must consider the spatial dimensions of the story and the elements that form the backdrop to the meeting, all of which contribute to the iconic character of the narrative. In the first fifteen verses of Genesis, chapter 18, the scene is presented with a double focus: on one side, we have the tent of Abraham, which is mentioned five times (18:1, 2, 6, 9, 10); and on the other side, the tree, under the sheltering shade of which the sacred meal will be consumed; and is mentioned three times (18:1, 4, 8), the first of which is implied at the beginning of the narrative: 'the Oak of Mamre'. 'If you tend to be partial to the tree in preference to the tent, it is probably because God occupies this corner (sic) of the scene. The tent, however, in this story does not play an insignificant role'.[22] We like to imagine even a third space, the virtual vantage point enjoyed by the reader, favored by several bits of information over and above the actors on stage, as detailed above. Now, the first part of the narrative centering on Abraham's hospitality (Gen 18:1–8) unfolds almost exclusively under the tree outside, while the tent remains in the background. That said, the space between the tent and the tree is, symbolically, Abraham's progressive journey of discovering the identity of the mysterious pilgrims,[23] alongside his gradual involvement in the dynamics of the ritual of hospitality. In this sense, even Abraham's posture of repose at the door of his tent as the story begins, can be interpreted in a new way: not as a sign of total passivity

---

of view, what we have just said regarding the dignity of Abraham as clan leader does not contradict his use of the term *'ebed* (servant) in verses 3b and 5b, to describe himself. As with the term *'ǎdōnî* (my lord), it is a relational term that replaces proper names not explicitly mentioned in the story. As Luigi Di Pinto recalls, the combination of the terms *'ǎdōn-'ebed* characterizes the difference between personal service and submission; they are essentially expressions of Abraham's courtesy (*cf* L Di Pinto, 'Abramo e lo straniero', 739–740).

22. J-L Ska, *Abramo e i suoi ospiti*, 117.

23. The space-time dimension plays a decisive role in translating a theological and symbolic meaning into a call for relationship under the sign of difference. 'Between the threshold of the tent, Abraham's intimate space, and the '*agape*' tree, there is a distance to cover, a risk to take ... Between the microcosm of the tent and the tree however, lies the intermediate space of possible and fruitful communion: the triadic articulation dear to Levinas which does not abolish otherness to the point of assimilation but, on the contrary, demands it as a condition for dialogue' [C Monge, 'L'hospitalité d'Abraham: la confirmation du 'moi' des pèlerins', in *Seuils et Traverses 4. Colloque international et pluridisciplinaire sur l'écriture du voyage* (Ankara: Actes, 2004), 212–218 (213)].

but rather as an attitude of vigilance, alert to check any disharmony within his own person before he can be ready to perceive an 'other' in his difference and strangeness, and so go to meet him. The threshold of the tent is the border between one's personal boundary and the space where communication is possible: the nomad's tent must be always open, and its occupant awaiting the passage of interlocutors even at the seemingly impossible 'hottest part of the day' (Gen 18:1). That is why Abraham quickly leaves his sitting position and the confines of his tent to fulfill his duty of hospitality.

'They replied, "Do as you say"' (Gen 18:5b). This terse reply of the three pilgrims is in contrast to the very formal invitation of the Patriarch, and even more with the sumptuous preparations that it sets in motion. In actual fact, it is not just 'a little water . . . a little bread' (Gen 18:4–5) that Abraham is preparing to offer his mysterious guests! The biblical description becomes even more pressing, in a climate of increasing frenzy. Verbs built on the root *mhr* ('hurry,' three times in vv. 6a.6b.7b) and *rws* ('run,' already used in v 2 and then repeated in v 7) lend a particular pace to the scene and are very paradoxical if we compare it with other details reported in v 11: 'Now Abraham and Sarah were old, well on in years . . .' Names of places are associated with action verbs ('Ran from the entrance of the tent to meet them'; v 2 and 'Then running to the cattle, Abraham . . .;' v 7) accentuate the sense of urgency of the task and likewise, a strict division of responsibilities: kneading and baking is for women, the slaughter of livestock is a job for the men.

Even the details of the meal, the abundance and quality of which indicate both the generosity and the social rank of the host, are very interesting. "'Hurry,' he said, 'knead three bushels of flour and make loaves'" (v 6b). The bushel was a cylindrical container used for cereals; it becomes a measure of capacity (*seâh*) for which commentators have no united opinion (ranging from 7.3 liters to a maximum of 15) but which certainly indicates an excessive amount to care for the need to feed only three guests. While Sarah prepares loaves, Abraham takes care of the meat. Once again, the quantities are enormous: no one would kill a tender calf for only three people; a lamb or a goat would suffice,[24] especially since, as noted above, meat cannot be stored for

---

24. Quite noteworthy here is the parable of the two men, one rich and the other poor, told by the prophet Nathan to King David: 'When there came a traveler to stay, the rich man refused to take one of his own flock or herd to provide for the wayfarer who had come to him. Instead he took the poor man's lamb and prepared it for

The Structure of the Biblical Account 197

any length of time in these very hot countries. Furthermore, even more compelling is that the ritual of hospitality demands that the meat of a slaughtered animal be served only for the occasion and not preserved! Abraham serves this meat with simple and curdled milk which, especially in Syria and in Arabia, makes a refreshing drink called *leben*.[25] Commentators wonder why the drink offered is not wine, as the region of Hebron is wine country par excellence in Palestine. Gunkel remembers that Abraham and Sarah are presented as Bedouins who live in tents. Bedouins have no vineyards in fidelity to their nomadic lifestyle. According to another hypothesis, the cycle of Abraham would not have originally been tied to the region of Hebron.[26]

We offer two clarifications as we conclude the analysis of this scene of hospitality. '[T]hey ate while he [Abraham] remained standing near them under the tree' (Gen 18:8b). After the verses that describe the preparation of the meal, distinguished by the joyful hurriedness at the unexpected visit, the scene ends as it began: in silence and in a mood of repose. Nevertheless, the two situations at the antipodes of this story present important differences. Abraham is no longer sitting, but standing firmly beneath the tree while simultaneously conveying his availability and his deep respect for his guests. As is the custom among the nomadic peoples, the Patriarch does not partake of the meal with

---

his guest' (2 Sir 12:4). In Luke's parable of the Prodigal Son, however, the father displays a superabundant generosity like that of Abraham. The elder son, in the same story, emphasizes the enormity of killing a fatted calf to celebrate the return of an ungrateful son: 'He was angry then and refused to go in (. . .) 'Look, all these years I have slaved for you and never once disobeyed your orders, yet you never offered me so much as a kid for me to celebrate with my friends. But, for this son of yours, when he comes back after swallowing up your property—he and his women—you kill the calf we had been fattening' (Lk 15:28–30). We must point out that the Targum, quoted by Louis Ginzberg, goes even further in its description of Abraham's generosity: 'What that the guests saw set before them was a royal banquet, even more maGenificent than anything deserving of Solomon at the height of his glory' » (*Baba Metsi'a* 86b, citato da Ginzberg L, *Le leggende degli ebrei. II. Da Abramo a Giacobbe*, [Mlano: Adelphi, 1997], 66).

25. This is not merely a drink because the meat itself is not boiled in water but with *leben*, or even with *ğebğeb*, a serum obtained in the preparation of butter which, when processed into small pellets, may be salted and hardened in the sun (*cf* A Jaussen, *Coutumes des Arabes au pays de Moab*, 68).

26. *Cf* A Clamer, 'Commentaire de la Genèse', in L Pirot and A Clamer, editors, *La Sainte Bible*, XII voll, (Paris: Letouzey et Ané, I-1re partie, 1953), 283.

the guests nor does he pester them with an excess of attention, while maintaining his place as the 'pater familias'. Especially, according to the most pristine ritual of sacred hospitality, does Abraham withhold any misplaced curiosity regarding the identity of his guests. Not only did he provide everything super-abundantly, but the gratuity of his attention is confirmed by the fact that there is no indication that he had already grasped the true identity of the mysterious visitors. A second particular: there is no further mention of the loaves that Abraham had asked his wife Sarah to prepare. It is not easy to explain this fact, except to think that, in the Semitic and nomadic cultures, the loaves would take the place of plates and cutlery.[27] That is why they are not mentioned in the detail of foods served.

A reward for hospitality?

As we have seen, the first great narrative section of Genesis chapter 18 describes a domestic scene utilizing the typical features of pastoral culture (the countryside, the outdoors, the nomad's tent and the flock, the heat and the tranquility of the setting, the generous and courteous hospitality, the maGenanimity of the host, the celebration of the meal, the sense of satiety . . .). There is no special tension in the narrative, simply a recounting of the scene.

Box 6 The 'Tragedy' Of Barrenness in the Bible

In the Old Testament, in particular, barrenness was beyond doubt considered a curse if not a divine punishment (cf. Gn 16:2; Gn 20:18; 1 S 1:5-7). The law also spoke of it as a logical punishment for a prohibited consanguineous union (Lv 20:20-21). In Israel, one of the reasons that made barrenness an all but unbearable disgrace was the expectation of the Messiah: every woman hoped one day to give birth to the Liberator of the people! Sarah, Rebecca, Rachel and Anna were all partially barren (cf. Gn 11:30; Gn 25:21; Gn 29:31;

---

27. In Hebrew, the loaves are called ūgôt and are a kind of large round bread made without yeast (especially when it is intended to be consumed immediately) and only lightly baked (*cf* Lev 2:4) on the hearth or heated stones once the ashes have been brushed away (*cf* 1 Kgs 19:6). This last method is especially useful if there is haste (as is the case of our story of Mamre). The size of the loaves is to facilitate cooking and ease of transport.

Jg 13:2-3; 1 S 2:5). That they were able to give birth at least once was the sign of an extraordinary intervention of God and of God's divine favor. Given this supposition, we can better understand Christ's harsh judgment on Jerusalem, as he ascended the road to Calvary, already condemned and ready to meet his death: "For the days are coming when people will say, 'Happy are those who are barren, the wombs that have never borne, the breasts that have never suckled'"(Lk 23:29)! As for the question of barrenness itself, the Semitic ambient was most likely derived from Mesopotamian Law (the Code of Hammurabi). It was the custom for a barren woman to lend the maidservant to her husband, in order to remove her shame and to gain for herself the title of motherhood (cf. Gn. 16:2; Gn 30:3-4). The question was the woman's honor, not that of her husband (the Bible never openly mentions male sterility) who, for his part, could choose a second and third wife in order to provide numerous descendants (Gn 25:1). In the case of a polygamous marriage, in which a man married to a barren woman was permitted to take advantage of an alternative mother (hired or leased, we would say today), the relationship of the latter with her husband was not regarded as a real marriage contract (cf. P. Galpaz-Feller, "Pregnancy and Birth in the Bible and Ancient Egypt (Comparative Study)", in *Biblische Notizen, Beiträge zur exegetischen Diskussion*, Heft 102, München 2000, pp. 42–53).

[9] 'Where is your wife Sarah?' they asked him. 'She is there in the tent' he replied.[10] Then his guest said, 'I shall visit you again next year without fail, and your wife will then have a son.' Sarah was listening at the entrance of the tent behind him. [11] Now Abraham and Sarah were old, well on in years, and Sarah had ceased to have her monthly periods.[12] So Sarah laughed to herself, thinking, "Now that I am past the age of child-bearing, and my husband is an old man, is pleasure to come my way again![13] But Yahweh asked Abraham, 'Why did Sarah laugh and say, "Am I really going to have a child now that I am old?"'[14] 'Is anything too wonderful for Yahweh? At the same time next year I shall visit you again and Sarah shall have a son.'[15] 'I did not laugh' Sarah said, lying because she was afraid. But he replied, 'Oh yes, you did laugh' (Gen 18: 9-15).

The question posed by the mysterious visitors concerning Sarah suddenly changes the pace of the story (v 9). Abraham responds promptly and immediately receives the announcement of his wife's pregnancy (v 10). The story is complicated by Sarah overhearing the reference to herself in the conversation. The narrator adds the details of the relatively advanced age of the couple and Sarah's reaction, with her derisive laughter (vv 10b–12). The narrative tension reaches its climax with the ability of mysterious guests to scrutinize Sarah's thoughts (v 13) and the reference to the authoritative intervention of Yahweh (perceived as such only by the reader) to confirm the extraordinary prophecy just made—which could not take place except by the omnipotent and direct creative action of God (v 14).

We look more briefly at the salient features of the second narrative section of the chapter. The account is no longer directly concerned with Abraham's hospitality, but rather, with the consequences of his unconditional generosity. The story also finally reveals something of the identity and mission of the mysterious visitors.

The abrupt shift in the narrative, just mentioned, can be seen in the change in spatial dimensions. From a framework gradually moving in the direction of the tent to the tree, we now have a new framework running in the opposite direction: from the tree to the tent. The tent, like the tree, denotes not merely a physical place but is a symbolic key in the narrative technique: it serves to circumscribe the personage of Sarah and to define the mission of the visitors.[28] The center of attention passes from actions to words. The main actors are seen as transient guests and the main interlocutor becomes—no longer Abraham—but his wife Sarah, as if the visitors speak directly with her; cf. v. 15b (otherwise it is always Abraham who acts as intermediary). The tent fulfils a dual role: it hides and at the same time reveals the presence of Sarah; it is a place of intimacy, of interiority unavailable to outsiders, a secret place.

Until now, the story of Genesis 18 unfolded on two levels: the first, very symbolic and theologically evocative, was directed only to the reader who, as mentioned above, received additional information concerning the main protagonists; the second seems describes them discretely so that, at least initially, they had to be persuaded to experience so lavish a hospitality.

'Where is your wife Sarah?' The question, posed by the mysterious visitors, is surprising for several reasons. First of all because, ordinarily, it is the host who asks the first personal question of the guests, thus

---

28. *Cf* RI Létellier, *Day in Mamre, Night in Sodom*, 95.

introducing the dialogue. Second, if Abraham apparently does not know his guests, they, on the contrary, know of his existence and even the name of his wife, even though she had remained hidden from their eyes until that moment! For the first time, Abraham and Sarah experience the uncommon nature of the visitors who seem to have access to confidential information that only the narrator and reader are believed to have. It is probably also because of their exceptional nature that these visitors at Mamre dare to ask a question about the wife of a householder. To do so would be considered in poor taste in the nomadic Bedouin context.[29] Abraham answers apparently without hesitation but very briefly and without speaking the name 'Sarah'.

Verse 10 is crucial because it contains not only the promise of an unexpected birth (further proof of the extraordinary nature of the three passing guests who, aware of Sarah's sterility, predict that it will be surmounted); but also gives us a surprising spatial detail: the pilgrims' backs are turned to the entrance of the tent, as we see from v 10b ('Sarah was listening at the entrance of the tent behind him') and still are able to capture the Patriarch's wife's laughter mocking at God's promise. In this detail, we find the third indication of the all-knowing understanding of the mysterious travelers who can not only see into the tent behind them, but are also able to read the secret thoughts of the heart (Gen 18:15). Sarah imagined that she could listen to the conversation between the men and give free rein to her feelings without being seen, but she is surprisingly called out and her reactions unmasked. Verse 12, after yet another editorial insertion that provides the reader with information about the advanced age of the couple and the sterility of Sarah (v 11),[30] describes the disbelief of the woman by introducing the reader to her inner monologue. Sarah's laughter, reported as interior and secret, is actually an expression of

---

29. It should be noted that such a question probably falls in the category of a divinely stated rhetorical or trick question. Often, God does not await a response (*cf* Gen 3:9 and Gen 4:9) but intends to simply open a conversation or test his interlocutor. In this specific case, the question resembles a request for information; in reality, it helps create a situation favorable to the formulation of a blessing (*cf* H Rouillard, 'Les feintes questions divines dans la Bible', in *Vetus Testamentum*, 34 (1984): 237–242).

30. It is, obviously, to offer a motive for Sarah's disbelief, and to prepare for the definitive revelation of the identity of visitors who are able to transcend what are, at the human level, insurmountable obstacles. Yet this editorial interpolation is also a ploy to decelerate the pace of the story and increase the tension of the plot.

the inner struggle of a woman not only too old but never having been able to bear children.[31] This existential torment is expressed in a question which combines astonishment and disbelief: 'Now that I am past the age[32] of child-bearing, and my husband is an old man [. . .]' (v 12). The use of a simile accentuates the idea of old age; we might say 'tired of life.' Instead, the term *'ednâh*—'[. . .] is pleasure to come my way again!' (v 12c), as noted by Létellier, denotes not simply 'pleasure' but, more exactly, 'sexual enjoyment' (from the root verb *dn* which means 'to live voluptuously' . . . 'to delight in'; *cf* Ne 9:25). It is a notion, therefore, that expresses sexual gratification, the apogee of a happy marriage! It is an expression that is amazing for its strength, if one thinks of the contrast to the venerable age of the couple in question. Sarah seems to look not so much to motherhood as such, but to the pleasure of having sexual relations with her husband.[33] The paradoxical contrast between being physically 'threadbare' and the nostalgia for sexual pleasure defines the tenor of the incredulity expressed by this woman. This disbelief is reinforced by the laconic appreciation of the status of her husband, 'and my husband is an old man' (v 12b). The decrepitude of Abraham corresponds to the withered-ness of Sarah. All these considerations are the product of Sarah's thoughts, a monologue revealed to the reader who once again has information that will prepare him for the shock of v 13, when one of the guests demonstrates access to the same level of knowledge. At this point, the narrator identifies him explicitly with Yahweh, but does not yet say if Abraham and Sarah have finally arrived at the same awareness. A further question concerning Sarah is asked of Abraham—a question that moves the attention away from sexual enjoyment to the topic of motherhood in an elderly woman. 'But Yahweh asked Abraham, "Why did Sarah laugh and say, 'Am I really going to have a child now that I am old?'"' (v 13). There is a

---

31. Cf. the 6 xtra-page THE 'TRAGEDY' OF BARRENNESS IN THE BIBLE

32. The Hebrew term *'aharê belotî*, can be rendered 'worn out,' 'empty,' 'threadbare,' and is usually used in reference to old clothes.

33. The Bible is very explicit regarding the enjoyment of sexuality (*cf* Ws 7:2) considering it a fully legitimate part of marriage (Gen 18:12), while underlining the dangers of abuse (Pr 7). As for Sarah, the term *'ednâh* on her lips, while giving the impression of referring to the transports of a single act of love, may also be interpreted as 'the full strength of youth' or as an allusion to the menstrual cycle or even just simply to 'fertility'.

The Structure of the Biblical Account   203

slight change in the terminology: the bold allusion to sexual pleasure is replaced by the term 'motherhood', returning to Sarah a dignity more in keeping with that of an elderly woman. The mysterious guest understands exactly what the woman had called her husband: 'an old man'—but not exhausted (in the sense of impotent); we have here a psychological subtlety of some importance that will attract the attention of the Jewish commentators. Once again, another rhetorical question (v 14) is posed to Abraham; clearly rhetorical because the answer is given without waiting for one from the Patriarch. 'Is anything too wonderful for Yahweh?' Can God not possibly also grant a child to a couple advanced in years?[34] In this passage, there is the interpretive key to the whole story of Gen 18:1–15, a statement of trust in God's ability to fulfill his promises. That said, the ambiguity of the situation is not fully resolved: the mysterious guests answer the question so impersonally without exposing themselves directly, without even completely revealing their identity.

In Genesis 18:14 there is a combination of the difficultly and wonderment that sharply delineates the boundary between human limitations and the immensity of divine power. What is humanly impossible is possible for God and, therefore, a wonder to behold. We may never forget that the Word of God contains within itself a power that goes beyond human limitations and weakness. 'Is anything too wonderful for Yahweh?' In this rhetorical question there is an implicit affirmation of divine omnipotence. Moreover, the religious experience of Israel throughout their history can be summed up in the expression of an arduous journey of faith in Yahweh, who makes possible what is humanly impossible ('Who among the gods is your like, Yahweh? Who is your like, majestic in holiness, terrible in deeds of prowess, worker of wonders?' Ex 15:11). After stating God's omnipotence, which is the core of the message (v 14), Yahweh returns to the exigencies of the moment and takes control of the situation by reformulating the original promise expressed in v 10: 'at the same time next year I shall visit you again and Sarah shall have a son' (v 14b). This is not, however, a simple repetition of v. 10, because there are new elements. First, there is a reference to God's return to Abraham and

---

34. It is curious to note that the rabbinical interpretation of Rashi and of other great Jewish commentators is more oriented to the foreknowledge of God: "Is it impossible perhaps for God to predict the future?"

Sarah: 'At the same time next year', and not simply 'next year', as in the earlier verse. Secondly, the child's birth is the work of God's power. The conclusion of this story is surprising because it seems to take a step back: the conversation between Sarah and the guest continues with Sarah in denial of her emotion before this stranger who reads her heart[35]. Sarah wants to conceal her disbelief before a promise that seems absurd; we could also imagine her desire to retreat back inside the tent and never come out in the illusion of escaping the penetrating gaze of Yahweh. The guest's final word, very mysterious and quite brutal, ('Oh yes, you did laugh'; v 15b), places the story in the literary category of 'open parables', where the reader is called upon to draw his own conclusion[36]. Sarah's laughter, confirmed by the sharp retort of the guest, explains the origin of the name of the promised son Isaac (Isaac means 'laughter').[37] That the observation of Sarah's laughter is repeated (four times: 18:12, 13, 15a, 15b) is certainly emphatic and accentuates the importance of a term that will be recalled at the time of Isaac's birth ('Abraham named the son born to him Isaac, the son to whom Sarah had given birth [. . .] Then Sarah said, "God has given me cause to laugh; all those who hear of it will laugh with me"' (Gen 21:3.6); here is the etiology of the name Isaac). That said, there remain several questions. The first is derived from an overview of the two great narrative cadres of Genesis chapter 18: Genesis 18:1–9 and Genesis 18:9–15. Can one really profess that the announcement of a birth is a reward for a generously offered hospitality? To respond to this question we must be able to demonstrate the continuity between these two parallel literary units.

The literary motif of 'theoxenia', hospitality accorded to strangers who are, in reality, gods disguised as pilgrims or divine messengers of the gods, is widespread even outside of the Semitic traditions. We find many books of this genre in Ugaritic literature,[38] as well as

---

35. *Cf* RI Létellier, *Day in Mamre, Night in Sodom*, 102.

36. *Cf* J-L Ska, *Abramo e i suoi ospiti*, 125.

37. Isaac comes from root verb *sāhaq* 'to laugh'. Among the most reliable etymologies of Isaac, we find 'God makes me laugh for joy, makes [the parents] smile' (*cf* Gen 21:6); but the etymology also indicates a name of good omen: that God smiles and is benevolent (toward the newborn).

38. Paolo Xella has made an extensive study of the relationship between the Ugaritic poem *Dnil e Aqhat* and the story of Mamre, and had discovered surprising parallels. 'A summary analysis of the structures of the Ugaritic and biblical texts

in the Greek and Latin worlds.[39] In the Bible in particular, we are aware that on any given day something extraordinary might happen to upset the ordinary flow of events. 'Do not pass your servant by' (Gen 18:3b). Abraham invited his guests using the expression 'do not pass by'—an expression which is frequently used with reference to the appearance of Yahweh or on the occasion of a manifestation of grace (that is, 'the transforming action of Yahweh'), either directly or through the mediation of a prophet, a man of God.[40] In essence, the simple 'passing' of Yahweh is the preamble to the revelation of God's glory, and is the mediation of divine goodness, mercy and grace.

There is a parallel pericope in the Second book of Kings. In the earlier mentioned episode, the Shunammite woman also receives the 'passage of God' in the person of God's prophet Elisha. The latter often visits the woman and receives her generous hospitality (*cf* 2 Kgs 4:8-9); and her generosity is likewise rewarded by the arrival of an unforeseen son (2 Kgs 4:16). The link between the gift and the counter-gift is explicitly stated in this narrative, as we may just as well suppose in the story of Mamre:

> He [Elisha] said to his servant Gehazi, 'Call our Sunammitess' [. . .] 'Tell her this', Elisha said, 'Look, you have gone to all this trouble for us, what can we do for you?' [. . .] Gehazi answered, 'Well, she has no son and her husband is old.' Elisha said, 'Call her.' The servant called her and she stood at the door. 'This time next year,' he said, 'you will hold a son in your arms' (2 Kgs 4:11–16).

[. . .] leads us to conclude that the two episodes go back, in fact, to a common tradition, each representing two diverse processing moments (one polytheistic and the other monotheistic) of a mythological theme very archaic and widespread: 'the visit of a god who rewards with a gift, a grace, or a supernatural favor', *cf* P Xella, 'L'épisode de Dnil et Kothar et Gen. XVIII, 1-16', in *Vetus Testamentum*, XIII.4 (1978): 483–488 (484–485).

39. For a thorough study of these issues, refer to the first chapters of our previous work in French: C Monge, *Dieu hôte. Recherche historique et théologique sur les rituels de l'hospitalité*, (Bucarest: Zetabooks, 2008).

40. *Cf* Ex 33:18–23; 34:4–11a; 1 K 19:9–21; 2 Kgs 4:8–17; Ez 16:1–14, Hos 10:11–13a.

The literary similarities with Genesis 18 are clear evidence[41] and lead us to conclude that the promise to Sarah of a son is of the same genre of 'theoxenia benefaction', which is repeated several times in the biblical context as well as in profane literature. In fact, in ancient as well as in biblical literature, the same two-fold binomial of hospitality offered—reward/hospitality refused—punishment is evident. In essence, we can affirm a logical continuity between Abraham's hospitality (Gen 18:1–8) and the subsequent announcement of a birth (Gen 18:9–15). Yahweh is passing by and is persuaded by his servant Abraham to accept his hospitality; later Yahweh blesses him with the promise of a son. Abraham found grace (*hēn*) in the eyes of Yahweh and 'the God who passes by' bestows abundant mercy and kindness to those who are ready to receive it.

We are aware, however, that a certain recurrence of literary motifs cannot be compelling evidence of a direct link between a reward given as recompense for hospitality granted. It remains true that Abraham's hospitality is exemplary in that it is freely given without expectation of any reward; certainly not the promise of a miraculous birth. The mysterious guests, for their part, make the promise in absolute and sovereign liberty, recognizing but not dependent upon the Patriarch's generosity, in the free willingness of God to engage humanity in a fruitful relationship.

---

41. The Shunammitess shares with Sarah the condition of infertility; the promise of a son to the two women is expressed by almost exact formulas: 'At the same time next year I shall visit you again and Sarah will have a son' (Gen 18:14b); and 'This time next year [. . .] you will hold a son in your arms' (2 Kgs 4:16). Both women express doubt and concern at the unprecedented nature of these prophecies. In both cases, the promises are perfectly fulfilled. (*cf* J Van Seters, *Abraham in History and Tradition*, 204–205).

The theophany of Mamre in the Christian interpretation

We return to the most divisive issue in interpreting the story of Mamre: the identity of the three visitors received by Abraham. Debated for centuries, the argument was at one time more theological in nature but currently is essentially more literary. If it is Yahweh who has appeared at Mamre, how is this explained in relationship to 'the three men' spoken of in Genesis 18?

From a theological viewpoint, the question touches on the structure of the theophany, the dogmatic evolution of the concept of God and the divine-human relationship. However, more recently textual criticism has shifted the debate to the historical-literary level, questioning among other things, the unity of the text that we have inherited from tradition and its uniqueness as assumed by its editor.[1]

After presenting an overview of the various translations of the story in Genesis 18, we will examine in detail the question of the identity of the three guests of Abraham. This brief excursus into comparative theology will allow us to say more about the value of hospitality as a particular intimacy of the human person with God and, conversely, of God with the human person.

Different versions of the same story

The multiple historical translations of the first verses of chapter 18 of Genesis exhibit some differences in the name given to the mysterious

---

1. For a good overview of the problems encountered in literary criticism, *cf* Joseph Loza's valuable commentary on Genesis 18-19 (J.Loza, 'Genèse xviii-xix: présence ou représentation de Yahvé? Essai sur la critique littéraire et la signification du récit', in *Congress Volume Paris 1992*, edited by JA Emerton, 179–192).

guest[s] of Abraham: The differences are, for the most part, unnoticed but in fact they are very significant. The Italian translation of the Jerusalem Bible [BG]: 'Then the Lord appeared to him at the Oak of Mamre . . .' differs from the Masoretic version [M], as it does from that of the Septuagint [LXX], where the proposed term is θεὸς (God or Yahweh).[2] Only in the fourth century CE, does Jerome propose 'Lord' (Dominus) in the Latin Vulgate version [V], which in its turn had been inspired by the major translations of Targum of the Pentateuch. In fact, the Targum Neophytes I [N][3] speaks of 'the Word of the Lord'; the Targum Pseudo-Jonathan [G][4] mentions 'the Glory of the Lord', the Shekinah. Here begins the problem of textual criticism because all of these versions oscillate between the singular and the plural to describe the mysterious presence of Abraham's visitors. Beginning from verse 2, we find a plural that cannot be justified simply in the formal sense (this is not one person speaking of himself in the plural to make a more solemn intervention, but three men who speak as if they were one and act simultaneously: v 2 reads 'three men standing near him' [JB] and *stantes prope eum*' [V]). Successively, even if only one character speaks to Abraham, the alternation between the singular and plural continues: 'As soon as he saw them, [Abraham] ran from the entrance of the tent to meet them, and bowed down to the ground. "My lord", he said "I beg you, if I find favor with you, kindly do not pass your servant by"' (vv 2b–3). 'A little water shall be brought; you shall wash your feet [. . .] and you shall rest yourselves before going further' (v 4). 'They replied, "Do as you say"' (v 5b).

---

2. The English Jerusalem Bible version is '*Yahweh appeared to him at the Oak of Mamre*'.

3. The Aramaic versions of the Bible (Targum is a term that means translation) represent the first interpretations of the Holy Scriptures for use in the synagogues. The Targum Neophytes I is one of two full versions of the Palestinian Pentateuch, which—setting aside the Targum of Babylon (also called Targum Onkelos)—is one of the two sets of manuscripts of Jewish interpretation of the Pentateuch. There are, therefore, only two complete manuscripts of the Palestinian Pentateuch: the aforementioned Code Neophytes [N] found in the Vatican Library and dating from the second century and the Manuscript of London [L] (*cf* R Le Déaut, editor, *Targum du Pentateuque*, I, *Genèse*, coll. SC n°245, Paris 2006/19781).

4. This is a virtually complete manuscript, drafted very late (perhaps at the end of the thirteenth century or the beginning of the fourteenth) and erroneously attributed to a certain Jonathon ben Uzziel. It is written in Aramaic.

The story continues speaking of the visitors in the plural, until the return of the singular starting from v 9 of the LXX ('He said, "Where is Sarah your wife?"') and from v 10 in the Vulgate: "Then his guest said, "I shall visit you again next year without fail and your wife Sarah will have a son."' Then in verse 13, after Sarah laughs: 'But the Lord (*Dominus*) [in the LXX *kurios* from this point until the end of the story] asked Abraham, "Why did Sarah laugh . . .?"' The story then ends with a return to the plural: '[T]he men set out and arrived within sight of Sodom' (v 16).

The targums do not facilitate our task. Abraham looks up and sees three angels in human appearance (N and L) who are standing; in the London manuscript, it is noted that Abraham ran toward them, greeted them and turned to Yahweh: 'My lord, if I have found favor in your sight, let the glory of your Shekinah not rise from above your servant [this also in N] before I have welcomed these travellers.' Then follows the description of the preparation of the meal of hospitality, the meal itself followed by the announcement of the birth of Isaac, and the controversy concerning Sarah's laugh, as in the Genesis account. The conclusion of the story is somewhat more detailed. 'The angels who looked like men got up from there; the one who had made the announcement to Sarah went back up toward the sky while the other two looked down toward Sodom' [L] and Abraham went with them to keep them company [N and L]. From this description we can infer that the tradition of the Targum is moving toward a clear distinction of one personage over the other two in its interpretation of the theophany at Mamre as given in the second part of chapter 18 of Genesis. Moreover, even in the Christian Bible translations, the narrator, after having introduced us to the core of Yahweh's thinking (vv 17–21), continues somewhat enigmatically: 'The men left there and went to Sodom while Abraham remained standing before Yahweh' (v 22). The conversation which follows no longer mentions the two men who left and the Patriarch seems to be left alone before the Lord. François Boespflug proposes two hypotheses for interpretation:[5] either Yahweh is represented by a group of three men (which could explain the abrupt changes from singular to plural); or Yahweh is only one of the three and Abraham, having identified him,

---

5. F Boespflug, *La théophanie de Mambré (l'Hospitalité d'Abraham: Gen 18)*, a manuscript dated 2005.

210   *Strangers With God*

would turn primarily or even exclusively to him, ignoring the other two.[6] In this case, the Lord, accompanied by two angels, would have visited Abraham and all three would have appeared to the Patriarch in human form. Yet we can conceive still another interpretation and imagine that the Lord had manifested Himself in the guise of three men who speak with one voice; subsequently two angels would then be sent to Sodom. The first interpretation encouraged a christological understanding during the first centuries of the Church; the second, beginning from the end of the fourth century, inspired a Trinitarian interpretation and was preferred by those Fathers who were anxious to contend, by means of the Scriptures, against subordinationism[7].

The structure of a theophany

The celebrated account of Mamre revolves around how the Israelites perceive the presence of God in their midst. To analyse in greater detail the relationship between God and the three mysterious characters greeted by Abraham, it is useful to look at the structure of a theophany, which is generally not identified with the appearance of a superior creature who would serve as an intermediary of the divine.[8] Certainly, with the prohibition against creating cultural

---

6. The rest of the story seems to encourage this hypothesis: as is generally understood, the 'men who left there' would be those charged with punishing Sodom and once they departed only the Lord was left with Abraham (*cf* Gen 19:1).

7. Subordinationism is a heresy concerning the Trinity which teaches that the Son (Jesus) is subordinate to the Father (God) and the Holy Spirit as subordinate to both. How the Persons of the Trinity are related remains one of the major differences between the Western and Eastern Churches. Subordinationism developed between the second and third centuries and gradually disappeared after the Council of Nicaea in 325, with the condemnation of Arianism (which asserts that Jesus Christ is Son of God, created by the Father and therefore not equal to but subordinate to the Father).

8. We confine ourselves here to drawing a distinction between two related terms: *epiphany* and *hierophany*. Epiphany comes from the Greek *epiphaínein* which refers to the rise of the light and in the broadest sense means to show or to appear. In Hellenistic thought it means not so much the visible appearance of God but a rescue operation. This is the precise sense it is used in the Pastoral Epistles to celebrate the advent of saving grace and to differentiate the first coming of Christ from the second, the Parousia, at the end of time. Mircea Eliade offers a broader definition to the term hierophany. Generally, it means a manifestation of the sacred. (E Cothenet, 'Théophanie', in *Catholicisme*, XIV, coll. 1104–1109).

images of God (Ex 20:4, 23; Lev 19:4; Lev 26:1; Deut 5:8; Deut 27:15), the theophany occupies an increasingly important role in Israelite faith. Despite this, the word theophany does not appear in the Bible.[9] Instead, it is the Fathers of the Church who introduce it to the Christian vocabulary in the fourth century to characterize the liturgical feasts of Christ's 'manifestations' (Christmas, Epiphany, the Baptism of the Lord and the Wedding Feast at Cana) and to refer to his historical and final comings. Later on, the term assumes very different meanings, sometimes almost contradictory. It is used in the sense of apparitions or of visions, or even of revelations in dreams. A theophany may be, at the same time, a demonstration of divine favor (at the heart of worship or in a vocational context), or a manifestation of God's power (the warrior god who fights alongside his people and chastises the infidels . . .) or, and very often, through natural upheaval (Ex 19; 1 Kgs 19:11). A manifestation of God is an illumination, opening paths of encounter and demanding obedience to God's Word (this is the real meaning of the theophany par excellence, like the revelation of God's name in Exus 3). In general, the biblical narratives stage divine messengers, partly distinct and partly assimilated to God himself. There are countless treatises of angelology concerning these very mysterious figures that populate the biblical accounts, in both the Old and New Testaments. An angel, in the proper sense of the term *mal'ak*,[10] is a messenger, an envoy, an ambassador, to whom God entrusts a mission and who speaks, sometimes, in the name of God himself. There was much speculation in the past about this extraordinary figure, sometimes identifying him even with the

---

9. In the Greek world the term is used for the feast of Delphi, where the statues of Apollo and other gods were exposed for the veneration of the people.

10. This term, dating back to the ancient Semitic language, often occurs in the Islamic tradition and will therefore be familiar to the Muslim believer and reader of the Qu'ran. In the holy book of Islam, angels are completely submissive and obedient to God (Qr XXI: 19–20, 27). However, the encounter between the angels and human persons and especially between the angels and the prophets, is highly controversial. In Shi'a Islam, angels are closely associated with the imam, but the latter, along with the prophets, are considered more excellent before God than the angels who nevertheless share God's protection against sin and error. At the same time, it recalls elsewhere that the imams are guided and helped by the angels. (*cf* DB Macdonald, 'Les anges dans le Coran et l'Islam sunnite', in voce 'Malā'ika', *Encyclopédie de l'Islam*, VI, 200–203. W Madelung, 'Les anges dans le Chiisme'.

Second Person of the Trinity: a kind of anticipation of the Incarnation through incomplete revelations. Father Marie-Joseph Lagrange first introduced a distinction between the presence of a simple messenger and the more direct communication from God. He writes: 'The presence of God in the Ark was a personal presence, much superior to that *of malʾak* who was, certainly, an envoy of God but also only a simple agent'.[11] The difficulty is to distinguish a direct and an indirect communication with God. What is the origin of this mediation so often problematic and ambiguous? Father Lagrange has no doubts:

> The intimate representation of Yahweh portrayed through his *malʾak* is the fruit of a modern concept. It has developed [. . .] in view of a concern to maintain intact the sublimity and transcendence of God. It is for the same reason that there came to emerge a theory of the intervention of angels in prophetic inspiration, or rather, in the tangible perception of the message they received[12].

If God's direct communication with us through his Word has never been questioned (and this corresponds to the teaching of the prophets themselves), we must, nevertheless, define the relationship between God and the manifestations that precede and sometimes accompany the divine teaching (Am 7; Jer 1; Ez 40:3; Ez 44:2). Lagrange does not seem to depart from classical angelology. After stating that the ancient prophets, like Amos and Jeremiah, never bothered to investigate whether the appearances of Yahweh were mediated rather than immediate, his personal position is that, 'When God becomes visible and speaks in the first person, it is through the appearance of an angel'.[13] It is a position that reflects the theology of the Old Testament, but is radically surpassed in the New.

The letter to the Hebrews testifies to the overcoming of this logic in the Christian context, since the coming of Christ.

> What you have come to is nothing known to the senses: not a blazing fire or a gloom turning to total darkness, or a storm; or trumpeting thunder or the great voice speaking [. . .] What you have come to is Mount Zion and the city of the living

---

11. M-J Lagrange, 'L'ange de Yahvé', in *Revue Biblique Internationale*, XII (1903): 215.
12. M-J Lagrange, 'L'ange de Yahvé', 216.
13. M-J Lagrange, 'L'ange de Yahvé', 219.

God, the heavenly Jerusalem where the millions of angels have gathered for the festival [. . .] to Jesus, the mediator who brings a new covenant and blood for purification which pleads more insistently Abel's (Heb 12:18, 22, 24).

The more mature theological reflection on this issue remains however that of St John who, in the fullness of the biblical tradition, reiterates: 'No one has ever seen God' (Jn 1:18; *cf* also 6:46). Then, by way of contrast to the Jewish interpretation that makes of Moses the unsurpassed witness of the Glory of God, he announces that 'The Word was made flesh', the very revelation of divine Glory (Jn 1:14; 2:11; 17:1). In the same gospel, Jesus, at the end of his life, declares to Philip, 'To have seen me is to have seen the Father' (14:9b). A paradoxical vision because John invites us to contemplate Christ exalted on the cross.

Now, precisely in the light of the Christology of the New Testament, it is interesting to return retrospectively to the Old Testament revelation and to rethink the meaning of some of the ancient theophanies.

Genesis 18 and 32: the two 'human theophanies'

In a recent doctoral thesis Esther Hamori, an American researcher of Jewish descent, takes up a very detailed analysis of two chapters of Genesis, 18 and 32, proposing, among other things, a very bold definition of theophany.[14] A true theophany, according to Dr Hamori, has special features: It is Yahweh in person who appears under human appearances,[15] not traditionally as in a dream but in broad

---

14. EJ Hamori, *When Gods Were Men: Biblical Theophany and Anthropomorphic Realism*, her dissertation to obtain a doctorate in Philosophy in the Department of Hebrew and Judaic Studies, New York University, 2004. We will not fail to refer to the study of the aforementioned RI Letellier, *Day in Mamre, Night in Sodom: Abraham and Lot in Genesis 18 and 19*, as well.

15. Manifestations of natural phenomena which express the power of God cannot be excluded, of course. The storm and the earthquake at Sinai fall within this category of phenomena: 'Now at daybreak on the third day there were peals of thunder on the mountain and lightning flashes, a dense cloud [. . .] Then Moses led the people out of the camp to meet God; and they stood at the bottom of the mountain. The mountain of Sinai was entirely wrapped with smoke, because Yahweh had descended on it in the form of fire. Like smoke from a furnace the smoke went up, and the whole mountain shook violently' (Ex 19:16–18). The examples of the divine presence hidden in cloud or fire or wind are numerous (Ex 3:2; 13:21; 1 Kgs 19:11–12).

daylight; and in waking hours.[16] Certainly, in the Bible we find many manifestations of God: on the one side, as in Gen 12:7 and 17:1, it is stated clearly that Yahweh appeared to Abraham; or again, in Gen 15 we hear that God speaks to Abraham in vision and during sleep. Esther Hamori, following the opinion of most exegetes, insists that, in the texts of the Old Testament, 'God' and 'man' are two quite distinct worlds and sometimes even opposed to each another. In the book of Numbers: 'God is no man ['îš] that he should lie, no son of Adam [ben-'ādām] to draw back' (Nm 23:19).[17] Although the few biblical portraits of God we have are anthropomorphic, their aim is not to reduce the gap between these two worlds. Even so, still according to Hamori, there are two texts in Genesis where God, in manifesting himself to the patriarchs, is described as 'a man' (the precise Hebraic term is 'îš) who has concrete, non-metaphorical human traits. We refer specifically to the triad of characters in the story of Mamre (Gen 18–19) where the plural of 'îš, 'ănāšîm, is used; and to the personage who struggles with Jacob and makes him lame (Gen 32:23–33). According to Hamori, we have here two cases of 'îš theophany: a 'human theophany' or 'real anthropomorphism'. If the appearance of God in human form was already recognized by other exegetes, Hamori goes further and states that, in these two accounts, God appears not only in an anthropomorphic vision, but in the actual material body of a man and not just figuratively.[18] Now, this anthropomorphic realism as a means of divine-human communication, has not only never been conceived of in the classical categories for theophany,[19] but its usage is

---

16. This definition of a theophany is a clear distancing from the classic definitions such as that of Pseudo-Dionysius, for which a theophany designates a kind of spiritual elevation of the visionary to divine realities. (cf Pseudo Dionigi l'Areopagita, Gerarchia celeste. Teologia mistica. Lettere, a cura di Lilla (Roma: Città Nuova, 1993).

17. We find similar expressions of the ontological difference between God and the human in Hos 11:9 and Jb 9:32.

18. EJ Hamori, When Gods Were Men, 6.

19. We speak regularly of dreams, angelic creatures and even the glory (kābôd) of God, but never of a human form to represent God. Clause Wastermann, for example, says, that a too realistically human interaction, such as in Gen 18, cannot, by definition, be a theophany. Marie-Joseph Lagrange takes the position of a literary critic; 'The appearance of any sovereign to Abraham'—he says—'is fertile ground for speculating about the relationship between Yahweh and the angels. This idea does not even belong to our theme, because the mal'ak have not been mentioned. We shall resolve the difficulties, I believe, by distinguishing among the forms: one part resembles a human form (cf Gen 18:1-16a); the other Yahweh alone (cf Gen 18:16b–33)' (M-J Lagrange, 'L'ange de Yahweh', 220).

not even attested elsewhere in the Bible. Moreover, it is totally absent in the mythologies of the ancient Middle East.

To establish her theory, Esther Hamori analyses in detail the meeting at Mamre, as well as the struggle between Jacob and his mysterious visitor. (These two stories are not from the same source and their similarities cannot be attributed to a single author). Now, both Abraham and Jacob acquire very gradually the consciousness of being in the presence of a unique interlocutor but, despite this, they are active neither in manifestations of worship nor in the construction of altars to honour the divine presence they come to recognise. The many realistic details built into the two stories hint at a very human and immediate rapport between the patriarchs and Yahweh who pays them a visit. In Genesis 18 the guests accept the full ritual of hospitality, the ablutions and the convivial meal; in Genesis 32, the struggle between Jacob and his opponent is not simply a metaphor, as we surmise because the Patriarch was injured in one hip (v 26). In both cases, Hamori emphasizes that the theophany is recognised verbally rather than visually. In other words, there is nothing visual that would allow Yahweh to be distinguished from any other man. It is only because of what their mysterious interlocutors say that the Patriarchs come to understand that they are in the presence of a transcendent Being, without it ever being said openly.[20]

But returning to the story of Mamre and its most controversial passages: the real problem is to explain the nature of the mysterious guests, the alternation between the singular and plural, the progressive differentiation of one man among the three (the one who speaks in the first person addressing himself first to Abraham and later to Sarah, and who will suddenly be identified with Yahweh; *cf* Gen 18:22) and, finally, the departure of the other two toward Sodom, where they will quickly be identified as 'two Angels' on special mission Gen 19:1).[21] The insertion of the periscope in Gen 18:17–33 (the dialogue between Yahweh and Abraham on the fate of Sodom) is not, for Hamori, inconsistent with the overall narration, even if of a later drafting.

---

20. In Gen 1:13–14, 'Yahweh allows a glimpse into his identity by exposing Sarah's laughter, even though she was hidden from him; and in the affirmation, Is anything impossible to God?' (Gen 18:14). In Gen 32:28–30, the myserious personage manifests his identity by imposing a new name on Jacob (the act of naming is a divine prerogative) and by refusing at the same time to reveal his own (God's name remains mysterious because God's identity is inaccessible).

21. Paradoxically, the only one of the three that will always be called 'a man' (*'îš*)) is the one who enjoys special treatment and that will prove to be Yahweh himself.

216 *Strangers With God*

She sees it as one more proof that the editor was conscious of being in the heart of a theophanic narrative. We may thus consider the reference to Gen 13 as an essential prelude to chapters 18–19, because the forthcoming destruction of the two 'sinful cities' can already be detected. Again, Gen 13 testifies to the arrival of Abraham in Mamre and the building of an altar which eventually comes to pass.[22]

In her analysis of the repeated transition from singular to plural in Gen 18:1–15, Hamori rejects the theory of harmonization of two distinct sources (the first regarding the appearance of Yahweh in person and the other the sending of three angels). As an aside, there is a similar occurrence in 2 Kgs 18:17–27, the story of three messengers sent by the king of Assyria to convey a message to King Hezekiah at Jerusalem. In this episode the three persons speak as if they were one and the response of the king is as to one. Well! Never has a harmonization of two sources been suggested here. Harmonization would entail the juxtaposition of two different narratives: in our case we have a narrative of hospitality concerning simple divine messengers, alongside an announcement of the birth of a child to a barren couple.[23] Esther Hamori dismisses a third theory—in vogue among contemporary exegetes—which suggests an indirect presence of Yahweh in a mission entrusted to three angels: a sort of 'theophany through an intermediary'. This, however, does not explain the progressive distinction of one personage over the other two. It is precisely by parting from the classical portrait of an angel or divine messenger and proposing instead a theory of *''iš theophany'* that the American researcher bases her interpretation of our fundamental text.

In essence, the two characters who appear before Abraham in the company of Yahweh, and who are called at the same time *'ănāšîm* (men) and *mal'ākîm* (angels; *cf* Gen 19:2) have features completely new and in agreement with the realism of an anthropomorphic *''iš theophany'.* This sets them apart from classical angelology. Like the character identified as Yahweh, they make their ablutions, they rest, they eat and, once they arrive in Sodom, their physical appearance is underscored by a threat of sexual violence (Gen 19:5) and a number of other details relative to their relationship with Lot and his family (Gen 19:10, 16).[24] However, only Yahweh, in Genesis 18 as well as in

---

22. EJ Hamori, *When Gods Were Men*, 25–26.
23. Clause Wastermann is a foremost promoter of this theory (C Wastermann, *Genesi. Commentario* [Casale Monferrato: Piemme, 1990], 274).
24. EJ Hamori, *When Gods Were Men*, 133–146.

Genesis 32, is represented visually throughout, in anthropomorphic and realistic terms. (As already pointed out, the revealing element of the divinity that hides beneath the human form is of verbal and not visual order). In contrast, the two angels sent to Sodom, manifest their true nature with spectacular gestures and not merely in words long after being received in human form: they dazzle the men that threaten their lives and the lives of those who welcome them (Gen 19:11) and carry out their divine mission to destroy the cities of Sodom and Gomorrah (Gen 19:13). In short, they discover their angelic role while the heart of their mission is very different from those of most celestial creatures as described in the biblical texts.

Hamori's interpretation of the structure of the theophany of Genesis 18, seems to us quite revolutionary as compared to the very complex history of the Christian exegesis of this biblical story. This history we will now attempt to summarize briefly before focusing our attention on the Jewish and Islamic interpretations for further comparison. The American scholar seems to follow a path at variance with classical angelology, as well as with the Christological and /or the Trinitarian readings of the meeting at Mamre.

What could we salvage today of this theology revealed by the proximity of a transcendent God without a reference so essential to Christians; namely, the Incarnation of the Logos? Perhaps we might have here the premise for a more fruitful inter-faith dialogue, leading toward the encounter of a God who becomes neighbour to humanity, thus responding to human desires voiced throughout the entire history of religion.

The identity of the three guests in the history of Christian exegesis

One question has always preceded all Christian interpretations of Genesis 18: how can an appearance of God be possible? In a theological stance that presents God as transcendent and of an entirely spiritual nature, it is still necessary to admit that God can be manifest in visible forms that represent God or are directly dependent on God—credible because the Sacred Scriptures, the Word of God which cannot deceive or mislead, tell us that God appeared to the Patriarch Abraham by the oak of Mamre.

Box 7 The Interpretation of the Meeting of Mamre in The Protestant Tradition

The Commentary on Genesis by Martin Luther (1543) is the last major work attributed to the founder of Protestantism. In his exegesis of Gn 18, Luther manifests a great attachment to the tradition of the Fathers of the Church and, in particular, to Augustine: likewise, Luther is opposed to an interpretation based solely on a symbolic reading of the text. As for his interpretation of the theophany of Mamre, he acknowledges the divine presence in the three mysterious pilgrims but he negates a direct reference to the Trinity; or, more precisely, he does not correlate his exegesis of the Trinity with an allegorical reading of the text but, at most, to an interpretation of its hidden meaning (the occultus sensus as opposed to the historicus sensus, utilized sometimes as a polemic against the Roman Catholic Church). According to Luther, the biblical text holds an historical significance dialectically and a hidden rhetorical meaning only in the order of faith. Stated differently, he does not reject the Trinitarian exegesis of the Fathers, but states that it is intelligible only to those who, at the level of faith, access the hidden meaning of the text; for him, it is futile to imagine that the theophany of Mamre can prove the existence of a triune God to those without faith. For the rest, Luther emphasizes the fact that the Fathers had never wished to argue in favor of a strict identification of the three mysterious pilgrims with the three persons of the Trinity; and Abraham, for his part, did not fulfill his duty of hospitality because he had implicitly recognized a Trinitarian presence of God in the persons he received! At the same time, he finds it significant that God appeared to Abraham in three persons and not four or two and that Abraham, while seeing three, worshiped only one, thanks to an insight into the faith of the true identity of the welcomed guests. We find in John Calvin's commentary on Genesis some positions similar to those of Luther, even if the latter seems more hesitant to adopt the allegorical interpretations. Furthermore, Calvin seems more oriented toward a Christological rather than a Trinitarian exegesis of Gn 18; apparently it was the theophany in Sodom (Gn 19:2) that influenced him to adopt this interpretation. The father of the Reformation emphasizes at length the importance of Abraham's hospitality and the evidence of his charity in the human sphere because it was in human form that angels appeared to him (Abraham would have recognized them as messengers of God only at the end of the meal).

The theophany of Mamre in the Christian interpretation

As already mentioned in relating Hamori's interpretation, the more classical theological presentation of the dynamics of a theophany is that God entrusts the mission of being a 'lieutenant' of the divine presence to angels during the short time of an apparition; because the angels, being creatures, have at least a 'spiritual body' that can solidify and make itself visible under this or that form.[25] A second fundamental question is the meaning of an angelic form taken by the presence of God: the problem of the relationship, so to speak, between the 'original' and the 'intermediary'. This question will be of prime importance during the time of the great controversies, first the christological and later the Trinitarian, in seeking to understand the relationship of Christ to the Father. The debate on these questions is far from over: The Christian interpretation of Genesis 18 and 19 has continually evolved in the history of exegesis and of spirituality—due more to preoccupation with major questions of dogma than to the complexity of the text itself.

The first Christians commentaries inherit the influence of the rabbinical interpretation (which we will study in depth): it takes up the idea that Abraham would have seen only three angels, and it is considered absolutely unthinkable that God could have eaten at his table.[26] These interpretations had never really disappeared and at base were superimposed on the christological and trinitarian readings.

---

25. This theory was popular from the time of St Augustine to Pope Benedict XIV (We refer to F Bœspflug, *Dieu dans l'art. Sollicitudini Nostrae de Benoît XIV (1745) et l'Affaire Crescence de Kaufbeuren* [Paris: Cerf, 1994], where the author summarises the reflections of this learned pope, steeped in the writings of the Fathers of the Church up to and including Gregory the Great. We refer as well to another interesting contribution of GJM Bartelink, 'Tres vidit, unum adoravit, formule trinitaire', in *Revue des Etudes Augustiniennes*, 30 (1984): 24–29 (29).

26. This is the understanding of Origen, Clement of Alexandria, Chrysostom, Theodoret, and others. When Genosticism and Docetism (a doctrine which argued that Christ had only an apparent [φάντασμα] body without fleshly substance, thus excluding his human conception and birth, as well as the full reality of his passion and death) were prevalent and shared with Monophysitism the same fear of compromising the divinity of the Saviour by his full humanity, certain expressions easily become suspicious. Clement of Alexandria (150 CE), for example wrote that it would be ridiculous to believe that the Saviour would have to eat and otherwise care for his body. If he ate, it was not because he needed to but to prevent his followers from thinking he was a pure ghost (Stromata VI, 9). Statements such as this did not save Clement from the charge of Docetism by some of his detractors.

220   *Strangers With God*

Questions of a Christological interpretation have dominated the first four centuries of Christian history. The meeting at Mamre was interpreted as a 'christophany', an understanding that it would have been the Word that had been accompanied by the two Angels in the visit to Abraham.[27] The main purpose of this interpretation was to stem the aforementioned rise of Arianism and Subordinationism.[28]

Nearing the end of the fourth century and into the fifth, there was a gradual movement, later confirmed, towards a trinitarian interpretation of the appearance at Mamre; this reading did not dismiss identifying the three visitors as angels, an hypothesis encouraged in Hebrews 13:28:[29] the point in question revolves around the meaning of the threefold presence. In these three angelic visitors, Abraham would have contemplated a foreshadowing of the mystery of the Trinity. There were not lacking, even in this era, countless interpretive nuances in the Christological versions (for instance, the antenicene readings were still being circulated), as well as in those strictly theological. If John Chrysostom (345–407) makes no Trinitarian allusion nor distinction of the divine persons in his reading of

---

27. We cannot dwell further on this issue. It should however be made clear that this Christocentric interpretation established itself very slowly. Abraham, according to the authors of the first four centuries of the Christian era, would have seen God in person, rather than the Son of God, accompanied by two angels. Justin Martyr, in his Dialogue with Tryphon, will engage, as we shall see later, a long controversy with his Jewish interlocutor to pass from this thesis to a christocentric thesis, indeed!

28. The Nicene Fathers and protagonists of the First Ecumenical Council (325 CE) were the main actors in this school of interpretation. The Council condemned Arianism and gave the Son and Holy Spirit an equality of essence, but a subordination of order because both received their existence from the Father. Among the well-known names in this group we have: Tertullian (155–ca 220), Irenaeus of Lyon (ca 140–208) and Hilary of Poitiers (315–367) among the Latin Fathers; and Justin Martyr (ca 100–165) and Origen (185–254) among the Greeks. Origen's positions are, in truth, very ambiguous, especially if we consider an expression traditionally attributed to him and which will be taken up in the following centuries with very different meanings: '*Tribus occurrit et unum et adorat ad unum loquitur*'. According to his fourth Homily on Genesis at least, the author seems to recognise in this formula the presence of the Lord (sometimes God the Father) amidst two angels, but does not explain the meaning of the threefold presence with the worship and the dialogue taking place in the singular.

29. '[R]emember always to welcome strangers, for by doing this, some people have entertained angels without knowing it.' This statement may refer not only to Gen 18 but to Tb 5:4; Jg 6:11–24; and 13:3–23.

chapter 18 of Genesis, Eusebius of Caesarea (circa 265–339) provides a long theological reflection to justify the identification of one of the three persons with the Word of God, while Cyril of Jerusalem (315–circa 387) goes so far as to see in Genesis 18 a foreshadowing of the Incarnation and, even of the Eucharistic Presence of Christ[30].

If the first champions of a Trinitarian exegesis of Genesis18 are the Alexandrian school among the Greeks (in particular Origen as already mentioned despite all his ambiguities, Cyril of Alexandria and, much later, Maximus the Confessor) it remains that it is only among the Latins, especially Ambrose (339–394) and later Augustine (354–430), that it becomes known as an interpretive school in a stable and enduring fashion. However, before coming to adopt Origen's formula (*'tres vidit et unum adoravit'*), Ambrose of Milan will maintain for a long time that Abraham saw three characters, but worshiped only one, identified as the Son of God and not representative of the obscure Trinity[31]! But in other writings of the same period, the bishop of Milan seems to be directed manifestly toward a Trinitarian exegesis, such as in his *Abraham*:

> Abraham was sitting at the door, at noon. While others were resting, he was watching for guests to arrive. It is not by chance that God appeared to him at the Oak of Mamre for in fact he was ardently looking for an opportunity to practice hospitality. And turning to look—it is said—he saw three men standing before him. And, as soon as he saw them, he ran to meet them. Observe first of all the mystery of the faith: God appears to him and he sees three persons. One to whom God manifests himself sees the Trinity: one does not welcome the Father without the Son, nor profess the Son without the Holy Spirit[32].

---

30. For a more detailed study of all these interpretations, refer to our previous publication, in French: C Monge, *Dieu hôte. Recherche historique et théologique sur les rituels de l'hospitalité.*

31. Saint Ambrose, *De Fide*, I, 13, 80.81 (PL, X, 115A): 'Rex gentilis in iGene cum tribus pueris Hebraeis quarti quasi angeli vidit figuram; et quia praestare putabat angelis, Dei Filium, quem non legit sed credidit, iudicavit. Abraham quoque tres vidit et unum adoravit', cited in AD'Alès, 'La théophanie de Mambré dans la tradition des Pères', in *Recherches de Sciences religieuses,* 20 (1930): 150–160 (155), note 18.

32. Saint Ambrose, *Abramo*, in *Tutte le opere di Sant'Ambrogio*, Opere esegetiche II/II, introduction, translation, notes and indexes by Franco Gori (Milano-Roma: Biblioteca Ambrosiana-Città Nuova, 1984), I, 5, 32–33, 71–73.

It is important to emphasise that Ambrose speaks of a Trinitarian vision in the typological sense of the term: that is why, while retaining a distinction of persons, he alludes to one Lord. It is therefore much more correct to say that, with Ambrose and afterward with Augustine, there is an affirmation of the Theophany of Mamre as an appearance of three angels who symbolize the Trinity. Both of these authors clearly espouse the rabbinical interpretation of the triple angelic apparition. Augustine, in his *De Civitate Dei*, beyond clearly pronouncing a ruling in favour of a trinitarian reading, seems to be primarily concerned—for theological reasons—with rejecting a Christological interpretation of the Theophany. The criticism of Augustine is decisive: it is difficult to admit a revelation of Christ in human form before the Incarnation. His arguments are primarily exegetical: he cites the text of the letter to the Hebrews (13:2), that we have already mentioned, the fact that Lot himself addresses the two angels visiting Sodom as 'Lord,' in the singular, while Abraham converses with the third mysterious character who did not go to the doomed city. In short, the bishop of Hippo wants to underline that the Lord was not less present in the two angels who went to Sodom than in the one who remained to speak with Abraham. Even so, alongside these exegetical arguments, Augustine also advances a dogmatic and critical christological interpretation of Genesis 18, which seemingly fosters an Arian rendition: the privilege of invisibility belongs only to the Father, leaving to Christ (the Word), as a lesser sublime god, the task of appearing in human form. Augustine, while reiterating that every theophany is oriented to the Incarnation of the Son of God, also states that a rigorously scriptural analysis prevents the attribution of all theophanies to the sole person of the Word, as certain Fathers had done before then. Here the bishop of Hippo introduces a trinitarian allusion, veiled but no less real. Thus, because the three divine persons are one God and equally invisible, only a careful analysis of the scriptural text could permit the allocation of any given theophany to a specific person of the Trinity. Now, since in Genesis 18 there is reference to Abraham's three visitors as one in three and three in one; and since there is no allusion to a specific superiority of any one of them, why not assume that it is about recognising, in a visible form, a revelation of trinitarian equality and the unity and identity of substance in three persons? In the *De Abraham* of Ambrose, Augustine upholds this interpretation of the unity and Trinity of

God.[33] If, much later Thomas Aquinas himself will comment on the old formula, '*tres vidit et unum adoravit*', he will do so not so much because of an authoritative reference to Augustine or Ambrose, but because the formula had been introduced directly into the Roman liturgy.

If we have lingered on the analysis of the first six centuries of patristic exegesis regarding the Theophany of Mamre, it is because we find here all the richness of a debate that, in the following centuries, will no longer enjoy the same development or the same vivacity.[34] In the Middle Ages, after a long dispute between the christological and trinitarian interpretations of the theophany of Genesis 18, the second will more often be adopted in opposition to Aryan or semi-Aryan leanings, as already mentioned, towards subordinationism, and also with an eye to pastoral catechesis. The story of Abraham's hospitality often parts from an exegetical analysis to concentrate on seemingly endless details, especially in response to questions of iconographic translation. For example, in medieval theology there would be a prolonged debate trying to clarify if angels really eat or only pretend to do so, (we will return to this question in the rabbinical exegesis). Similarly, there would be much dispute about the identification of each of the three mysterious pilgrims comparing them to the individual persons of the Trinity. From these brief references we can infer that, until the end of the nineteenth century, there are no significant

---

33. *Cf* C Monge, *Dieu hôte. Recherche historique et théologique sur les rituels de l'hospitalité*, 455ff. After Gregor the Great (540–604) and Isidore of Seville (560–636), the formula, 'tres vidit et unum adoravit', is found in Bede the Venerable (ca672–735) and the theological works of Peter Damian (1007–1072), Rupert of Deutz (1075–1129) and William of Chammpeaux (1070–1121).

34. For completeness, we should also include a study of the iconographic traditions of both East and West. However, this would take us too far from our goals. Instead, we can simply point out that, for obvious reasons of iconography, the pictorial interpretations of Genesis 18 always prioritise the Christological interpretation. Moreover, from the twelfth century onward and especially in the late Middle Ages, the importance of Genesis 18 in art is restricted by the hermeneutical principle that the formation of the Old and New Testaments is deeply unitary and that the events and truths of the New Testament have been prefigured in detail in the Old (as Augustine recalled and is quoted by *Dei Verbum* 16: 'What is hidden in the Old Testament is made manifest in the New'). The hospitality of Abraham is often linked with the Annunciation whereas in the 'Bible of the Poor' it most often refers to the Transfiguration.

developments in the history of the exegesis of Genesis 18. There is only a rather persistent adherence to some fundamental propositions.

At the end of the nineteenth century the most critical readings of the biblical text—already timidly proposed in the 'humanist' interpretations of the Renaissance—are systematised, especially by the 'historical-critical' school of Germany. From Wellhausen to Gunkel, from Von Rad and Van Seters to Herbert Haag, the extraordinary contributions of these fathers of modern exegesis radically change our view of the story of Genesis 18–19, as does the rest of the Pentateuch. Structure of the text, language, literary genres and levels of redaction: there is increasing concern to scientifically verify the coherence of the editorial redactions in the context of the literary work as a whole. There is a return to the theory of the influence of pre-biblical traditions. Allegorical and typological readings are gradually dismissed. For example, there is the discovery that a visit of divine beings to a human family (like the visit of Zeus and Hermes to Philemon and Baucis, that inspired Rembrandt) and the destruction of a sinful city (see Troy) are literary motifs very common in Greek literature. Van Seters states that the theme of a divine visit is never mentioned in the prophetic tradition concerning the destruction of cities (Deut 29:23; Isa 13:19; Jer 50:40; Am 4:11). Thus there is strong reason to believe that the source is non-Israelite yet, notwithstanding, is integrated into the literary creation of Genesis 18–19.[35]

We have just illustrated an example of the research that characterizes modern exegesis. Today, no biblical scholar, at least not in the West, would be troubled over a Christological or Trinitarian reading of the theophany of Mamre. This defines a caesura in the history of exegesis, in particular between scholarly exegesis and Christian piety and, consequently, a further estrangement between Christians of the East and of the West.

Such radical changes are found neither in the Jewish nor Islamic histories of interpretation of the story of Abraham's hospitality. However, their perspectives, deeply rooted in the theology of these two religious worlds, offer us a very attractive exegetical approach. We will limit ourselves to the interpretation of the visit of the three pilgrims: can we still speak of a theophany even in the other Abrahamic traditions?

---

35. *Cf* RI Létellier, *Day in Mamre, night in Sodom*, 200.

The theophany of Mamre in the Jewish Tradition

Abraham: The man of God

In the Jewish tradition the story of Abraham's hospitality at Mamre is preceded by a lively account of his origins which deserves to be recalled. We are aware that the Patriarch was born in a milieu of idolatry soon after the events of the tower of Babel (Gen 11:1–9) during the time of Nimrod, the murderous oppressor mentioned in Genesis 10:8-9.[1] After having miraculously escaped a massacre of the firstborn in Nimrod's kingdom, Abraham came to a knowledge of the one true God by a kind of natural revelation, on his own, by contemplating the world and scanning the heavens.[2] Once established in belief, he gradually attained the heights of knowledge and wisdom and became a defender of the true faith by combatting idolatry (this motif borrowed from the Muslim tradition), as well as his father Terah, who was a manufacturer of idols in Nimrod's service. Terah was disinclined to follow his son along the path of monotheism and did nothing to prevent him from being delivered over to the tyrant and thrown into a furnace, as was Daniel and his companions (Dn 3).

---

1. 'Cush became the father of Nimrod who was the first potentate on earth. He was a mighty hunter in the eyes of Yahweh, hence the saying, "Like Nimrod, a mighty hunter in the eyes of Yahweh."'
2. 'For the moment, there are differing versions of the manner and cause of this conversion. Some say that Abraham discovered God when he was very young, after having taken refuge in a cave in the desert; others, more numerous, think instead that the father of believers first worshiped the stars before recognising, at the age of forty-eight, the only true God and creator of the universe' (J-L Ska, *Abramo e i suoi ospiti*, 30).

226 *Strangers With God*

Abraham escaped, however, unscathed, through God's intervention.[3] These legends deal with, and at times elaborate on, existing traditions and symbolic events that characterise the lives of all great personages who are in a privileged relationship with God: a threatened birth, striking signs of divine favour from their earliest years, a call to become a model for a people or for a multitude of peoples.

The midrashic comments on Genesis 18:1–15 are particularly insistent on stressing the link between the conclusion of Genesis 17 and the beginning of Genesis 18:1. Thirteen years after the birth of Ishmael, Abraham is ordered to inscribe on his body, and on that of all his male relatives, the sign of the covenant with God that takes its origin from this period (Gen 17:23–25).[4] Now, in the rabbinic tradition, God took the initiative to make a visit to Abraham on the third day following his circumcision, when the pain was most severe.[5] Here is an excerpt from the Talmud: '[Citing from Gen 18:1] which means: 'In the hottest hour of the day?' Rabbi Hama bar Hanina[45] says: It was the third day after Abraham's circumcision and the Holy of Holies came to have news [about his health]. The Holy of Holies made the sun shine brightly[46] so that this holy man would not be disturbed by guests.[47][6]

---

3. In some versions of this legend, the angel Gabriel is sent to save the Patriarch. This interpretation is based on a midrashic reading of Gen 15:7: 'I am Yahweh, who brought you out of Ur of the Chaldeans.' The Hebrew word '*ûr* can be in fact refer both to the city of Ur (in the region of the Chaldeans) and to a furnace ('*ûr*)) in Aramaic. This apocryphal story would then be based on a play of words (*Cf* J-L Ska, *Abramo e i suoi ospiti,* 31). Still others would translate '*ûr* more precisely as 'fire.'

4. Following circumcision, Abram becomes Abraham. He acquires a new name and a new identity, chastened and chosen. Having been set apart himself, he was able to draw others along the same path of God (*cf* G Dreifuss and J Riemer, *Abraham the Man and the Symbol. A Jungian Interpretation of the Biblical Story* [Wilmette: Chiron Publications, 1995], 57).

5. Details about the poor health of the Patriarch are important in attracting the reader's attention to the fact that he did not think, at the time, of acting prophetically or, more simply, of any imminent hospitality. He was not even in the best condition to devote himself to prayer or mystical ecstasy. In short, we have a general framework that emphasizes the gratuitousness of the divine.

6. TB, *Baba Metsia* 86b, cited by K Hruby, 'Exégèse rabbinique et exégèse patristique', in *Revue des sciences religieuses,* 47 (1973): 341–369 (363). The entry on 'the hottest part of the day' has several other rabbinic commentaries, always with very interesting details. A summary of these interpretations can be found in the writings of Rabbi Jacob Butts (1689–1732) of Constantinople. He is the

According to other midrash, God would have first manifested to the angels the intention to pay a visit to Abraham, and they would have tried to dissuade him without success.[7] Jean-Louis Ska says that the midrash establishes a cause and effect link between the episode of circumcision and the visit of the Lord, rather than simply being juxtaposed as in the biblical story.[8] Rabbi Elijah Munk explains that

---

author of the first Ladin commentary on Genesis, drawn up for the benefit of the Jewish populations of the Ottoman Empire who were unfamiliar with Hebrew. In the first volume of his work (1730), Rabbi Butts offers different interpretations of Genesis 18:1 and its unusual setting. The first is a kind of medical explanation: Abraham is suffering from a severe inflammation due to the circumcision and needs the warmth of the sun to allow the wound to heal and to avoid infection. A second explanation is given by a Sephardic sage: God had sent great heat on the earth because it would have been lacking in respect to his faithful servant if, while he was suffering, the rest of creation were perfectly at ease . . . (cf Rabbi Yaakov Culi, 'MeAm Lo'ez', in Rabbi Aryeh Kaplan, translator, The Torah Antology, The Patriarchs, 'VaYera', II [New York: Maznaim Publishing Corporation, 1977], 166). The Zohar or Kabbalah, the foundational text on Jewish mystical thought drawn up in Castile towards the end of the thirteenth century by Moses of Leon, has further interpretations of this introductory verse of Genesis 18. The formula 'the hottest part of the day' refers to the day of judgment, burning like a furnace to separate the soul from the body. Yahweh would therefore have been manifested to Abraham at the time when a man leaves this world—at the time of the great judgment—because the Patriarch could not leave this life without having first seen the Shekinah (the glory or presence of God). It must be stated that this eschatological interpretation is not very widespread among the great commentators of the Talmud.

7. This urgency on the part of God emphasizes the importance of the obligation to visit the sick: Rabbi Culi remembers that Yahweh did no more than what is ordinarily humanly expected (Culi, 'MeAm Lo'ez', 158). In Hebrew the precept of visiting the sick is called bokkur cholim: the one who does so is accompanied by a special blessing from God and is preserved from future suffering and punishment after death. Visiting the sick also means taking care of his material needs and, if necessary, being available to clean his house and performing other useful services. While visiting the sick it is necessary to sit at his side, never at his head, because that is where the Divine Presence, coming into his house, resides. We ought to pray to this same Presence, in no matter what tongue, that the invalid might be healed. When someone falls ill, family members must come to visit as soon as they receive the news (and friends the very next day); all others must wait at least three days. This is only the most significant portion of the precepts concerning the praiseworthy act of visiting the sick (Culi, 'MeAm Lo'ez', 159–160).

8. J-L Ska, Abramo e i suoi ospiti, 32. The continuity of the two episodes is attested, according to rabbinic interpretation, by avoiding Abraham's proper name and replacing it with the personal pronoun: 'Yahweh appeared to him . . .' It might also have been written this way to avoid placing the Patriarch in a dominant position with respect to God.

Abraham, after performing the rite of circumcision, feared that this covenantal sign might raise a barrier between himself and the others, condemning him to isolation.[9] According to Genesis Rabba,[10] Abraham openly complained about this situation of isolation: 'While I was uncircumcised travelers passed by me'—and Yahweh seems to confirm this impression because the story continues: 'While you were uncircumcised you were among the uncircumcised', replied the Holy One, blessed be He, 'now I and my household will reveal ourselves to you.'"[11] So the Everlasting One is manifested to Abraham so that he might understand God's closeness and the concern for his health after he was circumcised.

> The Talmud continues:

> When the Holy One appeared to Abraham, [he] was seated, as it is said [cf. Gen 18:2]. [. . .] [At the sight of the Lord], Abraham rose. The Blessed One [then] said, do not bother to get up! Remain seated! As [the Scripture, Ps 110:1] says: "Yahweh's oracle to you, my Lord, 'Sit at my right hand'" Abraham [then] said, is it permissible for me to remain seated while you are standing? The Blessed One said, do not trouble yourself! You are one hundred years old: remain seated.[12]

Although this quote speaks openly of a direct manifestation of the Everlasting One and Abraham apparently seems to be conscious of the identity of his visitors,[13] it is very strange that, while the context is that of an apparent theophany, there are no specific acts of worship, not even the construction of an altar, as generally happens in similar circumstances.[14]

---

9. *Cf* E Munk, 'La Genèse 18, 1', in *La voix de la Torah. Commentaire du Pentateuque* (Paris: Fondation Samuel et Odette Levy, 1976), 178.

10. This treatise is the oldest exegetical midrash: a systematic commentary on the Book of Genesis (*B'reshith Rabba)*. It contains very ancient material although its preparation period is uncertain.

11. T Federici, *Commento alla Genesi, Berešit Rabba*, XLVIII, 9, 376.

12. TB, *Baba Metsia* 86b, cited by K Hruby, 'Exégèse rabbinique et exégèse patristique', 364.

13. We may have here, as in the biblical account, an editorial note for the reader but this interpretation does not convey the idea that Abraham knows who his visitors are.

14. The answer to this objection, however, might be found in the sacredness of hospitality which, according to the Talmud, largely replaces every act of worship of the Divine Presence.

The theophany of Mamre in the Jewish Tradition   229

The issue is understanding who actually appeared to Abraham, because Genesis Rabba says: "'[Abraham] saw three men standing in front of him' [. . .] and 'saw' the Shekinah and 'saw' the angels . . .'"[15] It seems necessary to distinguish two moments in this event: in the first instance it is the *Shekinah* that is manifest to the Patriarch; in the second there are three angels. The *Midrash ha-gadol* clearly testifies: '[Abraham said]: "My lord, if I find favor with you, kindly do not pass your servant by' (Gen 18:3). He then asked the *Shekinah* to expect the arrival of the guests (the angels)'".[16] Rachi offers the same interpretation of Genesis 18:3;[17] we will return again to this theme when speaking of the Jewish and Muslim interpretation of the *Shekinah*.

It is quite beyond doubt that the greater majority of the rabbinical traditions consider that Abraham has seen both the Divine Presence and three angels. The problem remains of determining what the relationship is between these two presences or these two visions.

The *Shekinah* and the three messengers

We must recognise that the Christian tradition seems much more preoccupied with establishing an intimate relationship between the Divine Presence and the three mysterious personages than does the Jewish tradition, even to the point of identifying them.

According to Tryphon, whose sentiments are recorded by Justin in his famous *Dialogue*, the Jews would treat the relationship as one of pure temporal succession: God appeared to Abraham first, before the arrival of the three (angels). This view is supported by the Talmud and the *midrashim,* which speak of the passing of the Everlasting One (the *Shekinah* or the Word of the Lord, that is, the *memra*); after the first withdrew, then came the other three personages.[18] The Talmud,

---

15. T.Federici, *Commento alla Genesi, Berešit Rabba,* XLVIII, 9, 376.
16. *Midrash ha-gadol,* 53, cited by K Hruby, 'Exégèse rabbinique et exégèse patristique', 365.
17. *Cf* 'Genèse-xviii-Vayyêra', in *Le Commentaire de Rachi sur le Pentateuque,* I (Paris: Fondation Samuel et Odette Levy, 1964), 101.
18. Many rabbis, including Rachi, insist that Abraham waited for the Shekinah in order to accommodate the three pilgrims who appeared soon after: he describes, in essence, a temporal sequence between the two receptions. He also recalls once again the pre-eminence of hospitality and works of charity above the religious duty of conversing with the Divine Glory or the performance of an act of worship (we have already mentioned the Jewish vision of hospitality as a mitzvah or religious imperative that precedes the practice of worship.

230   *Strangers With God*

for its part, specifies the functions of the three angels; here is the story
according to the version of Pseudo-Jonathan:

> [Abraham] looked up and saw three angels appearing in human
> form, standing in front of him. They were sent to accomplish
> three tasks; because no angel can be sent to perform more
> than one mission. One angel was commissioned to announce
> that Sarah would give birth to a son; the second was to save
> Lot; and the third to destroy Sodom and Gomorra.[19]

Three angels are sent for three separate tasks to be accomplished,
then, because, as the commentators point out, the same messenger
cannot undertake two commissions at the same time (nor are two
angels ever charged with the same mission).[20] The angels, each in
its own competence, determine the progression of events, giving
the account its internal cohesion. They unfold the action of God
which manifests itself first of all by an intention or a plan (the
announcement of the birth of a son to Abraham and Sarah) and then
effective movement (deliverance and destruction). The three terms,
announcement, deliverance and destruction, must be comprehended
in a unified manner. We have here, perhaps, the beginning of an
answer to the question about the relationship between God and the
three messengers, especially as they appear to the eyes of Abraham.
We must return to the first verses of chapter 18 of Genesis, which
states: 'Yahweh appeared to him', then continues 'he saw three men
standing near him'. The interpretation of the story as a whole gave
rise to a vigorous dispute between Maimonides and Rabbi Ramban.[21]
Maimonides maintains that Abraham had a prophetic vision, as
stated in Genesis 18:1. The description of the visit of the angels, the
Patriarch's welcome, the care he gave them, his hospitality, as well as
the announcement to Sarah, are not actual facts but representations
of a vision described in detail.[22] While Ramban endorses the principle
proposed by Maimonides: that in the Bible, when we speak of seeing

---

19. R Le Déaut, *Targum du Pentateuque*, 185.
20. Cf. *Le Commentaire de Rachi sur le Pentateuque*, 101.
21. Rabbi Moshe ben Nachman (ca 1195–1270), better known as Ramban, is
    not to be confused with Rambam, an acrostic used for Rabbi Moshe ben
    Maimon, otherwise known as Maimonides (1135–1204), who was almost his
    contemporary. Ramban is the author of a voluminous commentary on the Torah.
22. Cf. Maimonide, *La guida dei perplessi* (Torino: UTET, 2005).

or hearing angels, it is always in the context of a vision, because angels are not perceptible by the human senses; this author also raises objections to this principle. There are several biblical scenes, he says, that, while appearing to belong to the genre of a vision, have surprise endings. For example, as in the case of the afore-mentioned Jacob wrestling with the angel (Gen 32), why, asks Rabbi Ramban, would Jacob have begun to limp at dawn, if he had only seen a vision and not been in an actual physical fight? Similarly, why would Jacob have said, 'I have seen God face to face and I have survived' (Gen 32:31) if he was only dreaming? Ramban explains the account at Mamre along the same lines: There are difficult aspects to explain in a classical vision, because angels are not normally detectable by the human senses. At Mamre, Ramban says, the angels were given ordinary human appearances, making possible to be seen due to their exceptional nature. God, therefore, sent his angels in human appearance to satisfy Abraham's desire, distressed that he had no guests to welcome after his circumcision: it would have been an *ad hoc* revelation and not a true prophetic vision.

The Hellenistic rabbinical exegesis: Josephus and Philo of Alexandria

The more literal exegeses of the twelfth and thirteenth century point back to the more allegorical interpretation of texts which arose during the time of Hellenistic Judaism; here Flavius Josephus and Philo of Alexandria are the major representatives. Firstly, according to this school of interpretation Abraham is considered more a righteous sage than a model rabbi. In other words, the Patriarch is described as the perfect example of a life ordered by the light of reason and faith (truthfully, the authors speak explicitly of religion), and it is in this perspective that one must understand the commentaries of Josephus and Philo concerning the meeting at Mamre.

Josephus (who died around 100 AD) devotes eleven chapters of the first book of his *Antiquities of the Jews*[23] to the ancestors of Israel, to demonstrate to the Greek world the excellence of the traditions of his people.[24] We bring our attention to the first part of the interpretation given by the Jewish apologist about the story of Mamre.

---

23. For an English translation of this work, see *The Works of Josephus: Complete and Unabridged,* translated by William Whiston, Hendrickson, 1987.
24. Cf J-L Ska, *Abramo e i suoi ospiti,* 37ff.

> (196) When God had thus resolved concerning the Sodomites,[25] Abraham, as he sat by the oak of Mambre, at the door of his tent,[26] saw three angels; and, thinking them to be strangers,[27] he rose up and saluted them, and desired they would accept of an entertainment, and abide with him; (197) to which when they agreed, he ordered cakes of meal to be made presently: and when he had slain a calf, he roasted it, and brought it to them, as they sat under the oak. Now they made a show of eating.[28]

This presentation, as Jean-Louis Ska observes, seems less lively and colorful as the original reading in Genesis: Josephus suppresses all the dialogue and his version becomes a kind of commentary of the narrator who elaborates on the material in his own way.[29] There is no reference to a solemn appearance of the *Shekinah*; the presence of the Most High is only alluded to in the judgment pronounced against Sodom. Josephus also disregards, in the first part of the story, any establishment of a direct relationship between the mission of the angels and the care of God for this faithful servant. Uncertainty about the true identity of the pilgrims is maintained to the end to create a very prosaic reading of the tale. The theme of hospitality toward strangers predominates over all others and the ritual of welcome holds center stage. One reported detail brings us to the heart of a

---

25. Josephus anticipates the intimation of divine judgement against Sodom between the account of the circumcision (*cf* Gen 17), to which there is no allusion in Mambre, and Abraham's hospitality. This arrangement makes it simpler and more straightforward than the biblical narrative concerning this issue. Two angels take leave of the Patriarch who then begins to intercede with the third in favour of Lot's city (Josephus, consistent with the classical rabbinic interpretation, highlights the double mission: one of the angels announces the impending birth of an heir to Abraham, and the others, the destruction of Sodom).

26. An alternate translation is 'courtyard,' which allows one to imagine Abraham being settled and well situated in his own house, as would any wealthy man of the first century BCE.

27. Josephus brings together the view of the reader and that of the main actor: How could Abraham regard as foreign visitors whom he had just seen in angelic form? Actually, the biblical text speaks first of 'three men' who only explicitly become 'two angels' when two of the three appear to Lot. The Jewish historian combines the two moments.

28. *The Works of Josephus: Complete and Unabridged*, 'The Antiquities of the Jews', Book 1, Chapter 11, 2.

29. Cf J-L Ska, *Abramo e i suoi ospiti*, 39–40.

The theophany of Mamre in the Jewish Tradition   233

centuries-old exegetical debate among the rabbis: have the three angels really eaten and drunk at Abraham's table? Josephus agrees with the majority of rabbis in saying that they only pretended to eat. The Babylonian Talmud is rather dismissive of the issue:

> R. Tanhûm b. Hanilaï says that a man should always follow the custom of the location. When Moses ascended to the [celestial] heights, he did not take bread;[30] and when angels descended from there to perform a[n earthly] service, they ate. Did they [really] eat? What do you think? Rather, they had the appearance of eating and drinking.[31]

The same idea is found in Genesis Rabba, which states that the angels, by accepting Abraham's invitation to a meal honoured his generosity, but only pretended to eat, although the food miraculously disappears from the table.[32] To further clarify this question, apparently critical, the midrash includes the story of the angel who appeared to Manoah, the father of Samson, to announce the birth of his son (Jug 13). The text states that Manoah wanted to entertain the messenger of God with a meal (13:15), but was categorically refused (13:16). The midrash questions the difference between the behaviour of this heavenly visitor and Abraham's guests:

> Why is it that the angels who brought Sarah the [good] news that she would conceive [a son] ate while this one [the angel who appeared to Manoah] did not? Because the angels who appeared to Abraham looked like ordinary wayfarers at first. When he brought them into his home and, according to his desire, invited them to eat, they did not want to refuse his hospitality. They delivered their message after they had eaten, [thus] avoiding a semblance of being paid for their message. But the angel [that appeared to Manoah] gave his

---

30. This is a reference to the episode of Moses' encounter on Sinai when, because he lived only by the presence of God, did not eat for several days (*cf* Deut 9:9). As a man, he could share, for a certain period of time, the prerogative of those living in the presence of the *Shekinah*. Analogously and inversely, the messengers of God could honor the meal of hospitality offered by Abraham, although they were not fed by it.

31. TB, *Baba Metsia*, 86b, cited by K Hruby, 'Exégèse rabbinique et exégèse patristique', 367.

32. T Federici, *Commento alla Genesi, Beresit Rabba*, 379–380.

234   *Strangers With God*

> message first; if he had eaten [later, with Manoah], it would
> have looked as though he had been rewarded for his message.
> Consequently, he refrained from eating.[33]

In fact, this text is not so much interested in whether or not angels eat, as it is concerned with the question of dissociating prophetic service and angelic mission from any need to reward them. If it is God who is the origin of these messages and not the messengers themselves, then it is God first who we must thank, if possible, by offering the worship of a sacrificial victim (such as, among others, Abraham himself will do).[34] This midrashic reflection is nevertheless interesting because it highlights the need to honour generous hospitality. It is not inconceivable that, in this exceptional circumstance, the angels themselves may have been able to eat what Abraham offered them, rewarding him in this way for his generosity.[35]

Philo of Alexandria (13–54 CE) speaks of the patriarch Abraham in several of his works. He is a master of an allegorical interpretation of the facts, offering to the reader of the Bible stories of its protagonists in his own exclusive manner and beyond mere human perception. Speaking of the meal at Mamre, Philo seems to offer a kind of compromise between the more radical exegetical positions. In the section of his *De Abrahamo* consecrated to this scene (which is too lengthy to take up in its entirety), our author distills the essentials of his allegorical exegesis. With even greater liberty than Josephus, he ignores many details in his presentation. This negligence permits him to cast into evidence only that which he intends to highlight. In the first part of the story (Gen 18:1-8) there is a gradual shift from a

---

33. Cited by K Hruby, 'Exégèse rabbinique et exégèse patristique', 368.

34. This explanation does not apply to Manoah, the future father of Samson, and his wife. They, in fact, had not recognised a messenger of God in the angelic presence (Jug 13:16b), which is why they wanted to reward his service. Once they discovered his true identity during the offering of a sacrifice of praise, they realized that they had escaped death despite having seen God face to face (cf Jug 13:20–23).

35. On this question, Genesis Rabba noted curiously that Michael and Gabriel trembled at the prospect of having to eat at the table of Abraham (49, 14); but Yahweh comforted them, promising to send them a spirit that would have consumed all the food before the eyes of Abraham, without the Patriarch realizing a supernatural intervention (for further details on this topic, cf D Goodman, 'Do Angels Eat?' in *Journal of Jewish Studies*, XXXVII (1986): 160–175).

literal to an allegorical reading. The episode at Mamre is presented as a simple humanitarian act and Abraham is made a model of dedication.[36]

> [. . .] One day, at noon, seeing three travellers whom he mistook for men—they were closer in nature to God but in a concealed manner—he ran up to them, insistently asking that they not pass by his tent and share his hospitality, as dictated by custom. They, realizing the sincerity of his purpose—less by his words than by the thoughts of his heart—agreed without hesitation.[37]

The beginning of this narrative provides a perfect framework for a Philonian formulation: it insists on the utter sincerity of the generosity of the host who welcomes that cannot be refused and, at the same time, is totally discrete with regard to the identity of the visitors, not saying much even for the sake of the reader. Following are further comments not mentioned earlier:

> The three guests rejoiced exceedingly because of the ardent welcome with which they were received and the quality of the meal their host had prepared for them; their emulation was intense and unlimited: they offered him a reward that exceeded his expectations, promising the birth of his own rightful son the following year. This promise was given by the mouth of one, the most important of the three, because the three speaking together would have seemed less wise.[38]

Philo diverts attention from the meal as such (after having stressed, however, its abundant generosity), as if to avoid the debate on the eating habits of the angels.[39] It is the level of the exchange that is highlighted:

---

36. As Jean-Louis Ska states very well, Philo, respecting the details and intentions of the biblical account, traces the actions of Abraham, which are gradually communicated like a virus to the characters that surround him (J-L Ska, *Abramo e i suoi ospiti*, 44).
37. J Gorez, editor, *De Abrahamo*, nn 107–113 (Paris: Cerf, 1966), 68–69.
38. J Gorez, editor, *De Abrahamo*, n 110, 69.
39. Indeed, Philo says that the angels are nourished by the magnificent generosity and benevolence of Abraham and not by the food that is actually spread on the table. The idea is clarified as follows: '[. . .] The banquet was as it should be, the guests celebrating by showing their host the artlessness of those who eat well,

The guests give back to Abraham, who had welcomed and honored them beyond the requirements of human conventions, the reward for his hospitality, which likewise surpasses mere human expectations. Abraham practiced hospitality, which was an act of humanitarianism, but 'believing, at first, that the guest or guests he welcomed were only human, Abraham actually received and acknowledged the deity. Instead of mere humanitarianism, he exercised piety'.[40] By invoking the very identity of the visitors, Philo attains the culmination of his exegetical investigation and, for this reason, abandons a simple literal exposition for allegory. What did Abraham see, then, by the Oak of Mamre, according to Philo?

> In fact—he writes—at the center, as some, close to the truth, would say, he saw the Father of the Universe, who is called in Sacred Scripture, 'The One Who Is' while at his side were the oldest power and the one closest to his being, the creative power and ruling power. The name of the creative power is God. It is through him, in fact, that he defines and arranges the universe. The name of the ruling power is Lord—as is right for the one who governs and commands all that exists.[41]

In this metaphysical explanation, Philo comes to speak of the One without specifically mentioning the Trinity because, ultimately, the Three are always One Being: the center in its own essence with its two main activities at its side (creation on the left and sovereignty over the

---

turning towards him without congratulations and giving the discourse required by the occasion. Another remarkable thing was that, without having taken drink, they appeared as men who drink and, without having taken food, looked as if they had eaten. Yet that is secondary. The most important thing, the most extraordinary, is that although incorporeal, they took on human form in order to grant a favor to a righteous man. In fact, what other reason was there for this miracle than to allow this wise man to perceive, more clearly, that the Father had acknowledged that he was, in fact, wise?' (J Gorez, editor, *De Abrahamo*, n 117–118, 71–73). Philo wants to communicate to the reader the idea of a God who, far from despoiling what is human, miraculously takes on the guise of a man, and by so doing, demonstrates grateful nearness to a person of faith who knows how to care for his fellow men.

40. J Cazeaux, 'Le repas de Mambré dans le 'De Abrahamo' de Philon', in M Quesnel, Y Blanchard, and MC Tassin, editors, *Nourriture et repas dans les milieux juifs et chrétiens de l'Antiquité* (Paris: Cerf, 1999), 55–73 (70).

41. J Gorez, *De Abrahamo*, n 121, 72–73.

world on the right). It is a surprising interpretation that allows our author to explain, to some extent, the continuous passage of the text from the singular to the plural. The fact that Abraham invites a guest (in the singular) to accept his hospitality (Gen 18:3), despite having seen three persons, offers an unprecedented interpretative key to the encounter at Mamre as a sort of irruption of the divine (of which unity is the characteristic feature) that surpasses the human welcome. Cazeaux writes:

> Abraham is seated at 'noon'—for all around and about him the One is paramount. The account of Genesis continues with the story of Lot being rescued from Sodom as Sodom is unprecedentedly chastised. Here we see the two distinct powers [the two angels] acting alone. It is the anticipation of the following episode, the destruction of Sodom and the rescue of Lot, that gives Philo warrant to interpret the meaning of the number three here.[42]

Conclusion

Let's return to the initial question on this path to the heart of the rabbinic exegesis of the theophany at Mamre, that is, the relationship between the three mysterious personages and the Divine Presence itself. We could say that, in his allegorical interpretation, Philo is significantly close to the Christian reading of the Fathers. The *Shekinah* or presence of God is not only an inaugural appearance, rather, incorporates a threefold angelic apparition. From Philo we understand Zohar's commentary on Gen 18:16[43] more easily: that Abraham fulfilled his obligation as a host to accompany his guests part of the way to Sodom. A question arises: if Abraham knew that the three mysterious pilgrims were angels and not just passing travelers, why did he accompany them? Rabbi Eleazar said:

> Although Abraham knew, he acted toward them according to ordinary custom. He received them into his house as is done with guests; everything depends on it. Now—continues Rabbi Eleazar—while walking alongside them, the Holy One, blessed

---

42. J Cazeaux, 'Le repas de Mambré dans le "De Abrahamo de Philon"', 72.
43. 'Then the men got up and went towards Sodom; and Abraham went with them to bid them farewell.'

be He, was revealed to Abraham, as it is said: 'Now Yahweh wondered, "Shall I conceal from Abraham what I am about to do?"' (Gen 18:17). The words 'Now Yahweh', designates He and His Court because the Holy One, blessed be He, went with them. Come and see: when a man accompanies his neighbour to his home he awakens the *Shekinah* to join him and walk along the way with him to protect him. That is why a man should escort his guest to his home; by doing so he unites him to the *Shekinah* and the *Shekinah* to him.[44]

The presence of God, of which no mention had been made during the festive encounter with Abraham and Sarah and their mysterious guests (indeed it seems to have been withdrawn in favor of the hospitality shown), had never ceased to be with His servant Abraham; seemingly absent, it was One and Three in the action of God's messengers.

---

44. C Mopsik, translator, *Le Zohar. Genèse*, II (Paris: Verdier, Paris 1994), 79–80.

The theophany at Mamre in the Islamic tradition

Occurrences in the Qur'an: similarities and differences

The three great scenes of God's appearance to Abraham by the Oak of Mamre and the announcement of the birth of Isaac; Abraham's intercession on behalf of Sodom; and the story of Lot and the destruction of the city as found in Chapters 18 and 19 of the Book of Genesis, have important echoes in the Qur'an as well, although the latter is much more restrained and terse in its description. We propose the following Qur'anic texts according to a probable chronological order of revelation.[1]

We begin with Qr LI (called *al-Dhāriyāt*, 'The Scattering' (or twenty angels), 24–36:

> [24] Has the story of Abraham's honorable guests reached you?[25] When they entered upon him, they said, 'Peace!' He said, 'Peace, strangers.'[26] Then he slipped away to his family, and brought a fatted calf,[27] He set it before them. He said, 'Will you not eat?'[28] And he harbored fear of them. They said, 'Do not fear' and they announced to him the good news of a knowledgeable boy.[29] His wife came forward crying. She clasped her face and said, 'A barren old woman?'[30] They said, 'Thus spoke your Lord. He is the Wise, the Knowing.'[31] He

---

1. If we accept the hypothesis of Noeldeke (*cf* T Noeldeke, *Geschichte des Qorans*, G Olms, Hildesheim 1961), each of these texts belong to all three of the periods in which manual redaction of the Qur'an took place. Now, knowing that the composition of the *suras* is so complex and that these latter may contain fragments attributed to different periods of preparation, it may be methodologically useful to consider the accounts of Abraham's hospitality in the Qur'an according to a generally chronological progression.

240   *Strangers With God*

said, 'What is your business, O envoys?'[32] They said, 'We are sent to a people guilty of sin.'[33] 'To unleash upon them rocks of clay.' [34] 'Marked by your Lord for the excessive.'[35] We evacuated all the believers who were in it. [36] But found in it only one household of Muslims.'

The second reference is from Qr XV (*al-Hijr*), 51–60:

[51] And inform them of the guests of Abraham.[52] When they entered upon him, and said, 'Peace.' He said, 'We are wary of you.'[53] They said, 'Do not fear; we bring you good news of a boy endowed with knowledge.'[54] He said, 'Do you bring me good news, when old age has overtaken me? What good news do you bring?'[55] They said, 'We bring you good news in truth, so do not despair.'[56] He said, 'And who despairs of his Lord's mercy but the lost?' [57] He said, 'So what is your business, O envoys?'[58] They said, 'We are sent to a sinful people.'[59] Except for the family of Lot; we will save them all.'[60] Except for his wife. We have determined that she will be of those who lag behind.'

The third reference, especially important, is from Qr XI (*Hūd*), 69–76:

[69] Our messengers came to Abraham with good news. They said, 'Peace.' He said, 'Peace.' Soon after, he came with a roasted calf.[70] But when he saw their hands not reaching toward it, he became suspicious of them, and conceived a fear of them. They said, 'Fear not, we were sent to the people of Lot.'[71] His wife was standing by, so she laughed. And we gave her good news of Isaac; and after Isaac, Jacob.[72] She said, 'Alas for me. Shall I give birth, when I am an old woman, and this, my husband, is an old man? This is truly a strange thing.'[73] They said, 'Do you marvel at the decree of God? The mercy and blessings of God are upon you, O people of the house. He is Praiseworthy and Glorious.'[74] When Abraham's fear subsided, and the good news had reached him, he started pleading with Us concerning the people of Lot.[75] Abraham was gentle, kind, penitent.[76] 'O Abraham, refrain from this. The command of your Lord has come; they have incurred an irreversible punishment.'

We cite one last quote taken from Qr XXIX (*al-'Ankabūt*, 'The Spider'), 31–32:

> [31] And when our envoys brought Abraham the good news, they said, 'We are going to destroy the people of this town; its people are wrongdoers.'[32] He said, 'Yet Lot is in it.' They said, 'We are well aware of who is in it. We will save him, and his family, except for his wife, who will remain behind.'

The account in the Qur'an is in many ways very similar to that of the Bible.[2] The plot, for example, is virtually identical and the stories sometimes coincide in detail.[3] But if the similarities are undeniable, neither are there differences lacking.

The text of the Qur'an, as compared to the Bible, is extremely concise and moderate: it does not directly name the guilty people soon to be destroyed; there is no link between the circumcision of the Patriarch and the scene of hospitality at Mamre;[4] Sarah is always and solely identified as 'the wife of Abraham;' nor does the Qur'an specify either the number or the identity of the personages seen by Patriarch[5]. Among the features specific to the Qur'an we note that the suras do not precisely locate the incident and the setting is very

---

2. It is certainly not easy to say whether or to what extent the *suras* of the Qur'an have been inspired by Gen 18 or taken from other sources common to the same biblical or midrashic traditions. It is similarly difficult to prove, one way or another, whether or not it is a different version of an identical original event. However, neither is it absurd to think that it is; a certain compatibility of the stanzas would seem to prove it. The fact that the same biblical text has been taken, as it is, with some more or less important variations in more than one *sura*, produces an inter-textual quality within the Qur'an itself. That is why it is not without interest to approach the various texts of the Islamic tradition chronologically.

3. The great commentators of the Qur'an, such as Al-Tabarī and Al-Ya'qūbī, repeat almost verbatim some passages from the Talmudic tradition, limiting themselves to merely adding a short explanation or adaptation of elements easily known in the Jewish tradition, for their Islamic audience.

4. On this question we refer to R Firestone, *Journeys in Holy Lands. The Evolution of the Abraham-Ishmael Legends in Islamic Exegesis* (Albany: State University of New York Press, 1990), which also underlines the difficulty in an Islamic context to conceive of a God who will travel solely to visit his faithful suffering servant (55).

5. Some commentators have seen Michael and Gabriel among the angels; others have identified them as Michael, Gabriel and Raphael, appearing as a young man of great beauty.

242   *Strangers With God*

static (only twice is there any indication of movement: once when the messengers enter Abraham's dwelling—Qr XV, 52 and Qr LI, 25; and again when the Patriarch leaves and returns with the roasted calf—Qr XI, 69). There is no description of the preparation of the meal of hospitality; the menu is limited to a roasted calf and no loaves. Despite the Patriarch's desire to intercede, there is no trace of it on behalf of the city to be utterly destroyed; for it would seem as if he were trying to bend the will of the Lord. Abraham is reproved for his veiled attempt and, unlike what happens in the biblical version, the Patriarch does not insist, but submits; he is the model Muslim, showing perfect submission, the personification of an original monotheism which pre-existed both Judaism and Christianity.[6] Therefore, the economy of the details described and the simplicity of language in the story as told in the Qur'an is not necessarily at the expense of the strength of the message. In this sense, we do not totally agree with Jean-Louis Ska when he speaks of a certain psychological limitation in his description of the personages in the Qur'an.[7] An excellent article by Anthony H. Johns devoted to *Mafātīh al-Ghayb* ('The keys of the unknowable'[8]), a Qur'anic commentary by Al-Rāzī[9] whose title

---

6. Cf E Platti, 'Un Credo musulman', in *Le Monde de la Bible,* 115 (1998): 58 e Id., 'L'islam, "la religion d'Abraham"', in *Le Monde de la Bible,* 140 (2002): 39.

7. 'The Qur'an allows the personages less psychological space and they are first of all instruments of the divine will' (J-L Ska, *Abramo e i suoi ospiti,* 74). While the second part of the statement taken alone merits repeating, the delicacy of certain psychological and pedagogical traits which touch on the interpersonal relationships of the actors in the scene is quite surprising!

8. An expression in the Qur'an (Qr VI, 59) referring to the Word of Revelation that is most frequently replaced by the formula *al-Tafsīr al-Kabīr* ('The Great Commentary').

9. Fakhr al-Dīn Al-Rāzī is among the best known of Islam's theologians and exegetes. Born in 1149-50 at Rayy (now Iran), he died in 1209 in Herāt in today's Afghanistan, where he is still venerated at his tomb. The works of Al-Rāzī are encyclopedic, but the greater part of his texts is on the *kalām* (literally, the Word, or speculative theology), philosophy and exegesis. His most significant work remains the *Mafātīh al-Ghayb* (French edition Bulak 1279–1289/1862–1872, 6 volumes, Le Caire 1310/1892, 8 volumes. It was republished in 1327 of the Islamic era that corresponds to 1909 of the Christian era) in which the author imparts his entire culture, alongside his philosophical and religious thought. This work belongs to the genre of a commentary; in it the author often tries to connect the Qur'anic verses and, for each question asked, expounds the differing opinions of merit. For further details about this author and his works, we refer to GC Anawati, 'Fakhr al-Dīn al-Rāzī', in *Encyclopédie de l'Islam,* II, 770–773 and to R Arnaldez, 'L'œuvre de Fakhr al-Dīn al-Rāzī, commentateur du Coran et philosophe', in *Cahiers de Civilisation Mediévale* 11 (1960): 307–323.

is already very evocative (*Al-Rāzī's Treatment of the Qur'anic Episodes Telling of Abraham and His Guests: Qur'anic Exegesis with a Human Face*[10]), inspires us with the following considerations.

Al-Razi and the pedagogy of a transcendent God

Al-Razi presents a fresh look at the account of Abraham's hospitality and the announcement of the punishment due to Sodom as he analyses, phrase by phrase, the Qur'anic *suras* from an Islamic perspective. The author's learning goes well with his style as a great preacher and a spirituality that reaches the heights of mysticism. We limit ourselves to highlighting only a few aspects. There are, first of all, elements which restore a certain substance to the dynamics of the hospitable encounter which, in comparison to the biblical account,

---

Box 8 Divine Omnipotence and Human Psychology in the Context of the Qur'an

It is a common literary device for the bearer of bad news to carefully prepare its recipient to accept it nobly by first announcing glad tidings or simply by softening the offending blow with consoling words or gestures, so as to mitigate the pain aroused. This is especially true of the Qur'an (sura XV, 52–56 is not an isolated incident). If the human actors in the Qur'an, on the one hand, often seem at the mercy of divine omnipotence; on the other, their reactions and emotions are not concealed but described in a very lively and unconventional style. For example, Sarah's reactions, the wife of the patriarch Abraham, as presented in the Qur'an, are much more expressive and explicit than those more discretely depicted in the Bible: she cries out, she grasps her face, she shows her feelings openly (cf. Qr LI, 29; Qr XI, 72). The Qur'anic description has the merit of presenting the mood of the characters very effectively, if concise: as in the fear that takes hold of Abraham after he notices that his mysterious guests did not eat the roasted calf that he had brought in their honor. Al-Ṣan'ani recalls that if a guest does not accept the offered food, the host will think, firstly, that he did not value it or considered the meal not well prepared. Secondly, the rejection of a friendly gesture is of such gravity that

---

10. *Cf* AH Johns, 'Al-Rāzī's Treatment of the Qur'anic Episodes Telling of Abraham and His Guests: Qur'anic Exegesis with a Human Face', in *Mélanges de l'Institut Dominicain d'Études Orientales*, 17 (1986): 81–114.

one could legitimately fear the evil intentions of the welcomed guest. Al-Rāzī emphasizes the delicate psychological response of the angels that attenuates the effect of their behavior, seemingly disrespectful of the Patriarch's generous hospitality: after having reassured him, they announce the birth of a child, a boy, wise (features that reinforce the uniqueness of the gift), delaying the moment of the complete manifestation of the terrible message of the impending doom of Sodom and its inhabitants. Yet their pedagogical sagacity, aimed at reducing the impact of the divine Otherness on human perception, does not eliminate the immeasurable distance between the two worlds. In a Qur'anic context, any anthropomorphic view of God's universe, any attempt to grasp what is beyond the visible, is not even conceivable as a form of imperfect, temporary or strict analogical interpretation. Access to the invisible passes solely through a radical asceticism of the visible and not by any mediation of the visible. In other words, according to the Islamic view, God is, by intention, radically inaccessible except to one who contemplates God's name and God's actions. Even so, it cannot be forgotten that no name renders in fullness the essence of God, although some names, such as 'the Merciful One,' reveal one of the attributes of God's essence.

seem quite neglected in the Qur'an, as already mentioned. Guests and visitors, says Al-Razi, are honored in several ways. Abraham responds appropriately to the greeting of the pilgrims, still unknown strangers (Qr LI, 25), and places himself at their service in a state of confusion and anxiety, as well as of surprise at the unexpected visit ('When they came to him and said, "Peace", he replied: "Truly for us, we are afraid of you"' (Qr XV, 52). The exchange of greetings is critical in ceremonial hospitality and especially in an Islamic context. If the classic formula *al-salām 'alaykum* ('peace be upon you') establishes a relationship of trust and mutual respect between believers,[11] the greeting the visitors addressed to Abraham and that the Patriarch

---

11. 'Early on it was widely thought that the greeting *salām* was an Islamic institution. This is true only to the extent that this salutation was recommended by a verse revealed in the last period at Mecca and in two passages of the Qur'an of Medina (Qr VI, 54 and Qr XXIV, 27)'; *cf* Van Arendonk-Gimaret, entitled 'Salām', in *Encyclopédie de l'I-slam*, VIII, 947–949 (947).

The theophany at Mamre in the Islamic tradition 245

reciprocates in turn (Qr LI, 25; XI, 69) is simply *salām*.[12] Al-Razi devotes several pages analyzing this particular detail, pointing out that the word *salām* taken alone is undefined: it is a bidding of peace with no further qualifications, as if simply a daily greeting carrying with it no implication toward the eternal. In his commentary on Sura XV, Al-Razi resumes this reflection explaining that the angels greeted Abraham with a simple *salām,* then waited for the Patriarch to ask of them on whose behalf they were bringing the greeting. Surprisingly, Abraham's first response is polite but quite cautious: since he is not yet certain that his visitors are among the chosen servants of God, he does not have the right to wish them the peace that comes from God using the complete formula *al-salām 'alaykum*.[13] We insist on these observations of Al-Razi because he suggests the idea of a divine pedagogy that imparts knowledge of the identity of God's emissaries and their message only gradually to his servant Abraham. If the angels, at the onset of their appearing, had invoked the gift of God's peace, says al-Razi, Abraham would have been perplexed at their presence. Instead the Patriarch, after receiving the good news of the birth of his son Isaac, asks his mysterious guests: 'What good news is this, now that I am advanced in age, what is this good news?' (Qr XV, 54). The response, still concerned to mitigate the impact of the manifestation of the divine presence on the Patriarch, is retrospectively, proof of the progressive pedagogy adopted by the God of the Qur'an: 'I give you good tidings in Truth: do not be disheartened' (Qr XV, 55). After having confirmed that the grace of the birth of a child is the result of the direct intervention of God, the angels make Abraham understand that this gift is offered to allay if not to eliminate his discouragement. Yet, this statement is interpreted not so much as a reference to Abraham's past; rather, the reaction of the Patriarch itself explains it: a friend of God (*khalīl*) cannot be dismayed even at the prospect

---

12. *Sura* XV, 52, as compared with the other *suras* referring to the same incident, presents a variation: Abraham does not return the greeting but rather manifests his anxiety in the face of strangers who come into his house unannounced and without waiting to be introduced by him (*cf* AH Johns, 'Al-Rāzī's treatment', 94).

13. This formula is considered, among other things, the greeting addressed to the blessed at the moment of their entrance into Paradise. Similarly, those who are at the top of Mount Arafat (the mountain of the pilgrimage to Mecca and the intermediate place between Heaven and Hell) shout *salām 'alaykum* to the inhabitants of Paradise (Van Arendonk-Gimaret, under 'Salām', 947).

246   *Strangers With God*

of dying without posterity, he who was already of very advanced age ('And said [Abraham]: "And who might be discouraged at the mercy of his Lord? No one, other than the lost!"' (Qr XV, 56). Abraham, the 'gentle, kind, penitent' man (Qr XI, 75), was instead being prepared for the prediction of the inevitable punishment of Lot's people, the real purpose of the mission of the mysterious guests.

These hints of an exegetical analysis of the Quranic account allow us to highlight a narrative structure that accommodates—but not exclusively so—an assertion of the absolute and unquestionable will of God. That being said, it cannot be denied that the presence of God in the Qur'an bears characteristics very different from those described in the Bible.[14] It is indisputable, for example, that in the Qur'an God never appears on the scene, but instead sends emissaries to Abraham and Lot. 'The transcendence of God', writes Jean-Louis Ska, 'is clearly affirmed and there can be no confusion of plans between the divine and the human worlds'.[15] This transcendence of God is demonstrated in the human world by peremptory orders that do not admit of a rejoinder.[16] We have already mentioned Abraham's debate with Allah about the fate of Lot's people; it is also true that God immediately prevents any attempt at intercession: 'O Abraham, refrain from this. The command of your Lord has come; they have incurred an irreversible punishment' (Qr XI, 76). In the biblical account, on the contrary, the divine personage knows of a kind of inner debate: for example, already in Gen 18:17–21 God asks whether or not to reveal to Abraham the plan to punish the inhabitants of the city of Sodom; then God goes down to ascertain the gravity of the outcry against the city, and finally, to formulate a definitive judgment. None of this transpires in the Qur'an. In the Qur'an God is completely sovereign;

---

14. This last Qur'anic extract taken from *Sura* XXIX, belongs to a very different style which, in this case, witnesses a lack of vital communication between the Creator and humanity, a lack often noted in the Qur'anic revelation.

15. J-L Ska, *Abramo e i suoi ospiti*, 75. The concern to assert the transcendence of God causes the Qur'an to emphasize the distance between God and the creature. 'There is nothing like Him' (Qr XLII, 11). 'You know what is in my soul, and I do not know what is in your soul', Jesus says to God (Qr V, 116).

16. As Jean Louis Ska recalls, the expression, 'the command of the Lord' or 'the decree of the Lord' is repeated three times within a few lines in *sura* XI (Qr XI, 73.76.82); and the announcement of the birth of a son to Abraham, as well as the decision to destroy Sodom, are in fact real ordinations more than simply the relaying of information (*cf* J-L Ska, *Abramo e i suoi ospiti*, 75–76).

it is God who makes the determinations and no one censors the decisions. While human persons will have to answer for their actions (Qr XXI, 23), God's intentions are always realized and are not held accountable to anyone. This greatness and omnipotence of God, recalls Jacques Jomier, is expressed in the Qur'an through the root *a'jaza* ('to reduce to impotence'[17]): which makes one think that the statement, 'what is owed to God', occurs, almost inevitably, at the expense of 'what is due to humans' However, is this unknowable and incomprehensible God, consequently, too distant to be accessible to the human person or to inspire their own willing hospitality?

These considerations, just barely touched upon, allow a glimpse into the radical paradox of two terms essential for the Muslim faith and that always exist on the horizon of the religious thought of Islam: *shahāda* ('testimony' or 'witness' and consequently 'profession of faith')[18] and *ghayb* ('absence' and, therefore, that which is hidden and mysterious). Beginning from an understanding of this paradox, we would like to draw some conclusions about this chapter devoted to Abraham's meeting with the God who came to him as his guest.

Conclusion: a God who must be experienced!

'There is no god but Allah' is the classic formula of the Islamic faith that expresses, first of all, an action about which an 'eye witness' attests to what he or she has 'seen' (*shahāda*). This assumes a physical presence to the event or fact attested, or in other words, an experience! The Theophany of Genesis 18, with its simple anthropomorphism, transmits a firsthand experience of God which is among the greatest ever known, and which deeply marks the religious sense of all three Abrahamic religions. Once again one must remember that the story

---

17. 'They were superior to them in strength. But nothing can defeat God in the heavens or on Earth. He is indeed Omniscient and Omnipotent' (Qr 35, 44).

18. *Shahāda* is an action word, a verb which also means to be present, to see with one's own eyes, to witness an event, to testify, attest and certify [. . .] *shahāda*, then, can mean, first of all, 'what is there' and therefore 'what is seen'. Another very common meaning is 'to bear testimony,' that is, to make a statement by which the witness of an event attests to the reality of what was seen, although in the religious and theological sense its usage does not go that far. Here *shahāda* designates the Muslim profession of faith, an act of declaring: 'There is no god but God, and Muhammad is the messenger of God' (*cf* D Gimaret, in 'Shāhāda', in *Encyclopédie de l'Islam*, 207).

of Abraham is not characterized by a revelation of the unity of God, as certain commentaries of the Talmud or Qur'an (and even for some time the Christian interpretation) would have us believe, but rather by a call, a blessing, and a divine promise; in short, all happenings that point precisely to an experience of life.[19] This experience is properly mystical because it demands a detachment, a separation from all things and, above all, because it draws the soul into the solitude of God. Every revealed religion is founded in a mystical doctrine because mysticism is the privileged way that unites the believer to God who is manifest to the human creature who opens himself to God by faith. What is humanly impossible, is possible to God, in an act of sovereign liberty. The initiative always belongs to God. The mystical experience of Abraham is dependent on the divine election, gratuitous and unforeseeable and, up to this point, the great Abrahamic religions converge. But when it comes to specifying the details of this divine initiative, differences arise. Returning to the Islamic perspective which concludes this journey of interpretation of the meeting at Mamre, the way of the Qur'an is paradoxical by the need to witness an Absence, or said otherwise: to witness the mystery of God, in itself inaccessible and humanly unknowable (cf. Qr LXXII, 26). This task, however, in a purely human perspective, is doomed to failure: how does one think to witness the seeing of a vision of an Absence? 'It is He who sent down tranquility [*sakîna*] into the hearts of the believers, to add faith to their faith' (Qr XLVIII, 4). This is a revolutionary event: the religion of absolute Transcendence envisions an explosion of *sakîna*, by which a person finally experiences the gratuitous proximity of the Unknowable ('We created the human being, and We know what his soul whispers to him. We are nearer

---

19. As Divo Barsotti rightly recalls: 'The religion of the patriarchs is not dependent on metaphysics, but on an experience: they do not know whether idols are in vain, but they do know that God is, that Yahweh actually exists. The religion of the patriarchs is the recognitionion of the reality of God. And this reality is established not by a process of reasoning but more precisely because God is manifest and has appeared. The patriarchs have not speculated about God; their religion does not presume a theology, but a revelation, an experience. The development of theology, in fact of dogma, is nothing other than a profound analysis of this experience. The very history of revelation itself is undoubtedly due more to a deepening of a single identically human experience rather than of different experiences: the experience of God' (D Barsotti, *Il Dio d'Abramo: l'esperienza di Dio nella Genesi* [Firenze: Libreria Editrice Fiorentina, 1952], 366).

to him than his jugular vein'; Qr L, 16). The 'religion of Abraham' differs from those of primitive peoples: certainly not in the worship; probably not even in the idea of God nor in an ethical conception of life, but for the fact that this God enters directly into the story. Before this 'invasion' of God, humankind is as a single unit—in the sense of each not unlike the other. Instead, the human personality, far from being amorphous or fading into oblivion, becomes stronger and more powerful in experiential contact with God, even to aspiring to recapitulate the universe and the whole of creation in itself. In the same way, the call of Abraham sets him apart from others in order to transform him into the father of all! Consequently, it is not in the Patriarch's monotheistic or Trinitarian conscience that we find the meaning of the encounter at Mamre; instead here, at Mamre, Abraham experiences an accompaniment to the first step into the mystical experience of God, that irreducible Otherness that is the basis of every encounter. In other words, at Mamre Abraham gradually becomes aware of being in the presence of God but with no thought of any metaphysical questions: 'One or three?' Or, 'why alternate between the singular and plural?'[20]

In general, we situate ourselves from both a speculative and metaphysical perspective concerning the meeting at Mamre, giving birth to innumerable questions about the identity of the mysterious pilgrims and their relationship to God. Abraham has experienced what might be called 'radical otherness' and allows himself to be transformed by the experience to become 'the exemplar of the perfect host'.[21]

Undeniably—as we have analysed and delineated—there are differences in the interpretations given by the three Abrahamic religions to the invasion of the Divine Presence at Mamre; as well as to the relationship that develops between the host who welcomes and the three guests who are welcomed. Yet we must also emphasize that Abraham's experience itself plays a unifying role. We believe, with

---

20. In exactly the same way, Abraham will not speculate on the intentions of God in asking for the sacrifice of his only son; instead he returns the child back to the One from whom he had so freely and mysteriously been given him.

21. Again as Barsotti recalls: 'Abraham saw and knew the One upon whom Augustine and Thomas speculated, perhaps even more brilliantly than they—his soul, stirred and in awe, appraises, more than do the utterances of Thomas and Augustine, the grandeur of God' (D Barsotti, *Il Dio d'Abramo*, 366).

Divo Barsotti, that there can be no true experience of God as 'One' and 'wholly Other' unless there is a clear and conscious adherence to faith in the one God. The reason is very simple: an experience of 'the One' is not yet to recognise 'the One!'[22] Once more, monotheism demands a speculative analysis, however elementary, of this unique experience which we call an experience of God. If the call of Abraham and the festive gathering at Mamre following the circumcision of the Patriarch inaugurates the history of Israel, it does not, however, inaugurate God's Revelation, any more than it is the end point of this Revelation. The Genesis account, as it is received in both the Talmud and in the Qur'an, affirms in Abraham's story the vital necessity, the imperative, of an experience of God without which it is not possible to become a witness of God's presence.

---

22. We cannot linger further on the debate typical of spiritual theology apropos the relationship between an experience and the knowledge of God. Here we limit ourselves to underscoring the fact that in both Jewish and Muslim theology, as in the Eastern Christian tradition, knowledge of God does not usually undertake a philosophical or theological course. Nevertheless, both philosophy and theology may provide the language to recount such an experience. This latter is a mystery of divine revelation and follows, therefore, directly from it. In other words, because the experience of God itself comes from God, no human elaborations of the idea of God are able to convey that Transcendence and the Sanctity experienced of that Other that we call God. Now, the reflections of spiritual theology that lie at the heart of the monotheistic religions tend to analyse the characteristics more than the content of the experience of God; moreover, the God that the mystics experience is always more than any representation we make of it. Even when we speak of the true face of God that is manifest in the life and witness of Christ in Christianity, we cannot say, even here, that this is the only possible image of God.

Epilogue

Theological Paths in the Light of Hospitality

We have attempted to capture the evolution of the idea of hospitality and its practice in the cradle of the three monotheistic religions of Abraham. Now, as we conclude this journey to the heart of the Semitic world and its social practices, it is the exclusively theological theme that should have the final word because reflection on hospitality cannot remain either at a practical and moral level on the one hand or, on the other, within the realms of the political and legal. Were this the case, the sacred character of this ancestral tradition would be completely abandoned, along with the themes connected with it. Among these are those evoked from the beginning of our journey of research: the correlation between otherness and 'ontological otherness' in those who are willing to forge a relationship with others, and especially with the 'Wholly Other', not in terms of owning the other but in the acceptance of the irreducible distance between a world more or less known (one's own) and the (accepted though unfamiliar) world of the stranger.

In our investigation we have essentially pointed out three basic levels of the practice of hospitality. We find, first of all, hospitality at the individual level, given between one person and another, where the other to be gladly accommodated is unknown and often unexpected: someone whom one has neither chosen nor planned to receive and who is placed before us more and more frequently, particularly in these disquieting times and in post-modern societies. Louis Massignon liked to say about the practice of hospitality that the host/ess must also necessarily endeavor to understand the other, as well as put aside any attempt to subjugate him or her. Paradoxically, in a surprising reversal of roles, the host/ess must also be willing to be welcomed by the guest! Moreover, the free gift of oneself with no thought of return, essential in every true encounter, makes of hospitality an offer that implies a hope: a hope that, by opening oneself to the other without expecting to be compensated, may, in being accepted, evoke a like gift of self in return. The second level of hospitality involves different ranks of organization (any group or city, nation, civilization) who are bound to care for particular categories of people in particularly vulnerable situations (widows, the sick or elderly, orphans, the poor in general . . .) or, more generally, strangers. Hospitality at this level gradually loses its character of a personal connection between individuals. It is no longer the first duty of every person or even the privilege of the leader of the group who, at most, may delegate it to another group member. To sum up, provision for the indigent gradually disappears from the purview of individual virtue to become a law of society: now the welcome becomes more professional and institutionalized; a reception fundamentally unilateral, granted as a service to others, and soon even bestowed for a fee. From this moment on, one enters into a system of consumption, in a type of economic logic. But there is a third level of hospitality that represents somewhat 'the ontological character of this practice.' This is the theological dimension that, from the beginning, we have tried to highlight. Speaking, in fact, of each of the three monotheistic religions—which may be extended to the non-monotheistic religions as well—we have observed that they can, consciously or unconsciously, practice a divine hospitality both theoretically and practically, in the sense of being both the subject and the object of hospitality; that is, according to the original, double meaning of the term 'hostis' which is understood as the giver as well as the receiver of hospitality. We find here, first of all, the key to interpret the entire history of the Old Testament: Yahweh adopts Israel as a Chosen People; but that courtesy must be extended to all others, as we have already extensively analyzed in the celebrated account of hospitality by the Oak of Mamre. In New Testament theology the ontological character of the practice of hospitality is enriched by the Trinitarian dimension: in Christ we are invited to receive the Father, through the action of the Spirit. In other words, human hospitality is enveloped in the same mystery of hospitality existing within the Godhead Itself.

It is clear that these three levels of the practice of hospitality are not so distinct and exclusive of one another; rather they intersect and, at times, are intermingled. Honor towards one's fellows is to honour the gods who themselves are identified with the stranger; actually, they cannot be hidden under the appearance of the wayfarer. In short, hospitality, very frequently, implicates the divine, even to the extent of allowing us to say that it is of its essence—and this not only in the Christian tradition. This observation, already supported by a long extra-biblical literary tradition, ratifies the possibility of developing an authentic 'theology of hospitality;' or, better, a theological vision that deploys hospitality systematically within the various branches of its study. This is certainly not to approach the important issues of theology simplistically or to introduce a substance-less topic but a theology which presupposes rigorous discipline and a strong commitment to some basic principles. We offer a summary of such principles from a reflection of Joseph Doré, theologian and bishop emeritus of Strasbourg, at the conclusion of a day of study dedicated to Henri de Lubac.[1] Mons Doré, seeking to capture from the teachings of de Lubac the conditions and modality of what could be called a 'theology of hospitality,' quoted in order: the need for a firmly rooted openness; the necessity for a discernment that precedes the reception; and the demand for a real courage that effects the engagement. As to the first prerequisite, it is understood that one cannot receive another without one's own good foundation and stable personal roots. This means being able to witness to what we in our turn have received through the channel of a living tradition, as a fundamental newness at the heart of the incessant changing of the times. The second condition recalls the need for a continuous discernment, the principle of which is Christ, the Truth itself, who is himself the measure of the synthesis: in as much as he is the bond of all creation, in him all flesh has access to the Word and, as Peter tells us in the book of Acts, 'For of all the

---

1. The reference is to a meeting held for the Faculty of Theology at the University of Strasbourg in November 2002, organised under the direction of Philippe Vallin and Jean-Pierre WaGener, both specialists in the thought of Henri de Lubac. The purpose of the study day was specifically to revisit the work of this great Jesuit theologian, emphasizing, first of all, his ability to be profoundly open to accommodating in his reflections Christian authors considered atypical, such as Origen, Pico della Mirandola, Joachim of Fiore, Teilhard de Chardin and others, rehabilitated in full right to the heart of Catholic theology; and not forgetting, in second place, the theologian of interreligious dialogue (especially in his studies on Buddhism), Henri de Lubac precisely. The Acts of the day of study in Strasbourg University were published in a special issue of the *Revue des sciences religieuses* [*RevSR* 2 (2003)]: 'Henri de Lubac, ou l'Hospitalité de la Théologie'.

names in the world given to men, this is the only one by which we can be saved' (Acts 4:12). Finally, in the presence of the first two conditions, one must be prepared for a commitment to the future and have the courage to accept an often surprising newness as a gift. 'Rootedness, discernment, commitment: this could be the program, or better, the path to a theology of hospitality'.[2] It is a question of identifying hospitality as the point of departure for all theology both in its content and its practice and not simply as an accessory exercise, because a Christian is saved not alone or independently of others.

In these final pages, I wish to make a few suggestions concerning a theology of hospitality specifically in the context of a theology of religions.

A theology of religions as a theology of hospitality

We cannot dwell here on the epistemological question of a theology of religions: it is a very recent discipline, the object of which is still being developed but it has already become the nerve center at the heart of Catholic theology. Around it, in fact, have been expressed a number of magisterial guidelines and, not infrequently, disciplinary sanctions.

Surely one cannot simplistically equate a theology of religions with religious studies: if there is a complementarity between the two disciplines (both dealing with the study of religions), the methodology and approach to the question of religious plurality are different. Religious Studies brings elements of observation, description, comparison; it evaluates the different religions and the phenomena related to them. The Theology of Religions, instead, is inscribed in the ambience of faith and cannot be separated from the presuppositions of faith! In short, its task is to interpret the data offered by religious studies in the light of faith, in our case the Christian faith. More precisely, it means to study the different religious traditions in the context of the history of salvation and of their relationship to the mystery of Christ and of the Church. Of course, a Christian theology is not a universal theology, situated at the point of intersection between all creeds. This admission of limitation, however, brings with it a new starting point and a challenge to do theology differently. And here we wish to affirm, as intimated by Claude Geffré, the epistemological status of a theology of religions where, a priori, faith is not opposed to

---

2.   J Doré, 'Pour une théologie hospitalière. Conclusions théologiques', in *RevSR*, 2 (2003): 253–261 (261).

respect for others who believe differently[3]. It is important to reiterate the conviction that only a profound rootedness in one's own faith identity can insure a better understanding of another's faith, that of one's interlocutor. Such rootedness recognises that no human representation of God is adequate and it prevents one from either casting into doubt one's own understanding of God or from adhering superficially to the understanding of the other. We believe that an intelligent attitude, not carelessly or excessively comfortable, one that can allow another's gaze upon one's own universe of beliefs without sacrificing his or her ability to discern and judge, can be effectively represented by the disposition of the patriarch Abraham in the welcoming of the mysterious pilgrims at the entrance of his tent. Thus the very act of welcoming becomes at the same time an opening of one's horizon, known and recognised as one's own, to the horizon of the other not yet known to us, and an invitation to the one welcomed to open in his or her own turn, respecting the right time and an actual desire to share. In the celebrated scene in Genesis 18, the activity of the Patriarch and his guests beneath the shade of the Oak of Mamre and in the sharing of the sacred meal of hospitality, expresses precisely the need to find a neutral ground where their identities, neither forgotten nor deleted, are not, however, imposed on one another. The Patriarch demands nothing of the pilgrims in the intimate space of his tent; nevertheless, they, by probing the 'secret of the tent' (that is, the very heart of the identity of the other) finally reveal their mysterious identity: they grasp his deep desire for offspring which, when brought to fulfilment, will give back to Abraham and Sarah their full dignity in the eyes of their neighbours. From this brief analysis of the scene at Mamre in light of the theological significance of an altered posture in search of a 'neutral space' for an encounter in respect of differences, emerges an absolute necessary, if not to say, the condition for the existence of a Theology of Religions.

Beginning with the observation that, in a global world, interconnected and interdependent, religious pluralism is evident, the prophecy that Cantwell Smith made in the early 1960s: 'The religious life of mankind from now on, if it is to be lived at all, will be lived in a context of religious pluralism',[4] is now a fact. A first consequence of

---

3. *Cf* C Geffré, *De Babelà Pentecôte. Essais de théologie interreligieuse* (Paris: Cerf, 2006), 151.

4. W Cantwell Smith, *The Faith of Other Men*, (New York: Harper & Row, 19620, 11.

this is that 'the stolid conviction of holding to a possession of the truth while everyone else is wrong is no longer an option'.[5] Nevertheless, if, as is commonly believed, plurality is not an evil to be eliminated but a wealth of experience to be gained in all its fecundity, a claim for unity at all costs seems quite simplistic, if not fanciful. However, the proposal to make of pluralism a principal value, a true criterion,[6] was clearly rejected in the declaration of the Congregation for the Doctrine of the Faith, *Dominus Jesus*, because it was considered a 'relativistic theory'.[7] It remains, therefore, an indispensable need to question this new cultural climate characterized by a plurality of views and beliefs. It is also essential to think not so much about creating a new theology and its criteria but, rather, about the concrete experience of a new season of relations between religions, one which implies openness and mutual respect, the rejection of all forms of arrogance and intolerance, a path walked together in search of God and in the historical record of the revealed message. All this is to insist that a true pluralism can accept neither an inclusive discourse that eliminates all differences, nor a radical exclusion of religious paths other than one's own, which denies the existence of any common heritage. It is in this dialectic between inclusivism and exclusivism that the attempt to understand theologically the radical difference between divine and human reality is located, a difference that has not always been sufficiently safeguarded by traditional theology. As the Dominican theologian Christian Duquoc aptly observes, 'God, revealed in Jesus, has not made this particularity an absolute; [. . .] The original particularity of Christianity demands that differences remain real and not be abolished, as if God's manifestation in Jesus were the conclusion of "religious" history'[8]. Here we must rethink the relationship between the meaning of 'the Divine Mystery' on the one hand, and how it is used in the communities of faith and in interfaith dialogue on the other. It is the beginning of a complex process of dialogue, the players of which are situated as a new Abraham

---

5. E Schillebeeckx, *Umanità. La storia di Dio* (Brescia: Queriniana, 1992), 77.

6. Schillebeeckx, *Umanità. La storia di Dio*, 217.

7. Declaration of the Congregation for the Doctrine of the Faith, *Dominus Jesus, on the Unicity and Salvific Universality of Jesus Christ and the Church*, Rome, August 6, 2000, available at www.vatican.va/. . ./rc_con_cfaith_doc_20000806_dominus-iesus_en.html, accessed May 27, 2016.

8. C Duquoc, *Un Dio diverso. Saggio sulla simbolica trinitaria* (Brescia: Queriniana, 1985), 137.

summoned to stand at the threshold of their 'tent / identity' and be challenged by the visit / presence of the other: an attitude that may guide the theological direction of the interfaith issue. Now, does not the spirit of hospitality have as purpose the engendering of a liberality that allows one to recognise and respect the irreducible otherness of the other, over and beyond recognising, preserving and promoting their gifts? Mariano Crociata proposes an additional Theology of Hospitality in complementarity to the Theology of Religions.

Box 9 A Difficult Comparison

To delve into this particular area of the comparative theology of religions, we must realize that there are methodological precautions at stake because, even though the comparative method is a practical necessity in the field of human knowledge and has always been practiced by way of analogy (which specifically means comparison in theological circles), today there are many reservations concerning comparison per se in the theology of religions. In essence, this methodology is frequently based on assumptions and sectarian interests, even if not always declared as such. "In practice the comparison [. . .] too often leads to highlight only one religion, especially monotheistic Christianity, either by protecting it from every other comparative ambition or, more subtly, by permitting the comparison to better assert its differences." Having said that, Claude Geffré (*De Babel à Pentecôte. Essais de théologie interreligieuse*, Cerf, Paris 2006) insists that a Christian theology of religions cannot dispense its use of the comparative method. The challenge, then, is to learn to make proper use of it. The French Dominican theologian distinguishes, epistemologically, a comparative theology of religions from a comparative history of religions. In the first case, it is not enough to simply grasp the similarities and differences between religions, but to make a theological effort to really espouse an understanding of the way another faith community believes. For this reason, it is not only a comparison of the multiple expressions of each religious system but a search for the way each claims to place its own faithful in relation to the Absolute. Here again, Claude Geffré adds a crucial criterion for the comparatist practice when he states that one cannot compare isolated religious forms by highlighting similarities and differences. Religions must be taken as a whole. No one particular element can be understood extrapolated from the totality in which it is inscribed. We see from this that an interfaith theology can only be arrived at by a real integration of the respective faiths.

260   *Strangers With God*

> To the passage from an exclusively apologetic discipline to one that is fundamentally inclusive [i.e., a Theology of Religions]—writes Msgr. Crociata—is added in today's pluralistic world, evidence that there is divine, religious and cultural identity in an 'acceptance-of-the-other.' [. . .] Missionary witness and dialogue are two ways in which the Church is present in the contemporary world, and the spirit of concord and hospitality must animate all theological hermeneutics. In a world-wide theological discourse witnessing the emergence of authentic local theologies, a theology rooted in Europe loses its function, until now unchallenged, as the proponent of a universal theology. [. . .] In this perspective it is important to note that the apostolic exhortation *Ecclesia in Europa* considers non-Christian religions under the aspects of hospitality, immigration, coexistence and historical contribution to the formation of the European spirit[9]. [. . .] At this point, it reverses the theological opinion of a position of dominance among the religions and the claim to universality, the drawing up of tables and manuals, abstract and theoretical, in favor of learning new perspectives that arise from theological creativity in other cultural contexts and by its coexistence with non-Christian traditions. The emergence of a polycentric theology—a methodological contextualization of the one truth—requires a spirit of hospitality and participation.[10]

The sense of this long quotation is clear: the multicultural and multi-religious ferment is capable of setting off conflicts beyond that which can be contained by any religious or political hegemony. At the same time, this can be a great opportunity if the right to the existence of different languages, beliefs and ideals is recognised, if the acceptance and preservation of diversity—even that which is not necessarily understood—is valued and integrated into our lives.

Certainly, an 'option for hospitality' imposes a criteria of discernment; it is surely not an uncritical acceptance of all positions. Thus, to define dialogue as beginning with the notion of hospitality can be only a partial perspective and is not exhaustive. Even so, it does allow us to identify the effects of dialogue in terms of enrichment and the purification of one's faith (a purification which includes long

---

9. *Cf* John Paul II, Apostolic Exhortation, *Ecclesia in Europa* (June 28, 2003), n 57. *Cf* also nn. 19 and 46.

10. M Crociata, editor, *Teologia delle religioni: la questione del metodo* (Roma: Città Nuova, 2006), 82–83.

term prejudices as well; in short, it is the work of a lifetime, both personally and in an understanding of history).[11] Dialogue itself must be presented as a concerted effort towards consensus, guided by an appreciation of values, however limited, so that individualism and / or subjectivism does not deteriorate into total relativism.

To believe hospitably: Truth not as a substance but as a relationship

A 'pluralistic hospitality' is a task that opens to the future, but only if a drift toward relativism (or fundamentalism), which would undermine any possibility of social and cultural coexistence, is avoided. Once again, we believe that a Theology of Religions which systematically defines hospitality as an ethical category designed to encourage an encounter with our differences, would express a new awareness of the diversity and vitality of religious traditions.

This consciousness is not an end in itself but a stimulus to theological questioning on the significance of plurality within the one divine plan of salvation and amid the multiplicity of sincere paths in the human pursuit of God. Here we must make note of the crisis of 'tolerance' spawned by the ideas of secularism, rationalism and the Enlightenment, which seem today to have no logical foundation. Whatever is of vital importance is shared, not tolerated. Similarly, if one's truth is at variance with another's, there is no problem, either for oneself or for the other who may be in error; problems arise only when one tries to convince the other of the validity of his/her position. What sense would such tolerance make in allowing another license to ignore that which gives meaning to our lives, that which yields to happiness? *De facto*, a certain conception of tolerance is not an aid to recognition of the other, because there is in it no possibility of reciprocity.

Discarding then, a simplistic understanding of tolerance, the choice might be made for—in our opinion the most noble—'the neutralization of the conflict of absolute value' (in which all the religious wars have originated[12]), alongside a search for the lowest common denominator, for a consensus of guiding elements which

---

11. *Cf* R De Vita, 'Premessa', in R De Vita and F Berti, editors, *Pluralismo religioso e convivenza multiculturale* (Milano: Franco Angeli Edizioni, 2003), 25.

12. We speak in the past tense because modern violence now seems, with no false masks, to be unleashed mainly by economic factors, even if these latter will continue more or less under the deceptive appearance of religious conflicts of absolute value.

will include the cost of some sacrifice. Hans Küng's manifesto for a global ethic is situated in this order of ideas. As the Swiss theologian already stated, however, the risk that lies in this approach, which seems so reasonable and peaceful, is to aim for a harmony between the different positions, for a uniformity which eliminates any element of distinction—which is the basis of all true dialogue.[13] In this case, the adopting of a common denominator is purely conventional and arbitrary: risking a simple product of the will more than the force of an idea, or a belief.

Our path in the light of hospitality allows us to glimpse another way: the establishment of a relationship between two distinct entities who remain steadfast in their own truth. True Dialogue demands recognition of the other in him/herself, respecting their values and caring about them, until one can acknowledge that they also bear an element of the truth. As we may not try to reduce, harmonize or bring our own truth to the approval of others, so we may not diminish another's in their perception of the truth. Each speaks one's own truth and, in encountering the truth of the other, understands it as an investigation (literally translated as the Latin term 'research' or, more loosely, 'to come to'); and that, therefore, the content of one's testimony is not the truth itself, but one's perception of truth. This will not lead to indifference or relativism, but to the realization that one does not possess the truth but can only approach it by conjecture. Essentially, it is that truth which surpasses all of us that allows the possibility of meeting the other, with their own perception of the same truth, a perception that I need to bring me closer in my own turn to the one truth that grounds us both[14]. Here we touch upon a central theme of

---

13. There are multiple forms of aggression that can be the result of fear of another who happens to be different, regardless of whether or not force is used (seduction, for example, or diminishment by benevolence; *cf* P Claverie, *Petit traité de la rencontre et du dialogue* (Paris: Cerf, 2004, 36ff). Hans Küng is aware of the risk involved in bringing all differences into harmony when he says that there is no world peace without peace among religions, then adds that there can be no peace among religions without a dialogue that deepens and preserves their different foundations.

14. Pierre Claverie, martyred bishop of Oran, Algeria, loved to repeat: 'Not only do I admit that the other is a subject with his own rights and differences, free in his conscience, but I also admit that he can have a part of the truth that is lacking to me and without which my own search for truth cannot be said to be entirely complete' (J.J Pérennès, *Vescovo tra i mussulmani. Pierre Claverie martire in Algeria* [Roma: Città Nuova, 2004], 224).

the Theology of Dialogue. The first condition for allowing the desire for dialogue to take root and grow is a vision of truth as a relationship rather than as a substance that can be appropriated[15].

In these considerations, rather obviously pastoral, one can discern an overlay of Western philosophical thought which has taken a decisive step thanks to Hegel's insight that in order to be awakened to self-consciousness one needs an acknowledgment by another self-conscious being[16]. Yet, as already mentioned several times, this presence of the other bringing with it so great a gift coincides with the discovery of a disquieting estrangement and 'foreignness,' often perceived as a threat. It is an everlasting dialectic that resides not only in the practice of the virtue of hospitality, but also apprehended in the vertigo aroused by the human experience of God's presence, 'the Other par excellence.' And yet, it is God alone who enables the chasm of disparity to be surmounted without eradicating it, thus renewing the possibility of a dialogue between opposites. In other words, the 'God made flesh' of the Christian faith becomes the veritable new 'tent of hospitality': all persons in search of God among them come together in the very same locus where God and humanity unite.[17] The Gospel story of the appearance of the Risen One to the two disciples on

---

15. 'How can one imagine an authentic encounter with another, a non-dominating relationship reciprocally transformative, if truth is considered as a thing, as an asset that can be possessed? Each meeting would then be condemned to an impasse: I identify with my own truth; or, this other's truth is exclusively his / hers:' there is no middle way' (J Mouttapa, *Religions en dialogue* [Paris: Albin Michel, 2002], 111).

16. *Cf* F Hegel, *Fenomenologia dello Spirito,* V Cicero V, editor (Milano: Bompiani, 2000).

17. We well know that the major challenge of interreligious dialogue, from the Christian perspective, is the difficulty of opening a dialogue with others on an equal footing when, from the beginning, we place ourselves in the exceptional situation of claiming that our founder is not one mediator among many but the Son of God sent as the only Saviour of the world. It is then tempting to relativize this salvation in Christ. Since God alone saves, should we not admit that Jesus Christ is the way of salvation only for Christians? Now, according to the clear teaching of the New Testament it is certain that, from the first moment of creation, God brought an eternally universal plan of salvation to fulfilment in Christ, making him the Beginning and the End, the Alpha and the Omega. This does not mean that the mediation in Christ excludes other ways of salvation, on condition that one realizes that all other mediations, for example those of the Abrahamic religions, have a salvific value to the extent that they are mysteriously connected with the mediation of Christ.

the road to Emmaus (Lk 24: 13-35) perfectly illustrates this dynamic encounter between two individuals who find their identity because of the intrusion of a 'third between the two'. The unknown pilgrim is a true 'midwife', bringing to light not only the paschal mystery but also fragments of truth hidden in the search of the disciples fleeing from Jerusalem, because it is the Truth itself which comes to meet the human quest, always partial and uncertain, however sincere. Once again we speak of truth as a 'happening,' as a presence, as a relationship, and not simply as an object of knowledge. Once again we repeat that metaphysics is not disregarded but exceeded by ethical reflection: the unknown pilgrim, rather than reveal himself (he is recognised only after he disappears; *cf* Lk 24:31), reveals the human presence of the neighbour (in the necessity to return to the Jerusalem they were running from; *cf* Lk 24:33). This is not the destruction of the human in God, but the discovery of a new face of God in welcoming another distinct from oneself.

We cannot here fail to point out the difference between Christian theology and radical Islam. 'All things perish'—says the Qur'an— 'except His presence' (Qr XXVIII, 88); in other words, God manifests power by first annihilating (*fana'*)[18] the creature, then returning it to life for judgment. It is the extreme consequence of an anthropology exclusively and radically God-centered, which brings Massignon to clarify that 'the general trend of Islamic theology affirms God more by the destruction of beings than by their construction'.[19] But can we conceive of dialogue as a conversation between two persons, each irreducibly distinct, if the other is perceived as attacking one's very personhood? We hear Bishop Claverie once again, who says that the Word will be allowed to bridge the distance of separation and engender the possibility of encounter only by respecting the differences.[20]

---

18. This term belongs to the reflections of Sufism and is introduced by the great mystic al-Hallâj (922) to describe the mystical experience of identification with God. Two very similar definitions have been given for *fana'*: first, it means the loss of consciousness, including the consciousness of self, and its gradual replacement by the consciousness of God; secondly, it refers to the annihilation of the imperfections of the creature and their replacement with the perfections given by God (*cf* F Rahman, voce 'Bakā' wa-Fanā', in *Encyclopédie de l'Islam*, 980.

19. L Massignon, *La Passion de Hallâj* (Paris: Gallimard, 1975), IV, 631, cited by A Moussali, *La croix et le croissant. Le christianisme face à l'islam* (Paris: Edition de Paris, Paris 1998), 36.

20. P Claverie, 'Umanità plurale (Mons P Claverie, vescovo di Orano)', in *Il ReGeno*, 17 (1996): 538.

Finally, if dialogue is an essential dimension of Christian theology, then hospitality, as its complement, is the ability to live in a permanent state of conversion enkindled by the other; a kind of time of preparation for interreligious dialogue, an essential for creating the necessary trust that encourages the sharing of one's riches. Authentic dialogue is not to be seen as a Trojan horse by which one penetrates the fortress of the other, but an end in itself, a real necessity! Thus, 'to do theology in exile'[21] as invoked by the French theologian Christian Duquoc, is not a disadvantage but an implicit invitation to detachment; it is to claim no privileged position or distinction in the exchange with contemporary culture but rather to create a different way of life; to establish an identity open to relationship.[22] Theologically speaking, in this historic moment with its diverse cultures, ethnicities, religions, faiths and beliefs, it is not possible to speak directly about the God of Jesus Christ. It is first necessary to rediscover the theological dimension of what it means to be human. If a primary relationship with God cannot, before all else, be comprehended, the God of Jesus Christ will never be recognised. Western culture has long neglected this theological dimension of human-hood because historically the attitude of the Church has regarded theological discourse as opposed to the anthropology developed by the secular culture of Europe. It would seem that here there are the conditions for a decisive step toward the 'required coexistence:' living side-by-side while respecting differences and distinctions, directed toward a benevolent understanding of the perspectives of each and finally in mutual relationship. Coexistence, as a sign of reciprocal hospitality, will bring the Theology of Religions to the new level of a Theology of Religious Pluralism, where the questions no longer concern only the multiple approaches to God within the mysterious plan of salvation, but include possible ways of coexistence! This coexistence is an important advance towards integration and, above all, a step forward beyond mere tolerance.

---

21. The phrase is taken from the title of one of the last writings of the Dominican theologian, evoking the challenge of theological thinking in a context often 'inhospitable' and in a European culture alien for the first time to Christianity, but for all this, not alien to religion *tout court* (*cf* C Duquoc, *La teologia in esilio. La sfida della sua sopravvivenza nella cultura contemporanea* (Brescia: Queriniana, 2004).
22. *Cf* C Duquoc, *La teologia in esilio*, 97–99.

Moreover, there is an ontological, and not simply irenic, reason for an indispensable opening of each religion toward a relationship with the other: faith must necessarily point beyond itself because, first of all, its relationship with God is understood as its foundation and primary source. Now, the claim of a faith that stands as an absolute end in itself, negates the Absolute that is God![23] Only by intensifying the experience of this Absolute can that natural sense of insecurity inherent in every welcome of another who is different be overcome. The formula that seems most effective in conveying this dimension of hospitality is respect for and recognitionion of diversity as a source of enrichment. Moreover, it is only by intensifying the experience of the Absolute that the risk of a drift toward relativism can be averted, the result of the loss of the ontological value of diversity, intrinsically at the very heart of the triune God. The shocking fact of faith in a God who is both Three and One is the most sublime example that otherness is not to be cultivated as a value in itself, but has significance only within a sincere evangelical effort to build a visible unity[24]—which is not to be confused with uniformity. It is by ascending these theological-dogmatic summits that we may realize that the lovely gesture of hospitality is not simply an interaction between human beings but becomes a Covenant between the divine and the human. This requires a theological understanding of interpersonal relationships so that they become, on the horizon of a mutual hospitality, the place where the gift of one's very self may be exchanged, beyond and in place of an 'alms' resembling a substitute for the donor.

The sacred texts of the three Abrahamic religions, as we have extensively analysed, affirm that the care taken of the weakest is a measure of the moral character of a society (*cf* Ex 2:23; Lev 25:17–18). As a result, minority communities, such as Christians in the Middle East, are themselves a kind of moral barometer in the countries where they live, and can play a prophetic role against the dominant

---

23. Christ himself continually refers to the Father and does not absolutize his own particular historical experience, while at the same time referring to himself as the way to the Father for those who believe in him.

24. Without reflections such as these the meaning of the ecumenical journey cannot be understood; it would be as tempting to give up as it is gruelling to press forward. As John Paul II reminds us, the ecumenical effort cannot be content to put aside obstacles but must aim at a real sharing of gifts!

culture.[25] By alienating the other one ends up alienating oneself from a world into which one would want to be better integrated. The task of welcoming, however affects not only those in a situation of numerical majority. For Christians in particular, one of the gifts of the Holy Spirit at Pentecost is an extension of God's hospitality to the ends of the earth. This means recognition that all are now equally near to God and that the very presence of the other is the inalienable place where God is manifest. It is here that religions, in particular those derived from Abraham, as we have treated in this paper, can no longer be a place to defend their identity against a claim to diversity, but rather a 'frontier' to traverse, a reality that goes beyond itself, and which leads not only to a theology of dialogue but to a 'Theology in Dialogue' a methodology coextensive with theological thinking.

---

25. For a discussion of this issue in a Middle Eastern context, we refer to D Rosen, 'Cristianesimo e relazioni interreligiose in Terra santa oggi. Un paradigma di 'alterità', in A Melloni and G La Bella, editors, *L'alterità: concezioni ed esperienze nel cristianesimo contemporaneo* (Bologna: Il Mulino, 1985), 41–53; M Lahham, 'Cristiani ed ebrei in Terra santa', 56–61.

Postface

The English edition of this research on the practices of hospitality at the heart of the three Abrahamic religion's traditions and beliefs, comes out in dramatic coincidence with terrible conflicts at the heart of the West (the Ukrainian-Russian war) and of those lands that are the cradle of Semitism (the devastating conflict between Israel and Hamas). Speaking about the sacredness of human life, of an hospitality that does not take hostage, of the dialectic of gift in even a theological perspective, and, that is, some way revealing the face of the One God, seems almost insulting. For far too long, particularly in the Middle East, we have witnessed, in complicit silence, a massacre of children, young and old, as well as the uncertain fate of dozens and dozens of hostages dragged into the tunnels of the Gaza Strip and, finally, the 'total siege' imposed on the open-air cage of Gaza, which causes indiscriminate suffering to the population already affected, for decades and certainly not only since 7 October 2023, by the shortage of food, fuel and medical supplies.

In fact, these tragedies seem to be a confirmation of the disastrous consequences of the loss of reference to the other as a glimpse into the Absolute. We are confronted with the consequences of a total 'dehumanisation of the enemy' that increases, for both sides in the conflict, the tolerability of his death: a dehumanisation that makes even war crimes morally acceptable, sometimes disguised as legitimate defense that, in reality, appears much more like a disproportionate 'right to revenge'. Once again, inescapable questions arise about the meaning of life: why all this? Asking ourselves this question at a time when, as believers, we are often condemned to marginality, may seem absolutely distressing but, paradoxically, it can also become providential, because it offers us an opportunity for purification . . .

It is a question of emerging, once and for all, from an exclusively identity-based view of religious reference, which for Christians is expressed as a nostalgia for *christianitas*: that era that began around the 4th century with the Byzantine emperors Constantine and Theodosius, when the faith of Christ's followers became not only progressively majority but also hegemonic, particularly at the heart of the Western world, producing its own culture. The French Revolution certainly represented a decisive turning point for the end of this era. However, *cristianitas*, which has to do with the history of society, cannot be confused with Christianity, which is a religious fact inextricably linked to the event of the incarnation and the relationship with Christ, God with us. Likewise, the fanatical Islamism of those who are violent in the name of Allah cannot be confused with the faith of those who surrender to the One God. For some time, we are no longer simply experiencing a phenomenon of unstoppable secularisation, but also a disturbing alliance between atheists (defined in the West as 'pious') and self-styled believers who are attempting to restore religion to a hegemonic position even at a political level. This attitude, by the way, very easily takes on xenophobic, if not blatantly racist connotations.

Beliefs manipulated for political projects become mere discriminating factors of identity. New paths could also be fostered with a renewed understanding of the concept of culture, to be understood first and foremost as a true mediation between the particularity of individuals and the universality of the Common Good, between the singular nation and plural humanity. True cultural exchange is neither self-expansion nor self-absorption, but the deepening of an identity from the experience of the diversity of languages and beings. This exchange refers to a hospitable dynamic, that is, the capacity to remain oneself while in the effort to respect and welcome the irreducible diversity of the other. It is the paradoxical rehabilitation of the 'weakness' recognised, accepted, welcomed, overcome, to give birth to another type of transforming force. To be strong without being powerful. To be truthful without being fanatical. Having a sense for aesthetics without being aesthetic. Being true without being self-righteous. To be one without being the other. In short, in the complexity of our times, to reject the all too banal binary logic that hastily separates the good from the bad, feeding the machine of that 'world war being fought in pieces'. But overcoming

Postface 271

the crude polarisation that fuels the enemy's logic is only a first step, because a tolerant juxtaposition of diversities cannot be considered the real goal.

Coming back to that Holy Land of faiths, in these months again tragically wounded and outraged by blind violence, we cannot but think of the Holy City par excellence: Jerusalem. André Chouraqui, in his book *Vivre pour Jerusalem*, while denouncing a present of the Holy City chained, as well as often crucified by history, does not give up prophesying for her the call to become the land of encounter, when we would be able to recognise in every human being our brother, as Psalm 87: 5-6 makes us understand: «However, of Zion it will be said, "They were all born there, for the Most High himself establishes her." The Lord records in the register of the peoples, "This one was born there." . . ..».

Someone might recall here the tragic dilemma, the historical bipolarity that gives rise to the question: is it really city of encounters or simply city of coexistence, where so many people and situations touch each other without interpenetration? The Israeli writer David Shahar, already noted, several years ago, the fact that people live in different worlds that coexist, side by side, without inter-penetration, worlds that are sometimes present within the different belongings themselves: tension between believers and non-believers; tension between different communities. What does all this mean in relation to the mystery of peace, prosperity, joy, justice, fraternity that Jerusalem announces by its name, that the holy scriptures prefigure with extraordinary enthusiasm?

If we think about it, from the first decades of Christianity, one has the impression that the mission of historical Jerusalem at some point gets buried, or emerges in transitory forms, such as that of the pilgrimage, which speaks of the nomadic temporariness that is leitmotif of the Holy Scriptures and of the very vocation of the Chosen People. And so, the Jerusalem of mystery, bathed in God's saving presence, takes on new meanings, prophecy of an 'already and a not yet'. Questioning ourselves about Jerusalem as prophecy inevitably means questioning the relationship between the heavenly Jerusalem and the earthly Jerusalem; the Jerusalem of now and the Jerusalem to come. It is a question of understanding how to situate the value of sign and the value of reality in a reciprocal relationship, how to reconcile the historical and temporal dimension with the eschatological one.

It is not enough to hope for the hypothetical elimination of differences in the *eschaton*; the question is rather one of peaceful coexistence in history.

It is the problem of the Holy City of Faiths par excellence, but not only of it, where theoretical questions intersect with practical ones, where one point in common remains: what is the human in front of us? How do we establish and preserve what is truly human? We are aware that the definitive figure of the human is not yet given, because the promotion of the human is an ongoing process. However, spaces are needed, such as non-virtual but real-life workshops, for its construction in everyday life, in a context of mutual hospitality. Boundaries need to be redefined as 'thresholds', i.e. transition zones, because one can only achieve a reconciled relationship with ourselves only if we enter into a reconciled relationship with the other. Walls imprison those who build them.

****

List of Boxes

1.	The Other, The Stranger, The Immigrant: A Lexical Search	7
2.	Ancient Roads and Caravanserais	124
3.	Paul's Understanding of Hospitality: A 'Selective' Practice?	130
4.	The Compiling of the Qur'an: The Meccan and Medinan Suras	178
5.	Mamre: Site of the Encounter	191
6.	The 'Tragedy' of Barrenness in the Bible	198
7.	The Interpretation of the Meeting of Mamre in the Protestant Tradition	218
8.	Divine Omnipotence and Human Psychology in the Context of the Qur'an	243
9.	A Difficult Comparison	259

A concise bibliography

R. I. Letellier, *Day in Mamre, Night in Sodom: Abraham and Lot in Genesis 18–19*. BibInt 10. Leiden: Brill, 1995.

Derrida J., *Of Hospitality*, Stanford University Press, 2000

A. Arterbury, Andrew, *Entertaining Angels: Early Christian Hospitality in Its Mediterranean Setting*, Sheffield Phoenix, 2005

A. Yong, *Hospitality and the Other: Pentecost, Christian Practices, and the Neighbor. Faith Meets Faith,* Maryknoll, NY: Orbis Books, 2008.

A. Sutherland, *I Was A Stranger: A Christian Theology of Hospitality*, Abingdon Press, 2010

P.-F., De Béthune *By Faith and Hospitality: The Monastic Tradition as a Model for Interreligious Encounter*, Gracewing Publishing, 2002

J. W. Jipp, *Saved by Faith and Hospitality*. Grand Rapids: Eerdmans, 2017.

M. Dal Corso (ed.), *Religioni e ospitalità*, Antonianum, Roma 2021

M. Dal Corso (ed.), *Teologia dell'ospitalità*, BTC 196, Queriniana, Brescia, 2019

A. Shepherd, *The Gift of the Other: Levinas, Derrida, and a Theology of Hospitality*—Cambridge: The Lutterworth Press, 2014

F-Daou—N. Tabbara, *Divine Hospitality: A Christian-Muslim Conversation*, World Council of Churches, 2017

Some Articles

C. Monge, « Life Together: Lessons in Hospitality from Mamre », in *Toronto Journal of Theology* 29/1, (2013): 101–110.

_____ « Jalons pour une pensée théologique à partir de la condition d'étrangeté ontologique », in *L'hôspitalité*, Théologiques, Montréal, vol 25, 2 (2017): 37–60.

_____ « Le don de Tibhirine "Oser une communion spirituelle orante, en dépit des différences théologiques" », *in Collectanea Cistercensia* 83 (2021): 1–15.

_____ «Dieu hôte: le dialogue interreligieux à la lumière de l'hospitalité», Mélanges des Sciences Religieuses, Nouvelle série—T. 80—N°1 (2023): 89–105.

J. D. Safren, *«Hospitality Compared: Abraham and Lot as Hosts».* in *Universalism and Particularism at Sodom and Gomorrah: Essays in Memory of Ron Pirson.* Edited by Diana Lipton. Ancient Israel and Its Literature 11. Atlanta: SBL Press, 2012: 157–178

V.H. Matthews, 'Hospitality and Hostility in Genesis 19 and Judges 19'. BTB 22 (1992): 3–11.

N. MacDonald, 'Listening to Abraham—Listening to YHWH: Justice and Mercy in Genesis 18.16–33'. CBQ 66 (2004): 25–43.

D. M. Csinos, *Just Hospitality: God's Welcome in a World of Difference. Toronto Journal of Theology, vol. 27, 2011, p.* 300–301

Printed in the USA
CPSIA information can be obtained
at www.ICGtesting.com
CBHW030110170624
10126CB00004B/93